the
long distance
cyclists' handbook

SIMON DOUGHTY

Simon Doughty is a professional cycling coach and writer. Under his guidance riders have won medals and set national and world records in road, track, mountain-biking and cyclo-cross events. He has toured extensively and competed in most cycling disciplines, twice ridden the prestigious Paris–Brest–Paris randonnée, and crewed in the Race Across AMerica.

Dedication

For Linda, who has endured more than most

Published in 2001 by A & C Black (Publishers) Ltd
37 Soho Square, London W1D 3QZ

Copyright © 2001 by Simon Doughty

ISBN 0 7136 5819 3

A CIP catalogue record for this book is available from the British Library.

Illustration/acknowledgements
Cover photographs: Cassie Lowe on the Race Across AMerica 2000, courtesy of Simon Doughty
Internal photographs courtesy of Simon Doughty, unless noted on the individual photographs
Illustrations by Dave Saunders

Note: Whilst every effort has been made to ensure that the content of this book is as technically accurate and as sound as possible, neither the author nor the publisher can accept responsibility for any injury or loss sustained as a result of the use of this material.

Typeset in 10/12pt Minion Display

Printed and bound in Great Britain by
Biddles Ltd, Guildford and Kings Lynn

Contents

Get ready

Get set

Go!

Preface

I have written *The Long Distance Cyclists' Handbook* to provide you with ideas and techniques to make your cycling more enjoyable and efficient. I hope that it will give you an insight into making your cycling more rewarding, and that it will enable you to ride further, more comfortably and to stretch your own personal horizons. Whether you're dreaming of cycling 100 miles in day, undertaking a round-the-world tour, racing in ultra-endurance events or joining the growing numbers of people who enjoy the challenges and camaraderie of long-distance cycle rides (or randonnées), the experience and the rewards are as varied as they are abundant. Or perhaps you just love riding a bike and want a few tips to use in whatever style of cycling you prefer.

With such a broad spectrum of activities to cover you may find some sections of this book more relevant than others to your particular interests or level of experience. That is to be expected, as there is no definitive 'right way' to cover long-distance cycling. Use this book as a guide and adapt the suggestions given to suit your own preferences and circumstances. It's quite likely that you may discover some good ideas appropriate for your special interests in an unexpected area. Think laterally and I can guarantee that you will find the call of the 'long road' all the more alluring. I hope you enjoy it as much as I do.

In the book, equipment and planning are given significant prominence. Although many people will happily cycle without a thought to either subject, they are probably not riders who are concerned with improving their cycling or riding with greater efficiency. Attention to these details can help to avoid many pitfalls, and make the whole cycling experience both much more enjoyable and much more rewarding.

This book is arranged into three sections: 'Get Ready', 'Get Set' and 'Go!'. You don't have to read it from beginning to end; you can select sections according to your needs and interests. If you want to get a feel for what you are letting yourself in for, head straight to 'Go!' and read about the experiences of various events – from fixed-centre touring through to randonnées ranging from 200 km to 1200 km, and the Race Across AMerica (yes, it does have a capital M!) or wilderness cycling. 'Get Ready' covers the choice of appropriate equipment, and tailoring your bike for your needs. Don't worry if you don't take in all the detail at first, you can always come back to it later, perhaps when you feel more comfortable with other aspects of your riding. If you are planning a trip, wondering how to make life easier for next time, or have a problem to overcome, 'Get Set' should provide you with the answers you are seeking. The principles given here really are applicable to any cyclist, but how much you absorb depends upon your own needs and how seriously you want to achieve performance improvements.

I have defined 'long distance' as a minimum of a half-day ride (about 4 hours). For some people that could be a 25-mile sponsored ride or a charity event such as the 55-mile ride from London to Brighton where many riders take all day to cover the distance. For those who get the cycling bug and want a bigger challenge, randonnées or *sportive* events provide the opportunity and incentive to stretch your limits. The standard randonnée distance is 200 km (events are held from 100 km to 2000 km). These are non-competitive rides with a minimum speed limit of around 15 kph and usually a maximum speed of 30 kph. The route visits a series of 'controls' where the rider must have a card stamped as proof of following the route. The longer events of 300 km or more usually require some time spent riding through the night. Every four years the most prestigious 1200 km Paris–Brest–Paris randonnée is held in France, attracting around 3500 riders from around the world.

Sportive events are similar to randonnées, often covering around 200 km. The bigger events may have literally thousands of participants. They are not pure races but they do have a competitive element and many tourists often enjoy the opportunity to test themselves without having to push themselves to the limit – although at the head of the event it can be every bit as fast and competitive as any road race. Result sheets are published with riders' times, and prizes are awarded to category (usually age and sex) winners.

For racing cyclists, long distances really begin at 100 miles. Road racers have stage races (a number of single-day races held consecutively – anything from a weekend to the three weeks of the big professional tours of France, Italy and Spain – where the lowest aggregate time determines the overall winner). Recovery and stamina are key qualities for successful stage-race riders. Time-triallists also have events lasting 12 hours or 24 hours to test themselves. Riders are set off individually at one-minute intervals to ride alone and cover as great a distance as possible in the time allowed. As the distance increases, inevitably the pace drops and so these longer events often attract a number of 'endurance tourists' too.

Perhaps the ultimate long-distance race is the Race Across AMerica (RAAM). This gruelling marathon event is open to anyone who meets the qualification standards – and can find the essential support crew, finance and training time. The race is continuous, with the clock running until the rider reaches the finish line 3000 miles away on the opposite coast. The riders pedal over 20 hours a day for more than a week. Success depends on mental strength just as much as physical ability, resilience and an ability to stay awake. If RAAM was easy then everyone would do it, but fewer people have completed RAAM than have travelled in space.

Cycle touring is an excellent means of transport for anyone with wanderlust. You can cover more ground on a bike than walking, and yet you are travelling slowly enough and 'closely' enough to empathise with the people and the geography of the places you visit. In its simplest form cycle touring is a Sunday afternoon ride, but it may progress to longer rides, weekends away, cycle camping for a week to explore a new area or maybe a lengthy journey across countries or continents. There are commercial companies that will organise tours for you, taking your luggage from one place to the next, or you can suit yourself by carrying your belongings in panniers or a saddlebag, free to take whichever direction you wish.

Throughout the book, text boxes include useful information, tips and reference points. You should be able to find whatever you are looking for by using the contents list, sub-headings and index. The word 'he' has been used throughout the text purely for reasons of simplicity, and should be read to include 'he and she' in all cases. Long-distance cycling is a wide-ranging topic, and consequently space restrictions have limited the amount of content and detail that I have been able to include on many of the topics. A Further Reading section is included at the end of the book. I hope that there will be updated editions of *The Long Distance Cyclists' Handbook* in years to come – to keep you abreast of the latest advances in equipment, sports science and world travel – so I welcome your comments (www.sdsport.co.uk), especially if you would like more information on any particular subject.

Enjoy your riding. *Allez! Bonne route!*

Simon Doughty, March 2001

Acknowledgements

Many people have influenced the writing of this book but two mentors from my early club cycling days as a teenager have perhaps had the greatest affect. Firstly, Harold Coleman, for sharing with me his passion and fascination for the variety of cycling history, its technical aspects and its pure pleasures; and secondly Ray Craig, one of AUK's founder members, who taught me so much about long-distance cycling.

For the book itself, I must thank Penny Clarke and Hilary Lissenden for their belief in my original idea and their invaluable editorial input to bring my manuscript into a readily readable format. Dave Yates, frame builder *par excellence* and himself no mean randonneur, who supplied bikes for the illustrations but which regretably did not feature in all their glory (check his website for a glimpse of his talents). Fellow randonneurs and clubmates, Ivo Miesen, Chris Beynon and Paul Lawson, who willingly delved into their extensive photographic libraries for suitable pictures. AUK Chairman, Rocco Richardson, for his support of this project from the outset and to AUK champion Liz Creese for posing for the stretches on her bike. Cassie Lowe, of course, for her friendship and the invitation to join her and experience (in her words) 'the ultra-mack daddy ride of them all', and to Steve Born and the rest of the Cass Crew.

Other photographic contributors are acknowledged alongside the relevant pictures, but commercial organisations Bike Express and Zyro plc must also be commended for their prompt reactions to last-minute requests for material.

To all those people I have met along the road who have made my cycling so enjoyable, some of whom have given me snippets of their advice and experiences here and there – and to those riders who made me realise that you need a source of information, or suggested ideas and topics for this book – this book is for you.

Foreword

If you've got a bike and the inclination, this book takes you through every stage and all you need to know about being a long-distance cyclist. The world of cycling has become increasingly high-tech in recent years. The days of everyone with a single gear, fixed-wheel bike and a saddlebag are long gone. Long-distance competition may have declined over the years in favour of shorter, more easily absorbed events, but the challenge still exists, offering an opportunity for the 'stayers' to show their mettle. In fact, participation in ultra-distance riding for pleasure has never been greater, with audax rides (randonnées) and *sportive* rides attracting more and more people every year.

Today, there are many riders who prefer not to join a cycling club. The clubs always used to be the source of knowledge and guidance for novice cyclists – they still are – but 'privateers' can still benefit from the experience of others and this book will really help those people. It provides a thorough foundation for all aspiring long-distance cyclists. It also fills in the gaps where club cyclists perhaps don't know all the answers and it provides much useful information even for experienced riders whether they are tourists, randonneurs or racers.

There is no other book written in the last ten or fifteen years detailing the up-to-date knowledge, technology, style and opportunities in cycling but *The Long Distance Cyclists' Handbook* brings all of this within the grasp of any cyclist wishing to extend their personal horizons either for pleasure or competition.

I hope to see you all 'up the road' soon.

Rocco Richardson,
Chairman, Audax UK
March 2001

Get ready

1 Which bike?

Bicycles may look pretty similar at first glance, but they are as varied as fingerprints, each one designed for a different purpose.

Most people use one bike for all their cycling: utility rides to school, to work or to the shops; riding for pleasure; taking part in sponsored rides; or as their first bike to join a cycling club and begin racing. If you know the type of cycling you intend to do, such as touring or racing, you can select the most appropriate machine from the outset (*see* Table 1.1 and pp. 8–14). Invariably, though, even the most experienced riders tweak their choice of bike as their cycling activities or abilities evolve, or as new materials and components become available.

Table 1.1 Matching your bike to your cycling needs

	Touring		Audax[1]	Racing
	Off-road	**Road**		
Range of activities	• Day and charity rides • Camping or youth hostelling weekends or 1–3-week tours • Extended trans-continental touring		• Organised events (randonnées) of 100–2400 km and 'challenge rides' • Lightweight credit-card[2] touring	• Time-trials: 10 miles–24 hrs • Road records • Road races: single-day and stage • Ultra-marathon events, e.g. RAAM[3]
Distance per day	30–100 km	50–150 km	100–500 km	• 16–250 km in single-day events • 500–800 km in 24-hour races
Pace (kph)	5–20 kph	15–25 kph	15–30 kph	35–50 kph
Gears[4]	Usually 3 × 7, 8 or 9	Usually 2 or 3 × 7, 8 or 9	Usually 2 or 3 × 7, 8 or 9	Usually 2 × 9 or 10
Tyre size[5]	26 × 1.5–2.1"	700 c × 28–38	700 c × 23–32	700 c × 19–22
Luggage	Sometimes	Yes	Minimal	No
Mudguards	Sometimes	Usually	Usually	No
Lighting	Not often	Sometimes	For longer events	Only for 24-hour or similar

[1] See pp. 182–91.
[2] See pp. 11–12, 181.
[3] Stands for Race Across AMerica (see also pp. 190–7).
[4] See also Chapter 3, pp. 37–44.
[5] See also Chapter 3, pp. 24–31.

If your bicycle has to double up in its duties – say, touring and road racing, or touring and off-road riding – then you will have to concede a little performance in some areas, but that need not be a problem. Avoid the extremes of any cycling discipline and most bicycles can, with a bit of lateral thinking, be adapted for use in a variety of situations. Assuming your current bicycle is correctly adjusted to fit you (*see* Chapter 2, pp. 15–23), if you wish to adapt and improve it for riding longer distances the main areas to consider are gearing, wheels and luggage capacity. If, however, you need to change many parts on your bike it may be more economic to buy a new one than to upgrade a bike that is beyond its 'best-before date'.

Frame designs

All bicycles are a compromise between strength, stiffness, comfort, manoeuvrability, aerodynamics, weight, durability and luggage-carrying capacity. The bicycle must also be fit for its purpose. Just as you wear different shoes for running, hiking or going to work, so your choice of bicycle needs to be influenced by its intended use – whether that is to transport you across continents over a period of months, or as a performance machine for 200 km randonnées or 24-hour time-trials.

The Ultimate Universal Long Distance Bicycle does not exist. One rider's perfect bike may be totally unsuitable for someone else. Everyone has their own approach, but some common themes apply and there are a few methods which are generally accepted to be less suitable – although there will always be someone to prove otherwise! Figures 1.1 and 2.1 illustrate the main parts of a bicycle.

Comfort

You must be comfortable on your bike in order to ride efficiently for a long time. This applies just as much to racing as it does to touring (*see* Bike set-up, pp. 17–22, and Types of bicycle, pp. 8–14).

Light weight

Bicycles are propelled solely by your muscular effort. The heavier the bike and the rider, the harder it is to overcome the forces of inertia and gravity to get the bike into motion and keep it moving. Over a long distance, particularly in hilly areas, all this extra work will soon tire you out.

Durability

There is a degree of trade-off between reduced weight, durability and cost. Some very light bicycles are pared down to the minimum using ultra-light materials, but this can jeopardise their longevity. Shaving grams from a bicycle can be expensive when exotic materials like titanium, carbon fibre, magnesium or ergal alloy are employed. For many riders the cost of saving 200 g is not worth the cash – especially if you can perhaps lose even more weight from yourself just by exercising a little more or taking care over your diet (*see* also Chapter 6, Nutrition and hydration).

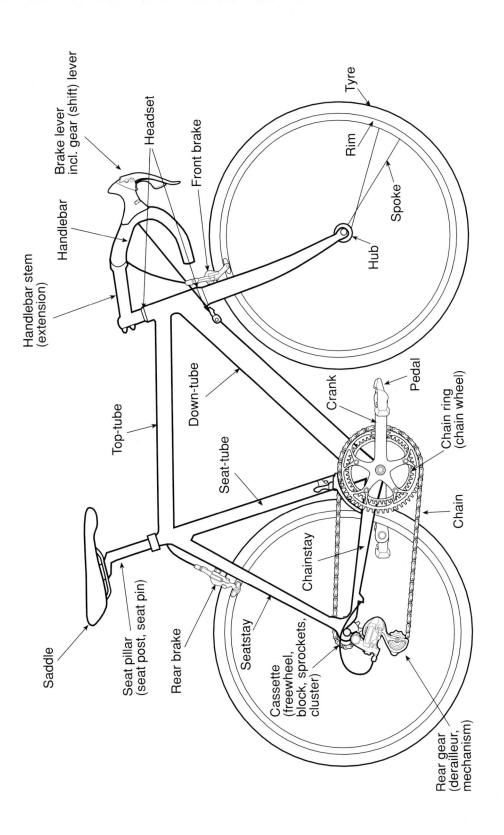

Figure 1.1 Component parts of a bicycle

Resistance forces

Minimise the forces of mechanical, rolling and aerodynamic resistance, and the easier the ride will be.

- **Mechanical resistance** is the friction created by the moving parts on the bike – the transmission (chain and gears), pedals, bottom bracket and hubs. Poorly maintained components make cycling more difficult; they will also wear out prematurely. Mechanical drag will increase if parts are badly fitted, damaged or inadequately lubricated.

- **Rolling resistance** is the effect of the tyres, their compound, construction and pressure against the road surface.

- **Aerodynamics** are most significant for the racing cyclist, because air resistance is the greatest force that a cyclist has to overcome (increasing exponentially and significant at speeds of 25 kph or more). This is less of an issue for touring cyclists, so you can happily cruise along in an upright position, with bulky panniers and loose clothing flapping in the breeze (although you might think differently about this force when you are battling into a strong headwind!).

Frame materials

All materials vary in their quality and one material is not always better than another. For example, a good steel frame can be lighter and stronger than a poor-quality titanium frame. Four principle materials are used for bicycle frame construction.

Steel

Frames made from lightweight steel are strong, durable and easily repairable. Steel is the most common material used by independent custom frame-builders. It is also a 'comfortable' material with a little 'give' in it when ridden. Companies like Reynolds (UK), Columbus (Italy) and Deda (Italy) all produce tube-sets with varying profiles and qualities – *see* also Useful addresses, pp. 204–6. Enquire with the company, their agent, your local bike shop or frame-builder for advice on the best tube-set for your needs.

Aluminium

Butted tubes

'Butted' tubes have less material in their centre to reduce weight, and have more material at their ends for stronger joints. 'Double-butted' means the tube has thicker walls at both ends. 'Triple-butted', however, means the butt is stepped into three thicknesses.

Aluminium is largely used by mass-producers, but former 'steel-only' frame-makers are beginning to use the material in response to customer demand. At around 40% the weight of steel, it has gained wide acceptance in the professional ranks in recent years. However, it has a lower fatigue life than steel so aluminium frames usually have very thick-walled tubes – or very large-diameter tubes with thinner walls – to improve the metal's strength and fatigue qualities. The resulting ride tends to be very stiff, which is desirable for racing but can prove uncomfortable over longer distances. Currently there are few places where aluminium frames can be repaired.

Most modern tube-sets use heat-treatments or have aluminium alloyed in different amounts with other metals to improve their characteristics. This has helped to enhance aluminium's status, and advances in material technology are making good framesets very affordable. However, the longevity of some aluminium frames is questionable.

Titanium
Possibly the ultimate material for a bicycle frame, titanium is nearly as light as aluminium but far stronger even than steel. It is impervious to rust or corrosion, has a 'springy' feel which it retains for life, and fatigue resistance which surpasses both steel and aluminium. However, it is very expensive to manufacture and work with, production runs are short, and few frame-builders use it.

Carbon fibre
Carbon composite frames are either made from tubes joined together using aerospace adhesives, or are moulded in a one-piece 'monocoque' design. Carbon fibre is best used in a moulded form, where the material can be varied to fine-tune the ride. The material is relatively expensive; most frames are designed for use in competition. Being a moulded construction, it is not easy to adjust the dimensions for a rider's individual needs, but by careful choice of components some carbon frames can be adapted to make excellent machines for lightweight leisure pursuits.

Protection treatments
Both steel and aluminium need protection to avoid rust and corrosion. Steel frames are usually painted or powder coated. Chrome-plating can be used for a tougher finish, but this is weighty and expensive to apply, so it is usually restricted to strategic locations – such as the dropouts and the right-hand chainstay, where paintwork is easily damaged by the hub axles or the chain. Chroming needs to be done with care if the tubes are not to rust away from the inside.

Aluminium frames can be painted or anodised (an oxidising process which protects the surface of the metal). Since titanium is resistant to corrosion, most frames are left bare and brushed or polished to a fine sheen – paint would just make them heavier. Similarly, carbon fibre doesn't require any extra protection but it does need to be handled carefully to ensure that the fibres are not scratched or damaged. Otherwise, potential stress points can be created in the material – possibly with catastrophic consequences.

Factory-made or custom-built
People have ridden around the world on heavy, mass-produced steel bikes with just a single gear or with simple hub gears (*see* pp. 37–44). But like any activity, if you're keen and 'into it', there is no limit when it comes to spending money. You must ensure that whatever bike you choose, it is fit for its purpose and is:

- your size and adjusted to fit you

- suitable for the use you intend for it

- well maintained

- appropriately geared for your type of riding.

Most people fit production-made bikes – many of which offer remarkably good value for money – and you can adapt almost any bike to any purpose. Experienced cyclists, though, may appreciate the benefits of a bicycle tailored to fit their needs with a made-to-measure frameset and personally selecting every last detail from the colour of the paint to the make of the bottom bracket.

Types of bicycle

Road touring bikes

The traditional touring bicycle (*see* Figure 1.2) has been refined over the years, but remains largely unaltered with the following characteristics:

· lightweight but strong frame

· usually made from steel alloy tubes, brazed or silver-soldered together with reinforcing lugs (though some are welded aluminium frames)

· 'relaxed' geometry – i.e. designed for comfort rather than quick response

· 700 c wheels with wide tyres

· generous clearances for wide tyres and mudguards

· cantilever brakes often preferred to regular side-pull brakes (*see* also pp. 44–5)

· triple chainset with wide-ratio gears (*see* also pp. 37–42)

· drop handlebars for variety of hand positions

Figure 1.2 Touring bike: lightweight but heavy-duty, and designed for a comfortable ride. These bikes are fitted with a wide range of gears and capable of carrying all your luggage in panniers attached to racks over the wheels

- pannier carrier
- fittings for mudguards
- two or three bottle cages
- fittings for lights
- 'low-rider' carrier eyes on the front forks (if front panniers are anticipated)
- pump peg – usually under the top tube but, less obtrusively, on the left-hand seat-stay or behind the seat-tube if there is room.

Mountain-bikes

Mountain-bikes revitalised the cycle market across the world in the early 1980s. Their upright position with controls in easy reach, wide-ratio gears and comfortable tyres made them extremely popular (*see* Figure 1.3). Their main features are:

- strong frames, usually welded steel or aluminium
- sloping top-tube and high bottom-bracket height for clearance over rough ground
- wide, chunky tyres
- 26" wheels (smaller diameter than 700 c)
- cantilever or V-brakes
- triple chainset with wide-ratio gears
- straight handlebars with all controls within easy reach.

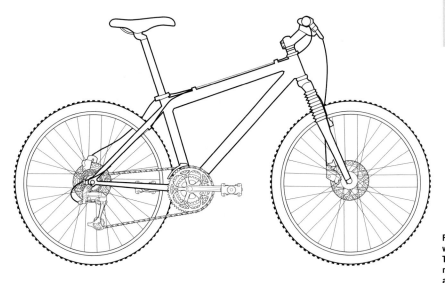

Frame ends or dropouts

There are two common styles of frame end or dropout (where the wheel attaches to the bicycle frame).

- Vertical dropouts are the best for both racing and touring frames. Their shape prevents the rear wheel from pulling to one side and the tyre then rubbing against the chainstay.
- Horizontal dropouts allow the rear wheel to be moved back in the frame if a bigger tyre is used, or if the wheel becomes buckled, but the distance is minimal. In a race the rider will either fit a new wheel from race service or abandon the event. Buckled wheels should not be fitted lopsidedly in the dropouts. This only puts more pressure on the wheel skewer and bearings and damages the hub.
- Both styles are available with threaded 'eyes' to take mudguard and carrier bolts, or without eyes for pure racing bikes.

Figure 1.3 Mountain-bike: shown here with front suspension and disc-brakes. These bikes can make exellent touring machines if fitted with smooth tyres and rigid forks

Many innovations, originally introduced for mountain-bike racing, have now become commonplace on even some budget mountain-bikes. These include:

- suspension forks
- rear suspension
- suspension seatposts
- disc brakes.

Unless you frequently ride off-road you don't need any major suspension parts. Suspension adds to the weight and complexity of the bike, and absorbs your energy. The big advantage of the 26" mountain-bike wheel is its strength, so you can load up your bike for touring quite comfortably with less fear of spoke breakages than with the traditional 700 c wheel. For road use, replace deeply treaded tyres with ones which have a smoother profile. These roll much more easily over tarmac and most are capable of handling brief off-road excursions too.

Racing bikes

There are several sub-divisions of racing bike (*see* Figure 1.4), with unique designs for time-trialling. Top riders even have special ultra-light bikes just for the mountains. The key features of regular road bikes are:

- strong, very light frames
- made from steel, aluminium, titanium or carbon fibre
- designed for quick handling response
- 700 c wheels with narrow (19–23 mm) tyres

Figure 1.4 Racing bike: road racing frames are now often made from aluminium – thin-walled fat tubes offer reduced weight and improved stiffness. Note also the narrow, lightweight wheels

- close clearances

- dual-pivot side-pull brakes

- double chainset and close-ratio gears

- drop handlebars for variety of hand positions

- gear shifters incorporated in brake levers

- may have concealed cable runs for aerodynamic or aesthetic reasons (though most mechanics prefer external slotted stops for bare wire cable runs)

- fittings for two bottle cages.

In Europe, professional cycle races often last 5–7 hours, so the riders need to be comfortable. Consequently, many professionals' bikes have more relaxed seat-angles than those used by most amateur racers in Britain and the USA. Having the seat-angle one or two degrees shallower is more comfortable and helps the riders sit back in the saddle for long Alpine or Pyrenean climbs, utilising more of the large muscles in the thigh to maintain a stable position and with less stress on the knees.

Audax or *sportive* bikes and credit-card touring

Bikes between the extremes of road racing and loaded-touring (*see* Figure 1.5): for those cyclists who prefer a lighter, faster style of riding but remain shy of full-on racing. Audax riding doesn't demand the high speed, strength and competitive edge of the road racer, nor is it the unhurried progress of the baggage-laden tourist. Characterised by minimal luggage and covering significant distances in a day – either touring from one guest house to another (often referred to as 'credit-card touring' in the US), or riding a randonnée or *sportive* event – the bike for this type of rider is a combination of the responsiveness of a racing bike and the comfort of a traditional touring bike. Its main characteristics are:

Figure 1.5 Audax bike: similar to road bikes, bikes for audax or *sportive* rides are lightweight and carry minimal luggage. Mudguards and a wide range of gears add to the comfort factor, and lights are essential for night-time riding

- strong, lightweight frame similar to the road-racing machine
- most commonly made from steel, although other materials are used
- slightly more relaxed angles for a little extra comfort
- 700 c wheels with 23–28 mm tyres
- clearance for medium depth tyres and mudguards
- fittings for two or three bottles, lightweight luggage, lights and a pump
- double or triple chainset for wide range of gears.

Compact frames

Compact frames with top-tubes sloping up from the seat-tube to the head-tube are common in mountain-bike design because of the added clearance they provide between rider and frame. (This is especially useful when tackling uneven ground if the bike is brought to a sudden, unexpected halt!) This design is now being adopted on the road in both racing and touring worlds (*see* Figure 1.6), with the hidden advantages that the shorter tubes use less material and are lighter, stiffer and can be made more aerodynamic. The bike's centre of gravity is lower, making it both more stable and quicker to manoeuvre, especially when cornering and descending. A long seat-pillar made from titanium or carbon fibre adds to the comfort of the bike.

Alternative bicycle styles

Strict guidelines dictate the design of bicycles used in competition, but for leisure cycling there are no such restrictions and many innovative models exist.

Figure 1.6 Compact bike: upward sloping frames became popular through mountain-bike designs, but they are now becoming more common for both racing and touring frames as they offer greater rigidity, lighter weight and a more stable, lower centre of gravity

Figure 1.7 The Moulton: this unique design is a miracle of engineering. The high-pressure tyres and suspension make it excellent for long-distance cycling – and one size really does fit just about everyone – but the best models do carry a premium price

The Moulton

The Moulton (*see* Figure 1.7) is a unique British-made, small-wheeled cycle (using 17" or 20" tyres) complete with front and rear suspension. First marketed at the beginning of the 1960s and then re-launched in the early 1980s, these machines have been used to break cycling speed records, ride across deserts and around the world. Their design – a triangulated web of small-diameter tubes – is strong, light, comfortable and practical; most models split into two parts for easier transport. There is even a dedicated Moulton Owners' Club (*see* also Useful addresses, p. 207).

The tricycle

Another peculiarly British machine is the tricycle. Trikes have great luggage-carrying capacity and are very stable at low speed (such as climbing steep hills when heavily loaded) or in icy conditions. They are slower, though, and they demand a totally different riding technique as compared to bicycles.

HPVs and recumbents

Human Powered Vehicles (HPVs) and recumbent cycles – in which the rider sits in a supine position, usually low-down and close to the ground (making these vehicles very aerodynamic) – are a small but growing niche. Various different designs exist with either two or three wheels. Opponents of recumbents quote the poor climbing ability and the safety issue against other traffic with the rider being so low. Their supporters counter these arguments with faster speeds downhill and on the flat, the stability of being close to the ground and the vehicle's unusual silhouette as positive advantages over regular bicycles.

Tandems

For togetherness on the road, there's nothing to match a tandem. Often popular with mixed couples because they enable two different power outputs to be married together – thus enabling male and female riders (or any unmatched pair) to enjoy cycling together – and when they are ridden by two powerful riders, tandems can be exceptional speed machines. A good-quality tandem can be expensive, but there is a wide choice of budget machines suitable for leisure and touring purposes.

In summary

Whatever your cycling style, your bicycle must be comfortable and reliable. Even professional racing cyclists have to be comfortable and will compromise the most aerodynamic position for one that allows them to ride for hours on end, day after day. It's no good taking a hammering from the road on Day One if your event lasts a week or more!

Few pros choose to risk failure by pushing the boundaries of material applications until they are convinced about a product's reliability. Exotic designs or materials in frames and components are far more common in British or US time-trials than they are in a Continental Classic race.

Before you invest in a specialist machine, you can use and adapt whatever bike you have. When you know which avenue of cycling appeals to you most, you can make an informed decision about buying a new bike. Don't be surprised if, in a few years' time, you have a whole fleet of different bicycles to cover all of your cycling pursuits!

2 Bike set-up

There are three contact points on your bike: the saddle, the pedals and the handlebars. These three points have to be adjusted to fit the bike to you. Unless custom-made, bicycle frames are supplied in standard sizes – although standard sizes can differ from manufacturer to manufacturer! You can then fine-tune the bike to your individual measurements by adjusting the position of the saddle and the handlebars.

Altering any one of the three contact points will affect the other two. Raising the handlebars will bring them closer to the saddle and change your weight distribution. Sliding the saddle forwards can reduce the reach to the handlebars but may compromise the pedalling position.

Frame sizes

Bicycles are made in different sizes because cyclists are different sizes. Bicycle frames are usually measured along the length of the seat-tube (*see* Figure 2.1 overleaf).

- Traditional British measurement: from the middle of the bottom bracket to the top of the seat-tube (*centre to top* or *c-t*). This can be misinterpreted, though, especially if the seat-tube is raised above the height of the top-tube.

- European method: from the middle of the bottom bracket to the centre of the intersection between the seat-tube and the top-tube (*centre to centre* or *c-c*).

These two methods differ by about 2 cm, but it can be more if large-diameter tubing is employed. Some manufacturers have their own methods of measuring and sizing frames, so when buying a bike or frame it is important you know exactly which points of reference are being used.

On a standard frame, where the top-tube is horizontal and parallel to the floor, the *length* of the frame is measured along the top-tube from the centre of the seat-tube to the centre of the head-tube. On frames with sloping top-tubes, the frame's length is measured as if it had a horizontal top-tube and the reading is taken where this line intersects the seat-post.

The bike should look and feel 'balanced'. As a general rule of thumb, on a well-balanced bike the length of head-tube is similar to the length of exposed seat-pillar. A tall rider will have a large frame, but he will also have more seat-pillar showing out of the frame. A small rider will ride with less seat-pillar exposed, and the frame and head-tube length will be shorter too. With the cranks horizontal, the top-tube should fall between your knees. If the top-tube is above your knees, the frame is too big – and *vice-versa*.

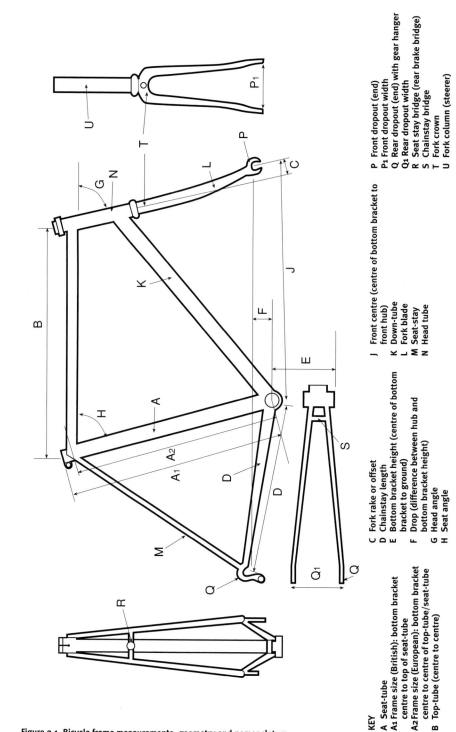

Figure 2.1 Bicycle frame measurements, geometry and nomenclature

KEY

A Seat-tube
A1 Frame size (British): bottom bracket centre to top of seat-tube
A2 Frame size (European): bottom bracket centre to centre of top-tube/seat-tube
B Top-tube (centre to centre)

C Fork rake or offset
D Chainstay length
E Bottom bracket height (centre of bottom bracket to ground)
F Drop (difference between hub and bottom bracket height)
G Head angle
H Seat angle

J Front centre (centre of bottom bracket to front hub)
K Down-tube
L Fork blade
M Seat-stay
N Head tube

P Front dropout (end)
P1 Front dropout width
Q Rear dropout (end) with gear hanger
Q1 Rear dropout width
R Seat stay bridge (rear brake bridge)
S Chainstay bridge
T Fork crown
U Fork column (steerer)

If in doubt between two frame sizes, choose the smaller one. This will be lighter, have a lower centre of gravity for better stability and manoeuvrability, and be stiffer and more efficient in terms of energy transfer.

Frame size and wheel size have no direct relationship. Standard road or touring bikes for adults have a wheel size described as 700 c. Shorter riders under about 160 cm (5'3") may require road frames with a smaller wheel size, usually 650 c (approx. 26") – although resourceful custom-builders can produce bikes with 700 c wheels for riders as short as 152 cm (5'0"). Universally, mountain bikes use a 26" wheel size that is a little smaller than the 650 c.

Your position on the bike will need to be altered according to the type of riding you do. A time-triallist racing 100 miles may be able to hold an extremely aerodynamic position for the 4 hours or so of that event, but he is unlikely to be comfortable in that position for a 24-hour race or be able to produce the varied power requirements of a road-racer. For long-distance riding, comfort is always a more important consideration than pure speed or aerodynamics, and that invariably means adopting a less extreme position.

> For a standard frame with a horizontal top-tube, choose a frame size about two-thirds of the your inside leg length. A frame with a severely sloping top-tube may be only half of your inside leg-length.

Sizing by numbers

Many different calculations have been suggested over the years to define the ideal riding position. The fact that there are so many different methods really proves that none of them is totally correct. All riders differ – in the length relationship between their limbs, their flexibility, and even in their perception of what is comfortable.

Saddle height

Correct saddle height (the longest distance between pedal and saddle) is essential both for efficient pedalling and to minimise the likelihood of injury. Seatposts can be adjusted up or down to alter saddle height. The exact height of your seat depends on many variables, making precise calculations very difficult. More commonly, the saddle is set close to an ideal height and then adjusted after riding.

The factors affecting saddle height are:

· foot size and length of toes

· rider flexibility

· pedalling style

· crank length

· seat-angle

· type of riding

· duration of ride

· terrain being ridden

· thickness of clothing

- type of pedal and shoes used

- unequal leg limb lengths

- compression of suspension parts used

- personal preference and experience.

As a starting point, sit on the bike with your heels on the pedals (*see* Figure 2.2). With one pedal at its lowest point – in line with the seat-tube – your stretched leg should be just straight and you should not rock on the saddle when you pedal backwards in this position. Ask a friend to check this by riding behind you and watch for any movement in your hips or spine. When you pedal normally with the balls of your feet on the pedals, you will have a slight bend at the knee. Usually, you *cannot* touch the ground with both feet when sitting on the saddle – but you should be able to reach the floor with the ball of one foot, without having to lean the bike over too far.

Adjust the seatpost by small increments – 2–5 mm per week – so that your muscles can adjust to, and cope with, the new position. Do not raise the saddle to a point where there is significant rocking of your hips, or where you are stretching to reach the pedals. If your saddle is set too high it can cause serious damage to your knees or tendons. You are likely to be very sore if you are sliding from side to side over the saddle to power the pedals (*see* also Chapter 7, pp. 82–3).

a

b

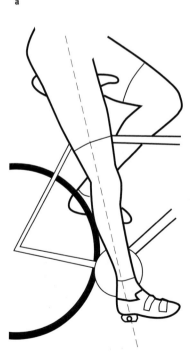
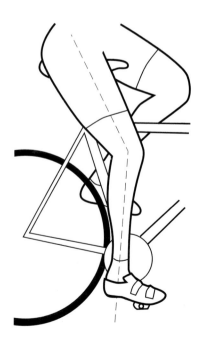

**Figure 2.2 Adjusting saddle height:
a) adjust the saddle so that your leg is straight with your heel on the pedal;
b) when you ride you will have a slight bend at the knee without undue rocking. This is a good starting position for achieving the correct saddle height**

Saddle position

Your saddle can be tilted or moved forwards or backwards on the seatpost. If you have long thighs (in proportion to your overall leg length) you will want to sit further back behind the bottom bracket (requiring either a shallower seat-angle, or a seatpost with more layback (*see* Figure 2.3a)). Riders with short thighs may prefer to bring their saddle further forwards (requiring a steeper seat-angle, or using a seatpost with less layback – or even an 'in-line' seatpost (*see* Figure 2.3b)).

The saddle should be level, but a tilt up or down of about 5 degrees is acceptable if that is more comfortable for you. If your saddle is tilted more than that, an upward raise to the front indicates that it is set too low; if it points downwards it is set too high. Women, however, may prefer a downward tilt to relieve pressure on their pubic area. The modern 'cut away' saddles go a long way towards alleviating this problem.

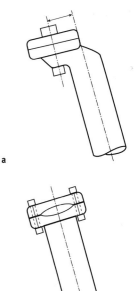

a

b

Figure 2.3 Seatposts: a) layack; b) in-line. By using a different seatpost you can achieve a different position on your bike

Knee over pedal spindle

As a guide, you can set your saddle so that your forward knee is directly over the pedal spindle when the cranks are horizontal ('quarter to three'). This setting is not imperative, since your knee is only in this position for 1/360° of a revolution, and then only if you do not slide forwards or backwards or get out the saddle.

Riding *style* has more influence on fore and aft positioning of the saddle than actual measurement. Riders trying to maximise power over a short distance – e.g. time-triallists, triathletes and track riders – may want to bring their saddle further forwards (*see* Figure 2.4a), but when you are riding over a long distance you will

Figure 2.4a Saddle position: the short-distance time-triallist pulls himself forward over the bottom bracket

Figure 2.4b Saddle position: the long-distance rider finds a more comfortable and powerful position by sitting further back over the rear wheel

usually find that setting the saddle further back is more comfortable (*see* Figure 2.4b). This is particularly true when climbing long hills. You may need to re-adjust the height of your saddle if you change its position relative to the pedals.

Handlebar position

Once the saddle is correctly positioned, your *reach* (the distance from the saddle to the handlebars) needs to be considered. This is the length of the top-tube and the length of the handlebar stem, but it is affected by the frame angles, seatpost and position of the saddle on the seatpost.

As with saddle height, there is no single correct measurement or calculation for determining the correct reach. To a large degree, correct reach is 'what feels right' and is influenced by:

- length of spine
- length of arms
- hand size and length of fingers
- rider flexibility
- type of handlebars

- riding style
- type of riding
- duration of ride
- terrain being ridden
- unequal arm lengths
- personal preference and rider experience.

Fine adjustment is achieved by selecting an appropriate length of handlebar stem and its position. You should be able to reach all parts of the handlebars and the brake levers comfortably for proper control of the bike (*see* Figure 2.5). Ideally, your back should be at an angle between 0° and 45° from the ground – i.e. absolutely flat for time-trialling and more upright for more relaxed riding. Your arms will be bent at the elbows, acting like suspension, absorbing the shocks from the road. If your arms are too straight and rigid you will soon tire from the constant vibrations of the road.

Figure 2.5 The classic road racing position – shown here 'on the drops' on a turbo-trainer: the rider's back is low and his arms are bent at the elbows for some shock absorption

For comfort, most road riders spend the majority of their time riding either on the 'tops' (the straight part of their dropped handlebars), or on the hoods of the brake levers, only dropping on to the lower part of the handlebars for more intense efforts. If you spend most of your time 'down on the hooks', your handlebars are probably set too high.

Table 2.1 Resolving positioning problems

Problem(s)	Cycling effect(s)	Reason	Solution(s)
• Difficult to reach the handlebars • Pains in back, shoulders, neck or arms	Bike control compromised; steering and braking very difficult	Overstretched	Reduce reach; change to shorter handlebar stem; change to frame with shorter top-tube (or steeper seat-angle); slide saddle forwards
• Sitting very upright • Feeling squashed or cramped • Knees hit the handlebars when climbing or sprinting out of the saddle • Pain in back, shoulders or wrists	Too much weight on saddle; too much weight on wrists 'Twitchy' steering Bruised knees	Too cramped	Increase reach; fit a longer stem; change the frame for one with longer top-tube (and/or shallower seat-angle); slide saddle backwards

It is usual to set the handlebars lower than the height of the saddle. This presents a smaller frontal area to the wind and improves weight distribution between your front and rear wheels. Leisure riders may prefer to sit more upright, for less back strain or less pressure on their wrists. Transferring *too much* of your weight from the front wheel to the rear wheel will make the steering very light, add to the stress on the rear wheel and increase pressure on your backside.

Ensure that your handlebar stem has enough length securely fitted into the fork column. Custom-built touring frames can have an extended head-tube so that your handlebars can be safely positioned higher than normal, without resorting to a large and ungainly frame size.

Foot position

Your pedals are the third contact point with the bike. For comfort and for maximum power, the balls of your feet should be directly above the pedal spindle – though some riders who prefer to 'twiddle' very low gears may set their feet a fraction further back. If you do not use any form of pedal binding your feet will find their natural position on the pedals. Toe-clips or 'clipless' pedals will vastly improve your efficiency but it is vital that your feet, ankles, knees and hips are all in natural alignment.

As a general rule, when viewed from the front your knees should move up and down in a straight line when pedalling. Any circular motion may indicate a problem with your foot position, but if you feel comfortable, don't alter anything. If your toes point outwards, you need to set up your cleats to replicate this foot position on your bike. If you get pains in the outside of your knee, point your toes outwards a little more. Similarly, if the inside of your knee hurts, adjust your cleats so your toes point inwards more.

Keep your feet as close to the cranks as possible without your heels or ankles hitting the cranks or chainstays. You may have to slide the cleats to one side of your shoes, even 'butcher' (physically alter) them, or space the pedal a little further from the crank with a thin washer for correct positioning.

An experienced coach, knowledgeable cycle dealer or clubmate may be able to help you set up your shoes and pedals. If you still have problems, however, seek a podiatrist who can prescribe wedges or orthotic insoles; these adjust the plane of your feet for more comfortable and efficient pedalling. (*See* also pp. 84–5, and p. 158.)

Measurements

Perfect bicycle fit is a matter of trial and error to achieve comfort depending on your experience and flexibility. You can get used to a position that is not necessarily ideal for you, and correcting it may initially feel uncomfortable as your muscles adapt to new positions. For this reason, it is best to make alterations to your position in small increments, usually no more than 2–5 mm at a time, allowing a week or two to get accustomed to the new position before you adjust it further (or back to its original location!). However, if your position is wildly 'out', then there is no harm in making larger adjustments to get 'on track' almost immediately.

Make a note of the relevant measurements on your bike using a table like the one shown below. This will help you should you ever need to replace or rebuild a bike, or if you change anything like the handlebars or seatpost.

Table 2.2 Make a note of the relevant measurements on your bike

Measurement	mm
(a) Bottom bracket to top of saddle	
(b) Saddle to handlebars	
(c) Drop from saddle to handlebars (may be negative)	
(d) Top-tube length	
(e) Handlebar stem length	
(f) Distance of saddle behind bottom bracket	
(g) Crank length	

These measurements may be slightly different on bikes used for different purposes, but if you find that you are much more comfortable on one bike than another, comparing these figures might reveal why this is the case – and help you to achieve comfort throughout your bicycle fleet.

3 Anatomy of a bike

Wheels and tyres

Wheels and tyres make the greatest contribution to the 'feel' of any bike. Your personal priorities – strength, flexibility, comfort, manoeuvrability, aerodynamics, weight, luggage-carrying capacity – determine what sort of wheel you should choose, though elements such as comfort can be greatly affected by your choice of tyres.

Quick-release levers

The quick-release (QR) cam (*see* Figure 3.1) used to secure wheels has been used in cycling for 80 years, to make wheel changes a very quick and simple operation.

The QR lever operates on a cam and is 'folded' into position. The thread on the skewer adjusts the QR lever and nut for different widths of dropout so that the lever is just tight when closed.

Wheel choice

For road racing, strong, lightweight, stiff wheels are required. Aerodynamics play their part but are not the roadman's priority, since much of the time he will be drafting behind other riders. If road-racing wheels are too stiff they will transmit every imperfection in the road surface on to you, battering you into submission before you reach the finish line. Standard road-racing wheels (*see* Figure 3.1) have small-flange hubs, 32 spokes (each one usually crossing three other spokes), and lightweight rims (about 400 g) of a box section or shallow aerodynamic V-section.

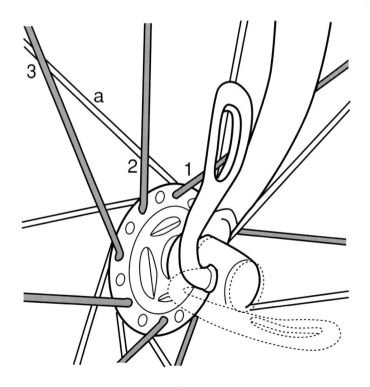

Figure 3.1 The quick-release (QR) cam: when on hubs these have an eccentric cam to 'fold' them into position and hold the wheel securely. Note the 'three cross' spokes: spoke (a) crosses three others (1–3) between the hub and the rim

Time-triallists can take advantage of fully aerodynamic 'disc' wheels (*see* Figure 3.2). Although heavier than standard road wheels, their smooth profile eliminates any turbulence created by the spokes. Unlike road races, where speed can fluctuate dramatically, time-trials are ridden at a near constant pace, making discs ideal. Disc wheels are prohibited in road races because of their susceptibility to side winds, and front discs are rarely used (often prohibited) because of handling difficulties. Their weight and inertia make them a poor choice for variable speed events anyway.

A good compromise is the deep-section wheel. Some use standard hubs (usually with fewer spokes); others have integral carbon blades replacing the spokes. Their open centre-section makes them much more manageable in difficult conditions. Rim rigidity is essential for low spoke numbers – so they are not often comfortable enough for long road events. Rims can have an alloy braking surface, but lighter ones may be all carbon-fibre and require special cork compound brake blocks.

Traditionally, riders selected their rims, hubs and spokes and had them built into a pair of wheels by a local wheelbuilder. Today the choice of ready-made wheels is quite bewildering, with technical claims and exotic styles of hub, spoke and rim – based on weight-saving, aerodynamics and strength – to tempt the keen cyclist. Eclectic spoking patterns and special rims such as those used by Rolf[1] and Shimano allow spoke counts as low as 12 or 14 per wheel. Vectran[2] spokes in Spinergy Spox wheels shave over 400 g from traditional wheel weights. Such esoteric equipment might be quite acceptable, even advantageous, in racing circles with a back-up team car at hand, but the independent long-distance rider needs to think about maintenance and the likelihood of replacement parts in remote areas.

Figure 3.2 Aerodynamic wheels on a time-trial bike: a rear disc wheel and a front tri-spoke. Note also the profiling of the frame tubes, seatpost, forks, stays, handlebars and stem to create the smoothest possible airflow around the bike

[1]Manufacturer of lightweight wheels with a unique 'paired' spoking pattern.
[2]Vectran is a strong, lightweight composite fibre similar to Kevlar.

How many spokes?

With more spokes in a wheel, the load is shared better and the spokes do not have to be overtightened. If fewer spokes are used, greater tension is needed.

The spoke holes (h) in 32- or 28-hole rims are further apart, so if a spoke breaks in a 32 or 28 h wheel then the rim will spring further out of true compared to a 36 h one.

Wheel choice for the randonneur or adventure cyclist should be tempered by the durability and availability of the component parts. Regular 36-spoke wheels are a safe compromise between strength and weight, and essential if you are going to do any loaded travelling, even with the stronger 26" mountain-bike wheels. A lighter rider with a smooth pedalling action might manage comfortably with 32 (or even 28) spokes but the gains of lighter weight and reduced turbulence of four spokes per wheel for leisure riding are small compared to the security and durability of 36 spokes per wheel.

Like the road-racer's wheels, the cross three-spoke pattern is ideal. You might benefit from crossing four spokes if you are heavy or carry a lot of luggage. Tourists can take advantage of the same quality hubs and spokes that the racing cyclists use, and sometimes even use exactly the same rims. However, heavier riders, or those carrying luggage, would be advised to use broader-sectioned rims together with fatter tyres. A broad tyre on a narrow rim may have its sidewall damaged, and a narrow tyre on a broad rim will 'bottom out' too easily and cause damage to the rim.

For more extreme riding, such as touring with extensive camping equipment, even stronger wheels with 40 or 48 spokes are a wise investment. These are not always easy to find, though.

Wheel size

After over 100 years of evolution the sports bicycle has become almost standardised with 700 c wheels. This size provides an excellent compromise between rolling resistance, strength, comfort and aerodynamics. Almost without exception, mountain-bikes have adopted 26" wheels. These are inherently stronger due to their smaller diameter, making them more suited to rough off-road riding.

The only significant variant on these two sizes has been the small wheel of the Moulton cycle and its derivatives (see also p. 13) which has managed to plough its own furrow and grow a dedicated band of followers within the cycling fraternity. The Moulton, which originally had 16" wheels and then more recently 17" and 20" wheels, combines some very clever and unique suspension applications. By using narrow tyres and rims designed to withstand high pressures, Dr Alex Moulton overcame the rolling resistance issue usually associated with small-diameter wheels. His design has the added advantage of low weight, quick acceleration and minimal air resistance, and it really opens up the frame to suit all sizes of rider and for easy load carrying.

Rims

Regard rims as consumable items. They do wear out, especially with more powerful braking systems. Modern lightweight rims roll better than their heavier predecessors, but at the expense of having thinner sidewalls and being less durable. Check your rims regularly for sidewall wear. If a rim wall feels at all concave, replace it. Rim walls are only about 1–2 mm thick, so wear of just 0.2 mm can have dramatic consequences especially when combined with high tyre pressures. Do not spend a fortune on rims, but it is worth buying good quality hubs as these can be re-built into wheels time and time again.

Deep V-section rims are very strong (*see* Figure 3.3a), but their extra metal makes them heavier and less 'forgiving' than standard box-section rims (*see* Figure 3.3b). For most leisure riders the box section, or very shallow V-section rim is the best choice.

For top racing performance most riders prefer 'sprint' rims (*see* Figure 3.3c) used with tubular tyres. These are lighter and stronger than the u-shaped profile of high pressure (HP) or 'clincher' rims. However, modern technology has brought tremendous advantages to regular tyres and many riders now prefer the convenience associated with clincher rims and tyres.

Spokes

The most popular spokes for lightweight bikes are 'double-butted' and made from stainless steel.

'Double-butted' spokes are thicker at both ends than they are in the middle – because spokes are stressed at the hub and the rim. Spokes rarely break in the middle of the blade. Plain-gauge spokes have the same diameter throughout their length. Using double-butted spokes saves about 170 g (6 oz) in a pair of wheels. This is a significant reduction of rolling weight. The marginal extra strength afforded by plain-gauge spokes is offset by this extra weight. However, if 'bullet-proof' wheels are required, then you may prefer plain-gauge spokes and these may be better in light wheels with very few spokes. Old spokes can be re-used when re-building wheels with a new rim, but if they have done long service in a wheel then it is wise to replace them and not risk fatigue fracture.

Aerodynamic spokes have flat profiles and some require special slots in the hub. 'Spoke nipples' (the threaded 'nuts' which secure the spoke to the rim) can be made in aluminium to save weight, but this is a soft material and only recommended for very special, lightweight wheels which do not see frequent service. For the vast majority of purposes it is best to use the standard and much more durable nickel-plated brass nipples.

Tyre selection

For a given load using the same tyre pressure, the sidewalls of a narrow tyre compress more than those of a wide one. As the tyre rolls, this deflection of the tyre shape absorbs energy; but the energy is not returned to the tyre as it regains its shape. The less deformity in the tyre, the less energy is absorbed. Hence the racers' desire for very high pressures in very supple tyres (high number of threads per inch, *tpi*).

Rolling resistance is related to the contact area of the tyre on the ground. Under a heavy load, a narrow tyre has a longer contact area with the ground and flexes a greater proportion of the tyre. Wider tyres have a shorter, rounder contact point with the ground and deflect less, making them suitable for use with heavier loads.

The optimum values for tyre width, diameter, suppleness and weight depend on the intended use and load.

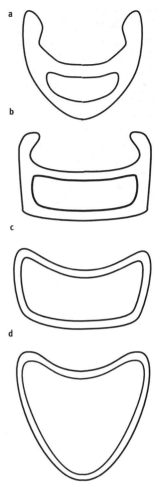

Figure 3.3 Rim cross sections: a) V-section; b) box section; c) sprint; d) aero-sprint

Table 3.1 The relative merits of wide and narrow tyres

	Disadvantages	Benefits
Wide tyres (>28 mm)	• Heavy, weight impedes acceleration and climbing • Cannot take high pressures • Greater deflection (twist), especially when cornering at speed • Feel unresponsive to the racing cyclist • Poor aerodynamic profile	• Less deformation when loaded, good at supporting heavy loads • Increased comfort and shock absorption • Wider tyres have lower rolling resistance*
Narrow tyres (<25 mm)	• Little shock absorption, may be uncomfortable especially over long distances • Poor load-carrying capability	• Light weight for better acceleration and climbing • High pressures essential • More likely to have supple casing • Responsive feel • Minimal deflection when cornering

*Compared to a narrower tyre of equal wheel diameter and same tyre pressure. Low tyre pressures increase rolling resistance.

Time-triallists often prefer very narrow 18 or 19 mm tyres, to hug the profile of their rims for least disturbance of the air. In fact, most would be better off using 21–23 mm tyres, as preferred by most road riders, especially in longer events. These give a significantly more comfortable ride; their handling properties – especially in wet conditions or on corners – are greatly enhanced; and they have a lower rolling resistance.

Tourists seeking comfort and load-carrying abilities need the cushioning of a fatter tyre. Choosing a tyre of much less than 32 mm could be disastrous, as its carcass will deform so much that either the rim will chafe the sidewall of the tyre or the tyre will actually 'bottom out' against the rim. A better choice for a touring bike with 700 c wheels are tyres with a cross-section of 32–38 mm, inflated in the region of 85 psi down to 60 psi. Mountain-bikes, or hybrid machines using 26" wheels, usually have wider tyres – either 1.25–1.8" with slick 'road' treads, or 1.5–2.3" knobbly tyres for off-road use. Here, recommended tyre pressures may vary from over 80 psi for the narrowest down to just 40 psi for the widest tyres used on soft ground.

For the randonneur wanting both comfort and performance, and carrying light loads, tyres in the 23–32 mm range are recommended. The narrower tyres are more performance-oriented with their higher pressures and lesser cushioning ability, but over long distances the smooth rolling and comfort afforded by the fatter tyre outweighs the performance issues required by racing cyclists.

Tyres have a five-digit ETRTO[3] designation. The first two digits indicate the depth of the tyre; the second show its *bead diameter*, i.e. what wheel size it fits. It is important to specify the correct diameter tyre to fit your rims. The most common size for lightweight bikes is 622 mm for 700 c tyres (various depths). The 26" size is divided between 559 mm for pure mountain-bikes – although there are plenty of road tyres to fit these rims – and 571 mm for 26" racing wheels.

[3]European Tyre and Rim Trade Organisation.

Table 3.2 Tyre and wheel sizes

ETRTO no. Bead seat diameter (mm)	French designation	Nominal size (in.) (rolling diameter × height)	Typical application
559		26 × 2	Mountain-bikes and derivatives
571		26 × ¾	26" triathlon and time-trial wheels
571	650 C	26 × 1¼	Utility bikes
622	700 C	27 × ¾ 28 × 1¼	Sports bikes – training, racing and touring
630		27 × 1¼	Older sports bikes
635	700 B	28 × 1½	Touring and utility bikes
642	700 A	28 × 1⅜	Utility bikes (British and US)

Tubular tyres

The tubular tyres ('tubs') favoured by racing cyclists can be made much lighter than regular high-pressure or clincher tyres. They are sewn together, fully encasing the inner tube, and the tyres are stuck on to 'sprint' rims with a special adhesive. Their round profile makes handling predictable, avoids the likelihood of impact punctures and permits higher inflation pressures. However, tubulars are more awkward to repair than regular tyres. Riders usually carry a spare tyre folded under the saddle, but after a roadside tyre replacement you should proceed with some caution as re-used tyre-rim adhesive is unlikely to create a perfect bond. Consequently, tubular tyres are best left for racing where close support is available for a complete wheel change.

Tyre treads

Many manufacturers offer tyres with different tread compounds. These provide better grip on the road when leaning the bike for cornering at speed, or perform better on particular surfaces. However, slick or treadless tyres are remarkably reliable in most conditions. Partly for customer reassurance, many sporting tyres have a light file pattern on the tread. Heavier treads are usually marketed as providing more grip in wet conditions, sometimes with grooves to help dispel water from between the tyre and the road surface – but these tyres can easily pick up flints in their grooves, making them more susceptible to punctures where the tread is thin.

Off-road tyres require deeper treads for traction on loose surfaces. If you are tackling a mixture of unmade roads and better surfaces, a heavy file pattern tread in the centre of the tyre with larger studs to the side is a good compromise. There is nothing worse than riding on some good 'black top' feeling like you're riding through treacle because of heavy, rough tyre treads which are not suited for the conditions (or *vice versa*). See Figure 3.4a–c.

Puncture-resistant bands

Kevlar composite or other materials are often incorporated under the tyre tread as a puncture-resistant band (*see* Figure 3.4d). Most are very effective, but they do add a little to the tyre's weight and make it less supple. For touring and commuting

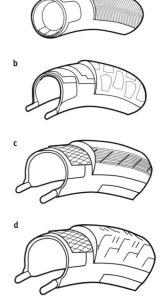

a

b

c

d

Figure 3.4 Tyre treads: a) road tubular – the lightweight inner tube is fully enclosed and sewn into the tyre casing, while a high-density weave makes the casing both strong and supple; b) lightweight 'slick' tread on a high-pressure or clincher tyre – popular for racing, training and fast, lightweight leisure rides; c) mountain-bike slick – change your chunky off-road tyres to a smooth, narrower profile for a really plush ride; d) Kevlar (or similar) band – positioned underneath the tyre tread, it can reduce many punctures

purposes tyres with this Kevlar band are popular, and even many racing tyres have some sort of proprietary puncture-resistant feature. After all, for the time lost due to a puncture and the energy used to chase back to the peloton, this small penalty is usually considered worthwhile.

Other puncture-resistant techniques such as expanding foams and gels have been tried, but generally these make tyres feel heavy and sluggish and they have not been adopted by 'performance' cyclists.

Tyre pressures

Having chosen your appropriate tyre width, follow the manufacturers' recommendations given on the tyre sidewall (*see* Figure 3.5). However, you may wish to adjust this for the circumstances. Racing cyclists commonly drop their pressure to 90–100 psi in wet races compared to their usual 100–120 psi for dry conditions. This gives a greater contact patch with the ground and provides a bit more security on slippery surfaces.

Inner tubes

Inner tubes should match the tyre size you are using. For 700 c wheels, the common sizes are 700 × 18–25 and 700 × 25–32. If you use too narrow a tube it will be stretched to its limit inside the tyre, be under greater tension and more likely to puncture. Lightweight latex inner tubes provide a very plush ride and their suppleness helps to reduce punctures, but the material does not to hold air very well, requiring inflation every few days.

High-pressure tubes have narrow 'Presta' valves and are almost universal on 700 c wheels. Mountain-bike tubes can have Presta valves or tubes with Schrader valves (as used on car tyres).

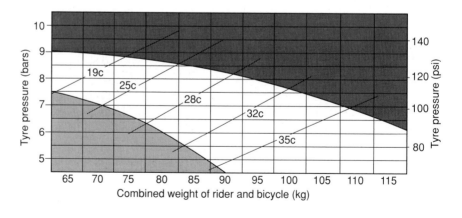

Figure 3.5 Tyre size and inflation pressures in relation to weight of rider and bicycle (adapted from Berto, F. J. (1988), *Upgrading your bike*, Rodale)

Over pressure   Recommended range   Under pressure

Rim tapes

Rim tapes prevent the inner tube from bulging into the spoke holes of the rim. Use a good-quality tape such as Velox or Michelin and make sure that it is the correct width for your rim. At a pinch, two or three layers of insulating tape may suffice, stretched so that it fully covers the spoke holes but does not interfere with the bead-seat of the tyre.

Fitting tyres and tubes

Use talc to lubricate the inner tube and edges of the tyre; this helps slip the tyre into place and stops the tube from sticking to the tyre wall. Carry spare inner tubes 'ready-talced' and wrapped in thick polythene bags to prevent them from getting damaged in your seatpack. Position the coloured label of your tyre next to the inner tube's valve. It is then easier to check where the cause of the puncture is in the tyre.

Handlebars

Lightweight racing and touring bikes use 'drop handlebars' which offer a great variety of hand positions for comfort, leverage and aerodynamics. There are subtle differences in handlebar shapes, some with an 'anatomic' section to keep the wrist in a more natural position when holding the lower part of the handlebar (*see* Figure 3.6a).

Choose your handlebars to fit you. Your arms should fall comfortably to the sides of the bars without being squeezed inwards or splayed outwards. Bars between 40 and 44 cm wide suit most adults, although women may prefer to use narrower ones if they are available. Choose a deeper shape if you want (and have the flexibility) to reach lower for greater leverage, a better aerodynamic position or simply if you have large hands.

Straight or flat handlebars are universal issue on mountain-bikes for better control over rough terrain. They can be fitted to road bikes (with appropriate stem and levers), though they do not offer as many hand positions – an important

Figure 3.6a Drop handlebars offer a variety of hand positions; 'anatomic' bars have a shaped section beneath the brake lever to make them more ergonomic

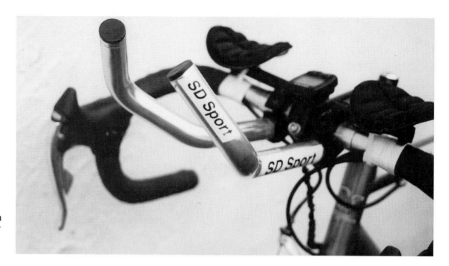

Figure 3.6b Triathlon (or aero) bars (with padded rests for the forearms) are often bolted on to regular drop handlebars to help the rider achieve a more aerodynamic tucked position, or sometimes just for comfort

consideration for long distance riding. 'Bar-ends' can help when climbing, and provide a more stretched out 'cruising' position.

Triathlon handlebars ('tri-bars' or 'aero-bars' – *see* Figure 3.6b) are typically a bolt-on accessory, with small padded rests for the forearms, enabling you to tuck into an aerodynamic position similar to downhill skiers. They also take pressure off your wrists and arms. Some practice and flexibility may be required to use these handlebars to their best racing advantage, but many tourists like them for comfort even if they are not adjusted to the extreme positions of the racers. Most tri-bars adjust for length, tilt, and in some cases height and angle too. They can be fitted to most handlebars, and bar-end shifters can be used on the ends of the extensions for convenience. As your hands are a long way from the brakes, tri-bars are barred from almost all massed-start racing and some randonnées too.

'Spinaci' bars (*see* Figure 3.6c) were designed to overcome the ban on tri-bars in massed-start racing. In essence, this is a two-piece additional mini-handlebar, bolted on to the front of the bike to replicate the aero-position of the tri-bar but

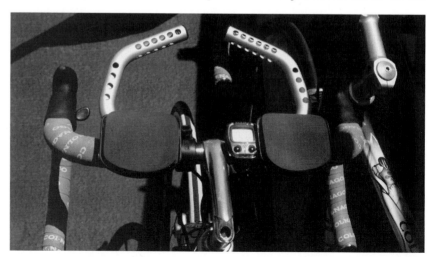

Figure 3.6c Spinaci add-on bars – drilled to save weight on a bike used primarily for climbing. The arm rests have been added for comfort, and note the handlebar computer too

usually without the padded arm-rests. Riders simply rest their forearms on the top of the regular handlebar. Needless to say, spinaci bars were also banned from road racing within one season. Some are still found on training bikes, and a few randonneurs and tourists use them to take advantage of the extra hand positions they offer as well as the extra space for mounting accessories.

Handlebar stems and headsets

Headsets – the bearing units at the top and bottom of the head-tube – allow the front forks to turn smoothly. There are two styles.

Standard headsets

Standard headsets (see Figure 3.7a) fit over the fork column and are adjusted and held in place by a threaded locknut. The handlebar stem sits inside the fork column, secured by a wedge or cone pulled upwards to expand its effective diameter to fix it in place. Handlebar height can be adjusted by 2–6 cm.

Aheadsets

Aheadsets (see Figure 3.7b) require a longer, unthreaded fork column. The headset slides over this and is held in place by clamping the handlebar stem *over* the fork column. When used with an aluminium or carbon-fibre steerer, this system can achieve significant weight savings (up to 400 g). However, there is very little leeway to adjust the handlebar height without buying a new handlebar stem of a different dimension. In theory such changes should not be necessary if you have your handlebar reach and height fully 'dialled in'. But for anyone riding much longer distances, overcoming an injury or with the slightest twinge of back pain, the ability to raise or lower the handlebars by a few millimetres could be crucial.

The best headsets have harder-wearing bearing surfaces, and are sealed to keep out dirt and improve longevity. Some use needle roller bearings: these spread the loads better and reduce pitting (or 'brinnelling') of the bearing surfaces as compared to headsets with regular ball-bearings.

The clamp of your handlebar stem must match the diameter of your handlebars. The best option is to buy the handlebars and stem from the same manufacturer.

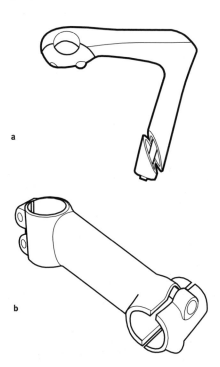

a

b

Figure 3.7 Handlebar stems: a) regular 'quill' stem for drop handlebars – the wedge at the base of the shaft is pulled upwards by the 'expander bolt' to secure the stem within the fork column; b) aheadset stem, which fits around a longer fork column and is secured by the two bolts at the back and an expanding cap (not shown) on the top of the stem

Tape

Handlebar tape provides padding, insulation and prevents your hands from slipping when wet. Cork tape is excellent, being warm, comfortable, durable and non-absorbent; but cloth or plastic tape, or foam grips can also be used. For extra padding, use double layers of tape, strips of neoprene or sections of old inner tube under the tape – but make sure this does not make the handlebar uncomfortably large to hold. You should be able to grip the handlebars so that you can touch the first knuckle on your first finger with your thumb without holding the bars too tightly.

Saddles and seatposts

Saddles

Your choice of saddle is very personal (*see* Figure 3.8). Gentle riding, sitting in a fairly upright position, will warrant a relatively broad saddle, often generously sprung or padded. If you prefer more 'performance' cycling you will probably find that a narrower, firmer, racing style is more comfortable, providing better support for long periods in the saddle. Modern racing saddles have a thick nylon base with a leather or synthetic covering over foam- or gel-padding. These saddles have almost totally superseded traditional leather saddles as they are generally cheaper, light (200–350 g), have no 'breaking in' period, are almost totally impervious to weather and need no special care requirements.

Despite their weight (600–800 g), leather saddles still have their followers because they literally mould themselves to the user's shape. However, this process takes years and a leather saddle has to be carefully looked after to retain its qualities.

Extra comfort is built into racing saddles by varying the thickness of the nylon base at strategic points, or varying the thickness of the padding material. This is done using nylon elastomers at the contact points with the saddle rails or by using materials with some inherent 'springiness', such as titanium, for the rails.

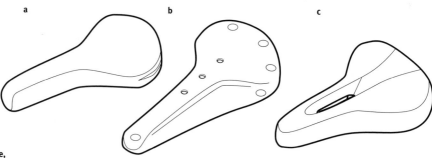

Figure 3.8 Saddles: a) racing saddles are narrow and firm but need to be comfortable for hours on the bike; b) despite their weight and need for care, leather saddles still have their devotees due to them moulding to the user's shape; c) women's saddles are shorter and broader than most men's saddles

Women's saddles tend to be shorter and broader, to better support the female pelvic structure. A characteristic of many women's saddles today is a cut-out in the nose of the saddle to alleviate pressure on the genital area. Such features are now found in some gents' saddles to overcome prostate numbness.

Saddle rails are usually made of steel or lighter materials such as aluminium, titanium or magnesium. You need to weigh up the pros and cons of light weight against durability and security very carefully before investing in one of the very light models. Being such a vital piece of equipment, comfort should be the over-riding factor when choosing a saddle. Highly popular are the ranges from makers such as Selle Italia with their Turbo and Turbomatic models, and the Rolls saddle from San Marco. The design leader in the cut-out style of women's saddles is Georgena Terry from the USA.

Seatposts

Seatposts (also known as seat pins or seat pillars) secure the saddle in place and allow its height, tilt, and fore and aft positions to be adjusted (*see* Figure 3.9). Most lightweight bikes feature seatposts with an integral clamp or cradle arrangement with one or two bolts to secure the saddle. The cradle may be set back from the centre line of the seatpost 'lay-back' or it can be 'in-line' (*see* Figure 2.3 p. 19). Depending on the design of your frame and your pedalling style you may prefer one type over another. *See* also Saddle position, Chapter 2, pp. 17–20.

For most road bikes, a total length of 200–250 mm is usually adequate. Mountain-bikes and compact road frames may require seatposts up to 400 mm long.

Suspension seatposts

Popular on mountain-bikes, suspension seatposts can be used on road or touring bikes to iron out the little vibrations encountered on poor road surfaces. Many users swear to being able to ride for longer and without the pains formerly endured.

Sizes

Seatpost diameters alter in increments of just 0.2 mm. It is vital that you choose the correct one to fit your frame, otherwise the post will slip or the seat-tube may be distorted in an effort to fit or secure it.

Some seatposts have an oval upper section in the quest for aerodynamics. Arguably, these are only of value

Seatpost safety

Seatposts should have a 'max' mark indicating the height that they can be extended out of the frame. A safe guideline is always to have about one-third of the length inserted into the seat-tube. The bottom end of the seatpost should sit below the junction of the top-tube and seat-tube.

For heavy duty use, especially if you suspend a weighty saddle-bag from the saddle, two-bolt design clamps are usually stronger than those using just a single bolt.

Be particularly careful not to scratch and damage a carbon-fibre seatpost.

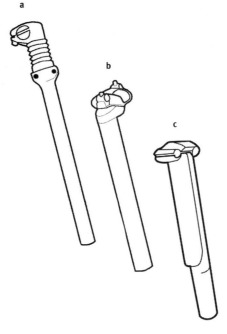

Figure 3.9 Seatposts: a) suspension – popular on many mountain-bikes but also used by tourists to reduce road-shock; b) traditional set-back road style with a micro-adjustable clamp for precise saddle positioning; c) aero-seatposts have a narrow, oval upper section for a smoother airflow under the saddle

where longer seatpost lengths are exposed – but in any case, the aero-section should never sit below the top of the seat-tube. Note that aluminium aero-profile seatposts are heavier than their round-sectioned cousins.

Pedal systems

There are numerous different pedal systems (*see* Figure 3.10). Many new bicycles are now sold without pedals, as suppliers recognise that customers have different preferences.

The simplest pedal is the 'rat-trap' cage. For any serious cycling these will be fitted with toe-clips and straps. Toe-clips help to keep your feet in position on the pedal; by tightening the toe-straps you can pull the pedals up on the backstroke in addition to pushing them down on the forward stroke. Racing cyclists use shoe-plates or 'cleats' on the soles of their shoes to help the process even further and avoid any possibility of pulling their feet out of the pedals when riding hard up a hill or in a sprint.

In the early 1980s the French ski-binding manufacturer Look introduced its clipless pedal, redesigning the interface of the pedal and shoe along the lines of a ski-binding. This system has been refined over the years but remains fundamentally unchanged, and copied with slight variations by other manufacturers such as Time. Very few racing cyclists now use toe-clips and straps.

The giant Japanese cycling component manufacturer Shimano applied similar ideas to off-road pedals, producing SPDs – Shimano Pedalling Dynamics. The principles are similar to the Look design but SPDs allow the cleat to be recessed into the shoe. This has great advantages for anyone who needs to walk or run as well as cycle (e.g. tourists, commuters, off-road riders). Tourists usually prefer the convenience of double-sided off-road pedals, but road-racers use just single-sided pedals.

Many riders enjoy a few degrees of 'float' in their pedals, allowing their feet to swivel slightly when riding and thus follow a more natural motion. On better pedal systems you can change the tension to adjust the force required to clip in or out of the pedal.

Figure 3.10 Pedal systems: left) racing shoes and pedal – shown here is the popular pedal and cleat from Look; right) the 'SPD' system developed by Shimano recesses the cleat into the sole of the shoe for easier walking by mountain-bikers and tourists

Gearing

The original bicycles in their modern, recognisable form had just one 'fixed' gear – a simple, toothed cog on the rear wheel with no capacity for freewheeling or changing gear. (Some riders still favour this form of transmission and it is still the only form of gearing used in competition on cycle tracks.) But when riders started to venture further afield they encountered different terrains, and wanted higher or lower gears according to the road conditions. This was achieved by either carrying spare sprockets with them and effecting a change at the side of the road, or having a wheel with a 'double fixed' hub – i.e. with two cogs of different sizes, one on each side of the hub. The rider then selected the gear he required by taking the wheel out of the frame and turning it around to use his chosen cog for the ground he was about to cover.

Variable gears were introduced to bicycles in the second half of the 19th century. The Sturmey-Archer hub gear has remained almost unchanged in 100 years (patented 1901) and the earliest derailleur gear was patented by Jean Loubeyre in Paris, 1895. The name was first used in a patent from another Frenchman, Charles Boizot, in 1910. The early gear systems were simple: 2-, 3- or 4-speed systems.

Today, most lightweight sports bicycles have derailleur gears, where the gear mechanism is situated underneath the sprockets on the rear wheel. A wire cable connects the mechanism to a gear lever on the handlebars or frame; this moves the mechanism across the line of sprockets and 'derails' the chain from one sprocket to another, in order to achieve different sizes of gear.

Multiple gears allow you to maintain an approximately even cadence (or pedalling rate) at all times – whether climbing up 10% (1:10) hills or cruising at 'evens' on the flat. The modern multi-gear cassettes of eight, nine or 10 sprockets have been a blessing for both racing-team mechanics and long-distance tourists. Team mechanics used to have to change the sprockets on every bike and all the spare wheels for each day's race. Not a quick task when looking after between six and nine riders in a team. Now, riders can have the full range of race gears available to them all the time. In the same vein, the tourist has a wider range of gear options available to him; he just has different chainwheels and a wider set of sprockets compared to the road racer.

Gear sizes

There are three ways to compare gear sizes.

Inches

In Victorian times, the biggest gear a cyclist could use on a penny-farthing was determined by the length of his legs! The introduction of the 'safety bicycle', with the use of different-sized chainwheels and sprockets to drive the bicycle, allowed riders of varying stature to compete with similar-sized gears.

Equating the two, the calculation is as follows:

$$\text{Gear size (inches)} = \frac{\text{no. of teeth (t) on chainwheel} \times \text{wheel diameter (inches)}}{\text{no. of teeth on rear sprocket}}$$

For example, riding a regular touring bicycle with a 48t chainwheel and using the 15t rear sprocket provides a gear of 86.4". One pedal revolution on this bike is equivalent to one wheel revolution of a penny farthing with a front wheel of 86.4" (over seven feet in diameter!). To use this the penny-farthing rider would need to have legs over 88 cm (40") long in order to reach the pedals!

$$\frac{48\text{t on chainwheel} \times 27" \text{ wheel}}{15\text{t on rear sprocket}} = 86.4"$$

However, the notation of wheel size is not strictly accurate and tyre sizes varying from 18 mm to 38 mm can have a profound influence on the mathematics. These figures are now little more than a benchmark by which to judge comparisons on the same bike.

Metres

The Continental expression of metres relates directly to the *development* or 'roll-out' distance. Simply wheel the bike backwards and measure the distance travelled as the cranks complete one revolution. This takes into account the different effective wheel diameters with different depth tyres. It is slowly being adopted by the English-speaking world.

$$\text{Gear size (m)} = \text{wheel diameter (m)} \times \pi \times \frac{\text{no. of teeth on chainwheel}}{\text{no. of teeth on sprocket}}$$

Teeth

You can refer to gears just by the number of teeth on the chainwheel and the rear sprocket – e.g. 48 × 16 (quote the chainwheel size first and the sprocket size second). This can cause confusion when alternative gears are offered in a similar vein. It's not immediately obvious that 54 × 18, 48 × 16 and 39 × 13 all produce exactly the same sized gear. Figure 3.11 shows how different combinations of chainwheel and sprocket size produce high and low gears. More commonly, people refer to gear tables rather than working out the mathematics each time (*see* Appendices, pp. 211–14).

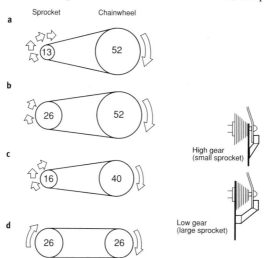

Figure 3.11 One revolution of the chainwheel results in:
a) 4 revolutions of the rear sprocket
b) 2 revolutions of the rear sprocket
c) 2.5 revolutions of the rear sprocket
d) 1 revolution of the rear sprocket

The actual gear size is affected by the outside diameter of the tyre. Two bicycles with the same chainwheel and sprocket combinations will have different gear sizes if the tyre sizes are different, but gear tables are useful for comparative figures.

Racing gears

The choice of gears for the road racer is fairly simple. Most domestic races are over less than 150 km, and few events are more than 200 km long. At racing speeds these will be events of 3–5 hours, largely ridden in a bunch of other riders of similar fitness and all travelling at the same speed. A 9- or 10-speed cassette (sprocket set) coupled with a double chainset will allow the road racer to compete on equal terms with all the other competitors in almost every event on the calendar.

The racer has 18 or 20 gears, with very small differences between them. In this way he can select the ideal gear for the occasion, whether he is powering along in a group at 50 kph, or ascending a long climb at 20 kph. The racer's top gear is typically around 120" (53×12, 9.4 m) and his bottom gear about 50" (39×21, 4 m). Occasionally some riders use an 11t top sprocket, or bigger chainrings of 54 or 55t, to provide higher gears that only the very strongest can use purposefully. Only if very extreme road conditions were anticipated would the racer be likely to change from these gear ratios.

For long-distance time-trials, or perhaps in flatter road races, riders may decide to use two chainrings with little difference between their sizes if they know that the lower hill-climbing gears will not be required. A 44, 46 or 47t inner chainring might be a good choice in a fast road race for the perfect gear selection.

In long-distance time-trials, few riders can pedal a very big gear for 12 or 24 hours, so for these events it is worth considering a more compact spread of gears – achieved by combining chainrings of say, 50–46t and the usual rear cassette of 12–21t sprockets.

Touring and randonnée gears

As a long-distance tourist or randonneur you may be faced with a 20% climb at the end of long day's riding. You could be very tired and you need gears that will enable you to tackle this obstacle. On the other hand, you might ride for days with a tailwind! To cope with all eventualities, tourists and randonneurs often prefer triple chainsets.

A good range of gears for the tourist is between 90" and 25" (or 7 m and 2 m). A typical touring chainset has three chainrings of perhaps 48–36–24t, although almost any combination is possible. Combined with a cassette of 12 or 13 to 28t (and sometimes even 32t or more) this provides a very wide set of gears in order to help the touring cyclist ride his bike loaded with luggage up hill and down dale, without undue stress, even if sometimes only at a very slow speed.

Randonneurs don't travel at the high speed of racers, so a very big top gear is unnecessary (long downhills are a good opportunity to freewheel and rest!); nor do they carry loads like the tourists, so extremely low gears are not required. A good recommendation for randonneurs is a triple chainset of 50–40–30t, or 48–38–28 – combined with a cassette ranging from 12 or 13t to a big sprocket of between 23 and

28t, depending on the rider's strength and style. This provides a range of gears from about 100" down to 35" (8.2 m–2.8 m) – or less than 30" (2.3 m) with a 28t sprocket – and the gaps between the gears are small and easily manageable.

Typical gearing recommendations

The following are some typical gearing recommendations for road racing, audax and touring. (For the mathematics of gearing, *see* pp. 37–8 and 211–14; and for comprehensive gearing tables, *see* Appendices.) The following tables show gearing in inches above and in metric (in italics) beneath.

Road racing

Chainwheel size		Sprocket size								
		12	**13**	**14**	**15**	**16**	**17**	**18**	**19**	**21**
53		119.3"	110.1	102.2	95.4	89.4	84.2	79.5	75.3	68.1
	m	*9.43*	*8.70*	*8.08*	*7.54*	*7.07*	*6.66*	*6.29*	*5.95*	*5.39*
39		87.8	81.0	75.2	70.2	65.8	61.9	58.5	55.4	50.1
	m	*6.94*	*6.41*	*5.95*	*5.55*	*5.21*	*4.90*	*4.63*	*4.38*	*3.96*

Audax

Chainwheel size		Sprocket size								
		13	**14**	**15**	**16**	**17**	**19**	**21**	**23**	**25**
50		103.9	96.4	90.0	84.4	79.4	71.1	64.3	64.3	54.0
	m	*8.21*	*7.63*	*7.12*	*6.67*	*6.28*	*5.62*	*5.08*	*4.64*	*4.27*
40		83.1	77.1	72.0	67.5	63.5	56.8	51.4	47.0	43.2
	m	*6.57*	*6.10*	*5.69*	*5.34*	*5.02*	*4.50*	*4.07*	*3.71*	*3.42*
30		62.3	57.8	54.0	50.6	47.6	42.6	38.6	35.3	32.4
	m	*4.93*	*4.58*	*4.27*	*4.00*	*3.77*	*3.37*	*3.05*	*2.78*	*2.56*

Touring

Chainwheel size		Sprocket size								
		13	**14**	**15**	**16**	**17**	**19**	**21**	**24**	**28**
48		99.7	92.6	86.4	81.0	76.2	68.2	61.7	54.0	46.3
	m	*7.89*	*7.33*	*6.84*	*6.41*	*6.03*	*5.40*	*4.88*	*4.27*	*3.66*
36		74.8	69.4	64.8	60.8	57.2	51.2	46.3	40.5	34.7
	m	*5.91*	*5.50*	*5.13*	*4.81*	*4.52*	*4.05*	*3.66*	*3.20*	*2.75*
24		49.8	46.3	43.2	40.5	38.1	34.1	30.8	27.0	23.2
	m	*3.95*	*3.67*	*3.42*	*3.21*	*3.02*	*2.70*	*2.44*	*2.14*	*1.83*

Off-the-peg bicycles often emulate racing machines, but professional riders can bowl along all day in gears that would make most people buckle in minutes, so the vast majority of cyclists will benefit from a lower selection of gears. For most, changing the standard outer chainring from 53t to something smaller – 52, 50, 48 or even 46t – still provides a high enough top gear. Couple this with a 39t or 38t inner ring – or even smaller if your chainset will accept it – for a much more useful selection of gears. Ignore the 11t top sprocket favoured by the pros, you don't need it. Instead, choose a cassette with a smallest sprocket of 13t or at most 12t (both mechanically more efficient and more durable than an 11t sprocket). Your other sprockets should range up to at least 23t to be useful – 26 or even 28t if you ride in very hilly or mountainous terrain.

For converting 'racing chainsets' into touring set-ups, French manufacturer TA makes a 'triple adaptor' chainring for use with double chainsets. This is a middle chainring that replaces the inner chainring on a double chainset. Its arms extend towards the center of the crank and are drilled to accept a smaller third chainring. You will probably need to use a longer bottom bracket axle and a different triple front changer to accommodate this.

'No-no' gears

It is unwise to make frequent use of the 'extreme' combinations of gears – i.e. the large chainring and the largest rear sprocket, and the small chainring with the smallest sprocket (*see* Figure 3.12). The acute chain-angle is inefficient and increases the rate of wear on both the chain and sprockets. Such extremes do really test the capacity and durability of the gear mechanisms. In practice, it may not be possible to use the inner chainring with the smallest two, or even three, sprockets because the chain either fouls the cage of the rear derailleur or catches on the middle chainring. This isn't a major problem, since there is often some overlap of gear size between the three chainrings, and the smallest chainring is usually engaged only for very steep or long climbs when the larger sprockets are also employed.

a

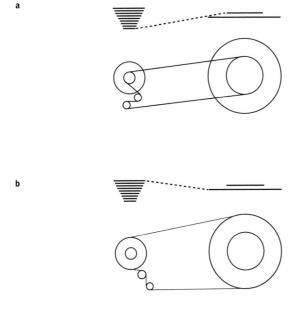

b

Figure 3.12 No-no gear combinations: a) small chainring and small spocket(s); b) large chainring and large spocket(s). These combinations are best avoided because the acute chain angle accelerates wear. On the small–small gear the chain may catch on the outer chainring or, depending on the rear mechanism, may even rub on itself. With the large–large gear, the rear derailleur is also put under considerable strain

Double vs triple chainsets

Changing gear with a triple chainset used to be notoriously unresponsive and most riders preferred the simplicity and reliability of a double chainset. However, the popularity of mountain-bikes led manufacturers to make great improvements in wide-ratio gear-changers, and triple chainsets have now been used even in the most elite road-racing circles. Some leisure riders do still prefer to use just a double chainset, usually coupled with a wide-ratio cassette: certainly it is a bit lighter, neater looking and easier to clean than a triple, but the use of wide-ratio cassettes can compromise the rear-gear shifts. Today, if you need a wider spread or better selection of gears, you can confidently use a triple chainset and its attendant front changer without any worries. If you still prefer a double chainset, consider one that can take smaller chainrings – e.g. 50 × 36, 46 × 30 or even 42 × 28.

Improved gear changes

For slicker changes, keep the differences between chainring sizes reasonably small. Better changes will be achieved with a difference of 10–14t between the chainrings. 16t is the maximum most double front changers can cope with. On a triple chainset, a difference of 10–12t between each ring is common.

Racers prefer close-ratio rear sprockets with increments of just one or two teeth between each sprocket – e.g. 9-speed, 12–21 cassette. This makes changing gear much quicker and easier than if using a cassette with 'jumps' of 3–5 teeth, and the gaps from one gear to the next are not too great. For leisure riders, 12–23 or 13–26 cassettes are a good compromise. Don't let slick gear changing dictate your choice of gear ratios; having *the right gear* available for your needs should take priority. Mathematics determines that the differences between teeth at the high end of the cassette (smallest sprockets) should be much closer than those at the low end (biggest sprockets). Most riders prefer single-tooth differences between the top two or three sprockets but can cope with 2–4-tooth differences between the larger cogs.

Have your most useful gear combinations as the middle three or four sprockets, whichever chainring you prefer. If you are always using the larger sprockets, you will benefit from having a smaller chainwheel. Conversely, if you are always on the 12, 13 or 14 sprockets, consider using a larger chainwheel, but try to keep your pedalling cadence above 85–90 rpm.

Bottom brackets

Most modern bottom bracket axles are cartridge style. Instead of separate cups screwed into the frame, with play in the axle and bearings being adjusted by the fit of the cups, the cartridge axle is pre-adjusted. It is screwed into place from one side of the bike as a single unit, and is then held in place by screwing in the second cup. It is a very simple and almost foolproof component welcomed by most mechanics for its ease of use and durability.

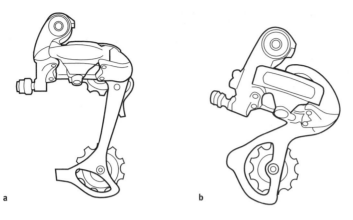

a   b

Figure 3.13 Gear mechanisms: a) bikes with wide-ratio cassettes or chainrings need a long-arm gear mechanism; b) racing bikes usually have a short-arm derailleur for more precise changes over the close-ratio gears

Gear levers

For years, gear levers were mounted on the bicycle's down-tube and kept in place by the tightness (friction) of their securing bolt. In the mid-1980s, Japanese manufacturer Shimano introduced 'index shifting' – 'clicking into gear' by precisely matching the amount of travel required by the lever to the distance the gear mechanism needed to move to engage the appropriate sprocket. Now, gear-shift levers are integrated into the brake levers for greater convenience, allowing you to change gear without letting go of the handlebars. This is safer, offers improved bike control at all times, and is quicker and easier so that it encourages greater use of the gears – helping you to maintain optimum cadence at all times.

Handlebar controls, or 'bar-end shifters' (*see* Figure 3.14b), plug into the ends of the handlebars and, until superseded by the integral brake-shift STI (Shimano) and Ergo-Power (Campagnolo) levers, these were always used in cyclo-cross where total bike control is essential. Now, handlebar controls are most commonly found on time-trial bikes, where riders use them from their aerodynamic

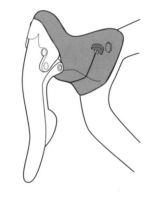

a

b

Capacity of gear mechanisms

Gear mechanisms have a 'capacity' (measured by the number of teeth of the chainwheels and sprockets). For front changers this is the difference between the largest and smallest chainwheel. A rear derailleur has to cope with the different chain length required over a range of rear sprockets plus that of the two or three chainwheels.

When using gear combinations that involve more than about 28t (combining the differences between the chainrings and the rear sprockets), a *long-arm* derailleur (*see* Figure 3.13a) will usually be required to cope with the extra length of chain required to manage the range of teeth on the sprockets and chainwheels.

Figure 3.14 Gear levers: a) combined brake/gear shift lever allows you to change gear and brake at the same time without letting go of the handlebars; b) bar-end shifters – simple and convenient – are now commonly used on time-triallists' aero-bars 'tri-bars' in order to maintain the best possible wind-cheating profile. Some tourists choose them for their reliability, simplicity and easy access, and they are sometimes used on tandems to operate a rear hub-brake.

Mountain-bikes have always had the gear levers mounted on the handlebars readily to hand, usually as a trigger device operated by thumb and fore-finger, although the SRAM Grip Shift using a twist-grip also has a popular following.

French firm Mavic has pioneered the use of electronic gear-changing with some success in the professional peloton. Their Mektronic system places gear-change buttons in multiple locations on the handlebar for easy access whatever hand-hold is being used.

Brakes

Choice of brakes

Like most racing components, the choice of brakes for the road racer is very simple: decide which manufacturer to use and buy according to your budget. Universally, racers use the compact and powerful dual-pivot sidepull brakes (*see* Figure 3.15a). The more expensive models have better quality castings and finishing, and may use materials such as ergal alloy, titanium or stainless steel. They may also have bearings on the pivots for improvements in modulation and control.

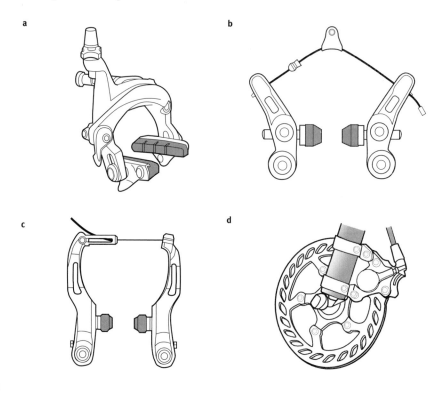

Figure 3.15 Brake design: a) dual pivot; b) cantilever; c) V-brake; d) disc

Since racing tyres are narrow (<23 mm) and there is no need for mudguards on the bike, racing brakesets can be very shallow (39–49 mm) – this keeps the calliper arms very rigid and braking feels very positive. The tourist or audax rider, however, will use fatter tyres (23–32 mm) *and* mudguards, necessitating brakes with a longer reach (47–57 mm) – though there are few good-quality brakes in this depth.

For bikes that use broader tyres or need very large clearances (e.g. mountain-bikes, cyclo-cross and 'rough-stuff' touring), sidepull brakes are impractical. Longer brake arms would flex too much under heavy braking pressure. So cantilever brakes are usually used, attached to special bosses on the frame and forks, with a straddle wire above the tyre pulling the two brake arms together (*see* Figure 3.15b).

V-brakes are a variation of cantilevers (*see* Figure 3.15c). Designed originally for mountain-bikes, these brakes are very powerful, but the correct levers must be used. Their compact design is especially useful on bikes with low seat-stays which might otherwise position cantilevers where the rider's heels can catch on them. V-brakes do not need additional cable stops or cable yokes, making them easy to set up, and most have a simple 'quick release' feature for rapid wheel removal.

Although accepted in mountain-bike racing, disc brakes (*see* Figure 3.15d) have yet to impact on road bikes. They are most likely to see service with tandems and on loaded touring bikes, where their superior stopping power can really be beneficial. Disc brakes are less susceptible to adverse weather. Since they do not operate on the rim, a damaged or untrue wheel can have a larger 'window of operation' before repair becomes essential, plus there is no heat build-up at the rim due to braking friction – which, in extreme circumstances and with normal brakes, could cause a tyre to be exploded off the rim.

Always remember that any very powerful brake can wear out brake blocks and rims very quickly. Check these regularly.

The most effective improvements in performance will come firstly from a better pair of wheels and appropriate tyres. After that, few changes will make significant differences. Upgrading to an expensive set of brakes, an exotic handlebar stem or a lightweight seatpost will have a negligible effect on how your bike feels. However, if you have a super-machine, then it's a shame to spoil it with cheap or heavy component parts. But shaving an extra half-kilo off a bicycle can be expensive when you need to resort to NASA-type materials!

4 Bike accessories

Bottles, cages and hydration packs

Most road and mountain-bikes have fittings for two bottle cages; on the down-tube and seat-tube. These need to grip the bottle firmly but be designed so that you can easily remove it when required. Some ultralight bottle cages are just too flimsy to hold bottles firmly enough, especially over rough surfaces. Nylon cages look ugly but most are surprisingly robust and efficient.

Bottles (French *'bidons'*) are plastic with a pull-out nozzle. Standard ones are 500 ml, and large ones usually 750 ml. A wide neck makes it easy to put in ice cubes and makes cleaning much easier too. Most (but not all) bottles are fully interchangeable between all makes of cage. Buy clear or light-coloured bottles so that you can keep a check on cleanliness.

Hydration packs

Research has shown how important hydration is, and new ideas for hands-free hydration have been developed for mountain-biking and other outdoor activities. Back-packs, like those from Camelbak and Platypus (*see* Useful addresses, p. 206), have a bladder and tube with a 'bit valve' (*see* Figure 4.1). Some models are cycling-specific, fitting underneath clothing for a smoother profile and even helping to reduce body temperature. You will tend to drink more with such packs, because of their ready access; this is good, but needs to be balanced against some disadvantages – such as the weight being carried, the fact that the pack is on your back, and sometimes that bottles are more convenient and versatile.

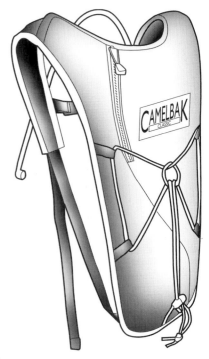

Figure 4.1 Hydration pack

Cycle computers

A cycle computer is a useful accessory, even if only for entertainment value on a long ride. The simplest ones provide basic information: current speed, trip distance and total distance travelled. Others show average and maximum speed, duration of ride, time of day, pace and stopwatch functions. More sophisticated models have sensors for cadence and altitude, or can be combined with heart rate monitors (*see* also Chapter 12, p. 139). Most are accurate to <0.5% and they can be very useful for navigation and pace judgement (*see* Figure 4.2).

Since handlebar space is always at a premium, compactness is a desirable feature. Check that the display figures are large enough for you to read them easily when on the move, and that you can operate the buttons when wearing gloves. Most computers have a magnet attached to the spokes, passing a sensor on the forks and a wire to the display unit on the handlebars; but cordless units are now being refined down to a convenient size.

Figure 4.2 Cycle computers are a convenient and useful aid for pacing and navigation purposes

Lighting

If you commute by bicycle or wish to ride at dusk, dawn or in darkness, good lighting is essential – for you to see where you are going, and for others to see you (*see* Figure 4.3a and b overleaf).

Light-emitting diodes

Light-emitting diodes (LEDs) have virtually replaced rear lights for bicycles. They are bright, reliable, lightweight, battery-efficient, compact and comparatively cheap. Many sizes and designs are available and there really is no excuse for any cyclist not having at least one of these lights available for emergency use. LEDs often have a flashing mode – ideal for drawing attention to your presence – but this can have hypnotic (or even epileptic) effects in the company of others, so most riding groups prohibit the use of flashing lights.

White LEDs have been made for front lights, but to date most have either a greenish hue to them or do not provide the spread and intensity of beam required to see the road ahead. They're useful as a means of recognising a rider, but have yet to be developed for illuminating the way ahead.

Battery lamps

Far better for illumination are battery lights or generator systems with filament bulbs. Alkaline batteries are almost essential for through-the-night performance. Lithium batteries are lighter in weight, last longer and perform better in a wider range of temperatures than alkalines, but their expense can be prohibitive. Some excellent, extremely bright, rechargeable battery systems exist. However, most have limited run-time – sometimes less than two hours – so are only suitable for shorter journeys. They can be very heavy and expensive too.

Legal lighting

Different countries have different legal requirements for bicycle lighting. In some countries the law has yet to catch up with advances in technology, and prohibits the exclusive use of LED lights despite their excellent performance.

Where LEDs are not yet legal, riders should only use them as a supplementary light.

Generators and dynamos

Generators or dynamos have seen a revival recently, with some good new products appearing. The simplest form of dynamo generator runs on the tyre sidewall. Most are lightweight with no 'drag' when off but noticeable drag when switched on – with the clear exception of the LightSpin system. Problems can arise in the wet when the pulley wheel may slip on the tyre, and some dynamos have even worn out a tyre sidewall in an overnight ride!

Dynamos that run on the tyre tread – usually mounted behind the bottom bracket in an effort to reduce drag and wear on the tyre – can work well in good conditions. However, most riders have to adapt them in some way to improve their performance, either by mounting them in places away from the original design concept, or by adding a pressure device to keep the roller in contact with the tyre when required.

Figure 4.3a Dual lighting system: here the small battery lamp is fixed under the handlebar and a dynamo lamp is attached to the fork crown

Possibly the best lighting solution is the new generation of dynohubs such as the Schmidt, weighing about the same as a set of battery lamps but much more reliable and with a greater power output. Their drag is negligible when not in use and minimal when providing power.

Figure 4.3b Modern dynohubs are popular with many randonneurs; they are reliable and their weight is similar to battery lamps

Table 4.1 Advantages and disadvantages of the different lighting systems

	Advantages	Disadvantages
Battery lamps (filament bulbs)	• Zero drag • Easy to remove when not required • Can be 'on' when stationary • Can double as torch or reading light	• Expensive to run • Can be heavy • Limited battery life • Need to carry spare batteries • Limited light output
LED	• Very bright to be seen • Very lightweight • Reliable • Long battery life • Easy to remove when not required • No drag	• Not good for front lamps • Suitable for rear lights only • Not legal everywhere
Dynamo (tyre sidewall)	• Good light output • Almost unlimited 'life' • Minimal running costs • No drag when 'off' • Wide price range	• May slip when wet • Can damage/wear tyre sidewalls • Inconvenient to remove • No light when stationary • Noticeable drag when in use
Hub generator	• Good light output • Minimal drag 'on' or 'off' • Almost unlimited life • Minimal running costs • Weight is kept low and in the hub centre • Convenient – 'always there'	• Expensive initial outlay • No light when stationary • Similar weight to battery lamps • Inconvenient – 'always there'

Head-torches

Petzl make the most widely available range of head-torches and the better models are fully waterproof with good beams. They are excellent for randonneurs studying a map or route-sheet in the dark, and handy for cycle-campers too.

In summary

It is a wise precaution to have at least two independent lighting systems on any bike used for extended night-riding. A small battery lamp can supplement a dynamo when stopped at junctions, and is essential for reading a map or working on a repair in the dark. Some dynamo systems incorporate a small stand-by light but the extra electronics can sometimes create more problems than they solve – it's best to keep your lighting systems simple. Handlebar plugs are an excellent location to carry spare bulbs.

By fitting two battery lamps you can manage if one lamp fails. You can extend the life of your batteries by switching from one lamp to the other every 20–30 minutes, and use both together for extra brightness when travelling fast downhill.

Halogen bulbs produce a whiter, brighter light, but must be handled with care and they do use battery power more rapidly than regular filament bulbs.

Night-riders continue to debate which system is the best, with some riders even making their own lights using ideas and components from other technologies.

Luggage

The independent long-distance traveller will need to carry some luggage. Exactly how much is a matter of personal choice and dependent on your journey – but curiously, little more luggage is required for a two-week tour than for a weekend away!

Ideally, all luggage should be carried directly on your bike. Avoid carrying luggage on your back whenever possible – the problems are numerous:

- your back will become hot and sweaty

- your centre of gravity is raised, making the bike's handling 'fragile', unpredictable or difficult

- weight on your back exerts more pressure on your backside and wrists

- getting out of the saddle or easing your riding position is difficult

- rucksack straps can restrict blood circulation to your arms and hands

- it can be difficult to look behind and check traffic conditions.

Having said that, sometimes it is convenient to carry something on your back – e.g. on short commuting trips or when riding off-road, where panniers can catch in the undergrowth or make the bike too heavy to lift over obstacles. Cycle couriers prefer the convenience of a giant shoulder-bag to swiftly load and unload their cargo, but a rucksack is generally better than a single-strap shoulder-bag. It distributes the load better across your back and shoulders, and it will not swing around your body at inopportune moments.

Consider about 35 litres as the maximum capacity for cycling. This should be ample for weekend adventure races or off-road events. Cycling-specific rucksacks have a sloping lid to prevent them interfering with a helmet; they sit a little lower on your back than a walker's rucksack, so that you can still look over your shoulder; and chest, waist and compression straps improve load stability.

Luggage construction

Most good-quality cycling luggage is made from heavy-duty Cordura or a similar derivative. This is a tough, lightweight and waterproof material, but zips and seams are susceptible to water ingress and so it is worth packing items in polythene bags to keep them dry. Use several small bags rather than just one large liner bag. Then, should one bag tear, you won't have everything getting wet. You can also organise separate bags for clean clothes, dirty laundry, shoes, food, etc.

When selecting luggage look out for the following:

- the number of pockets (two or three of reasonable size are usually adequate)

- reflective safety trim

- the quality of zips and buckles

- the security of the fixings

- loops for securing items on top of the bags

- ease of attaching and detaching the bags.

Mesh pockets on panniers are useful for keeping damp clothing away from other items (and for drying wet socks on the move!). Make sure that your bags will not bounce around in use. If necessary, use an elastic luggage cord ('bungee'), and tuck away excess strap lengths to stop them getting caught in your wheels or transmission.

Seatpacks, saddlebags and rackpacks

Seatpacks tuck neatly under the saddle, ranging in capacity from about 0.5 litres to 7.5 litres, and are good for essential items like spare tubes and tools for roadside repairs (*see* Figure 4.4). The larger sizes can take food rations and extra clothing too.

On longer rides you will need more space, for extra clothing or to stash away garments worn earlier as the day warms up. The traditional British saddlebag attached to the back of the saddle has largely lost its place to the 'rackpack' or 'top-bag' which sits on a pannier carrier (*see* Figure 4.5).

Randonnées are spent almost entirely 'on the road' and so can be tackled with no more luggage than a rackpack allows. When touring and stopping at B&Bs or youth hostels you will want to take more: 'street clothes' for the evening, a change of cycling clothes, toiletries and a towel. If you can't fit all of this into a seatpack or rackpack, add a bar-bag. This attaches to the handlebars – like a cyclist's glove compartment – offering easy access to anything required on the move (and a useful map-holder position). Do not put too much weight in the bar-bag as this may adversely affect the bike's handling.

Panniers range in capacity from around 25 litres to over 60 litres per pair. They need to be attached either side of a good, rigid carrier. Rear bags are wedge-shaped to clear your heels. The load should be balanced as evenly as possible on both sides

Figure 4.4 Seatpack: this size can easily contain all your roadside repair tools, two spare inner tubes and a lock. Note the identity tag attached to the zip, and the mini-LED on the back

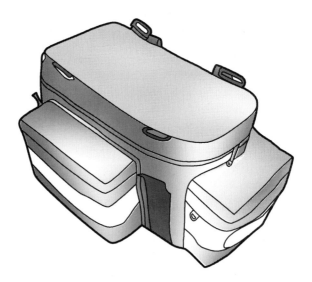

Figure 4.5 Rackpack: a neat and secure successor to the saddlebag. The pockets are ideal for organising your luggage, and extra hoops are useful for securing waterproofs, surplus clothing or the evening's food shopping

Table 4.2 Rackpacks vs saddlebags

Rackpacks	Saddlebags
Stable, having at least four well-spaced securing points	Less stable, with only three closely-spaced attachment points
Require a carrier to be fitted	May require a carrier to prevent bag from fouling back wheel or mudguard (not always essential)
Can be used on any sized bicycle with a rear carrier	Smaller riders may have problems if they do not have enough space to fix a bag under their saddle
No extra fittings required	Usually require bag loops on the back of the saddle. Few modern saddles have these, although some very neat bolt-on loops and specialist fittings are made
Most are easily detachable, so it is simple to keep your valuables with you when stopping for lunch or sightseeing	Fitting and removal can be a time-consuming affair (threading straps through narrow loops). Specialist fittings can make fixing and removing bags much quicker
Various sizes, from around 8 litres to 16 litres	Some saddlebags have a capacity of more than 20 litres

of the bike. Panniers keep the weight low down on the bike for greater stability, but any loaded bike will handle differently and may take a little while to master.

Luggage position

US carrier manufacturer 'Blackburn' (*see* p. 205) made an extensive study of the best locations for luggage on a bicycle and concluded, not surprisingly, that the best place to carry extra weight is as low down and as near the centre of the bike as possible. This study spawned the low-rider carrier which attaches to the front forks. Some riders, particularly on tandems, actually report better bike-handling response with low-rider panniers than when riding unloaded!

Expedition riders and tandem pairs may need to use every available position for luggage on the bike (*see* Figure 4.7). For convenience, many riders use a seatpack for their emergency tools whatever other bags they carry, and the bar-bag too can supplement any other bags.

Mudguards

In many countries mudguards hardly exist. However, in Britain's maritime climate and other places where rain is common, mudguards are extremely practical. You may choose to ride on a stripped-down bike in summer, but in winter especially, it is a good idea to have a bike equipped with mudguards.

For the majority Audax UK rides you are required to use full-length mudguards, although they are not required for similar events in most other countries. Few road-racing frames are designed for mudguards so you have to be creative when fitting them: cut them so that they do not foul the tyres under the fork crown or the seat-stay bridge; use very slim tyres; or accept that you may not be able to ride your continental road-racing jewel on these occasions.

Table 4.3 The 'pros' and 'cons' of mudguards

Pros	Cons
• Protect the bike from water, abrasive dirt and grit in poor conditions, prolonging the life of the frame and components	• Add weight to the bike
• Protect the rider from water, abrasive dirt and grit (especially backside, eyes and feet)	• May clog up in very muddy conditions
• Add a mud flap to the rear 'guard – riding in a group is much more pleasant for those behind!	• Are not aerodynamic
• Help to keep you and your bike clean in poor conditions	• If not adjusted properly can rub on the tyres
• Ideal location for reflective tape	• More awkward to reduce bike size for transport
	• Difficult to clean a bike thoroughly with mudguards fitted

Pannier carriers

The expedition cyclist relies not only on his luggage but perhaps even more so on his pannier carrier. The strongest rear carriers have four securing points and bolt to the frame, just above the rear dropouts and at the seat-stays. Three-point carriers (dropouts and brake bridge) can sway when loaded which makes the bike unsteady and rapidly fatigues the carrier.

Blackburn revolutionised cycle luggage racks in the late 1970s, with the introduction of aluminium carriers that were extremely strong and rigid due to their triangulated design, and nearly half the weight of existing steel racks. Despite

Blackburn racks costing double any other carrier, cycle tourists immediately saw their advantages and they still remain the market leader. The one criticism of aluminium racks is that if they break they are difficult to repair, especially if travelling in more remote areas. Consequently, some excellent, strong and lightweight carriers are now being made from tubular steel. Now these racks carry an even greater price tag than the aluminium ones!

For the truly ardent luggage-carrying cyclist, it may be worthwhile investing in a custom-built bicycle frame where the carrier is made as an integral part of the frame itself.

Pumps

A flat tyre can ruin a ride. Ideally you should possess two pumps: one to carry on your bike, and a heavy-duty 'track pump' kept at home. The track pump is a floor-standing model with a T-shaped handle and large barrel, capable of reaching very high pressures with ease. It is usually fitted with an accurate pressure gauge which removes the hard work from pumping up your tyres and ensures that – at least at the start of every ride – they are at the correct pressure.

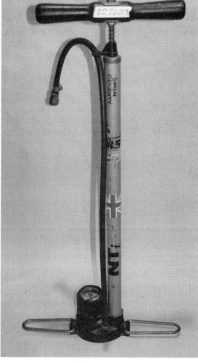

Figure 4.6 Pumps: left) frame-fit pump – readily accessible but out of the way on the seat-stay (note the peg at the top of the seat-stay); right) track pump – an invaluable aid to any cyclist, these floor-standing pumps have a large barrel and gauge for pumping up tyres quickly and easily to the correct pressure

Few discerning cyclists use the traditional pump with a separate hose. Instead they choose either a 'frame pump' or 'mini-pump'. Telescopic mini-pumps are neat and light, but their small volume makes it time-consuming and difficult to achieve the suitably high pressures required of most tyres. Frame-fit pumps for high pressures have a long, narrow barrel, and often include a lever to lock the rubber washer around the valve and prevent air loss when in use. For best results, buy the longest pump that fits your bike.

Trailers

When all the bike bags do not offer enough space to carry your essentials, you need a trailer (see Figure 4.7). Most popularly used by tandem riders, trailers can be loaded up to much greater limits, removing all of this weight from the bike's already stressed rear wheel. Of course, you still have to propel the load.

Single-wheel trailers have less rolling resistance and cope with rough surfaces much better. Child-carrying trailers usually have twin-wheels for stability.

Figure 4.7 The fully equipped tourist with a full complement of pannier bags, bar-bag and trailer. This tour leader was carrying equipment for his whole party! (photo: Ivo Miesen)

5 Cycling clothing

The most important items of cycling clothing are firstly proper cycling shorts and secondly shoes. After that almost anything can be used, although there are many advantages to using cycling-specific items. Road clothes tend to be close fitting and off-road garments usually have a looser cut. There is no rule dictating that you should choose one style or another. Many items of clothing are highly suitable outside their original design market – wear whatever you feel most comfortable in. The following pages cover the main pieces of cycling clothing, arranged in alphabetical order.

Eyewear

Sunglasses are now a major fashion accessory with a legitimate place in the cyclist's kit bag. The sun's rays can be harmful, wind can dry your eyes out and airborne dirt, dust, pollen and insects can all be potential hazards. So it makes sense to wear some form of eye protection at all times (*see* Figure 5.1). Clear or yellow-tinted lenses are ideal for low light conditions, with darker or mirrored lenses better for bright sunlight. The choice of styles and prices spans the spectrum. You don't need the latest, most expensive shades endorsed by sporting heroes or celebrities, but do look for light, comfortable glasses with interchangeable polycarbonate lenses which protect from both UVA and UVB rays.

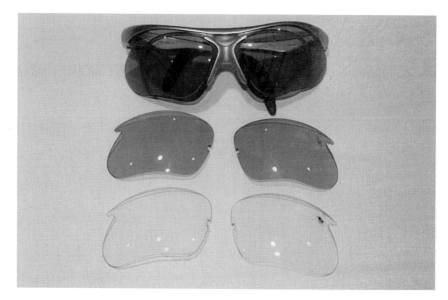

Figure 5.1 Eye protection – from the sun, wind, dust or other airborne objects. These glasses have interchangeable, lightweight, polycarbon lenses for different light conditions, as well as a prescription lens adaptor

Figure 5.2 Racing shoes with Velcro fasteners can easily be adjusted on the move. Note the minimalist short white socks too

Footwear

Cycling shoes have rigid soles to transfer power into, and protect your feet from, the pedals. Mesh panels are common for ventilation; these also keep weight down and drain water out.

If you use toe-clips and straps you can cycle in any stiff-soled shoe, provided that it fits inside the toe-clip. For 'clipless' pedals you will need specific shoes to accept the cleat that secures the shoe and pedal together (*see* Figure 5.2). Most shoe manufacturers accommodate a variety of – but not necessarily all – pedal systems (*see* also Chapter 3, p. 36). Check with your dealer that any new shoes you buy are compatible with your pedals and that they fit the shape of your feet. You may need to try on a few makes before buying!

Racing shoes leave the cleat exposed to lock into the pedal. With the stiff soles it's awkward to walk in them and wandering around in racing shoes can wear cleats very rapidly. Check your cleats regularly and expect to renew them at least once a year. The recessed cleat in mountain-biking and touring shoes (pretty much interchangeable) makes walking or running in these shoes very much easier. For additional comfort, the soles have a little more flexibility too.

Shoes can be fastened using laces, Velcro, ratchet straps or any combination of these, but racers and long-distance riders often prefer the convenience of the Velcro or ratchet systems that can be adjusted 'on the fly'. If you use laces, experiment with different lacing patterns, missing out lace-holes to give the most comfortable feel to the shoe.

It is useful to have a second pair of shoes a half or full size larger to accommodate two pairs of (or thicker) socks in the winter – or if riding in very hot conditions, when your feet can swell uncomfortably.

Overshoes keep the wind and water away from your feet to retain their warmth in the cold. These must fit over your shoes without being overstretched. With mountain-bike shoes you may need to buy overshoes a size or two larger to cope with their bulkier shape. If your shoes or overshoes are too tight they will restrict the blood-flow and your feet will actually become colder! You can wear an old pair of socks over your shoes, with a hole cut into the sole for the cleat, to do a similar job (just like the 'old days'!).

Gloves

Cyclists' fingerless gloves or 'track-mitts' have many functions.

- Padded palms reduce road-shock transmitted through the handlebars, and so alleviate pains in the wrists and sore hands.

- In a fall, the padding protects your hands from 'gravel-rash'.

- Gloves absorb sweat, providing a better grip on the handlebars.

- They're useful for wiping a sweaty face or runny nose on the move (many mitts have a towelling pad specifically for this purpose!).

Don't wear track-mitts over the top of other gloves – this just stretches them, rendering them a poor fit in warmer weather.

A useful tip on mitts

Most mitts fasten at the wrist with Velcro; when washing them, fasten the Velcro together to prevent it from snagging on other items.

Hats and helmets

The racer's cotton racing cap with a small peak still has its devotees, despite riders wearing protective helmets. The racing cap has much to recommend it: thin enough to be worn comfortably underneath a crash-helmet, it provides sun-protection (reverse it to protect the nape of your neck) and it will keep sweat from running into your eyes. It can help keep you warm in the cold (up to 75% of body heat loss is through the thin skin on the scalp); its peak can keep rain from your eyes; and it can provide protection from the glare of bright headlights at night. With such versatility it is no wonder that it refuses to go out of fashion.

Accidents are unpredictable, caused by any number of factors – slippery or poor road surfaces, animals, riding too fast for the conditions, inattention or drowsiness, sudden mechanical failure, carelessness of other road users, and so on. Fortunately, cycle-helmet design has improved dramatically and there are many light and well-ventilated helmets available. The better models have a simple harness at the base of the skull in addition to the chin strap to help keep the helmet in place, with plenty of vents to prevent overheating. A polycarbonate shell protects the polystyrene body from general wear and tear and they weigh around 200–300 g.

If it is to be of any value in an accident, your helmet must be properly adjusted to fit you. It should sit squarely on your head, not tilted to the front or rear. The straps should pass either side of your ears and the chinstrap should just feel tight when you open your jaw. If you rock the helmet gently on your head it should feel firm and just rock your scalp rather than moving over your head. Most helmets have foam pads to adjust the fit according to your individual head size and shape.

The polystyrene form of modern helmets is designed to compress or break in a fall, cushioning your head from any impact. Should you have an accident, it is important to replace the helmet even if there is no visible damage to it. Helmets need to be looked after carefully and not dropped, squashed or left in hot environments (like a car or in a window exposed to sunlight) where the adhesives used in their construction may disintegrate. Remember, it is just possible that this item might save your life.

Some aerodynamically-shaped helmets are merely aerodynamic fairings for better airflow over the rider and are not protective. These helmets can be very hot to wear – to minimise aerodynamic drag they rarely have any vents. They are limited to use only in time-trials and some track events, though competition rules may soon be changed to ensure that all headgear is protective.

Choose a white or light colour rather than a black or dark helmet. Light colours reflect the sun's rays and so reduce overheating, and they will make you more visible on the road. If you put any reflective material or stickers on your helmet check that the adhesives will not damage the helmet's shell or body. Look for helmets with ANSI 90.4 or Snell certification. Although not perfect, these tests do indicate that the helmets have passed minimum safety standards appropriate for competition, and as such most are suitable for long-distance cycling.

Jackets, jerseys and tops

Cycling jackets are cut closer and a little longer in the back and arms than other sports clothes, and may have rear pockets. Windproofing to the front and sleeves is useful for cold conditions, but the back is usually left unproofed to prevent you from getting too hot. Very thick or heavy jackets are not common, as there is greater benefit and more versatility to be had by layering-up with more thin garments than a few thick layers.

Figure 5.3 Cassie Lowe demonstrates perfect style – technique, position and dress – in the RAAM 2000

Clip-on braces

If your shorts or longs slip down in use, attach a pair of clip-on braces. It's what riders always used to do before Lycra or bib shorts were invented!

Cycling jerseys usually have three pockets at the back for ready access to small items, and a zip neck to adjust ventilation (*see* Figure 5.3). Most are made from polyester derivatives as these are hardwearing and easy to care for. Better jerseys are cut for the riding position; those cut for women are generally shorter in length, with narrower shoulders and shorter sleeves, often tailored at the waist and a little broader at the hem.

You can buy trade team jerseys with sponsors' names on, but plain or simply patterned jerseys are also available. Club riders can buy jerseys in their team colours. For safety, choose bright colours and avoid black or dark hues (but note that yellow is particularly attractive to many insects).

'Longs'

'Longs' or tights are cycling's equivalent of tracksuit bottoms – worn over shorts to keep your legs warm. Cut closer than other sports trousers to avoid snagging on the chain or front derailleur, many have a stirrup under the foot to keep them in place when riding. Wear this inside your shoe or it will quickly tear when you are off the bike. Lycra is the preferred material and, like shorts, longs can have a regular waist or be 'bib-tights'. Different thicknesses are employed for different times of the year. Unpadded tights are better than those with a seat insert. Wear regular cycling shorts as your base layer, then these can then be washed and changed and the longs worn again with a clean pair of shorts.

For times when the temperature is between zones or unpredictable, cycling has knee-length 'knickers', leg-warmers and knee-warmers. Knee-length knickers extend to just below the knee, usually worn in spring or autumn when the full warmth of longs is not required but you need to keep your knees protected from the cold (*see* Figure 5.4). In extreme conditions you can wear them underneath a pair

Figure 5.4 Riding at night and at high altitude calls for extra clothing: Cassie Lowe is well prepared for any eventuality in the RAAM 2000

of longs for extra warmth. Knee-warmers are a simple tapered tube of Lycra or similar material that tucks under the hem of your shorts to provide cover for your knees – useful to carry on many rides as they less bulky than other full leg cover. Leg-warmers are full-length leg-cover for use before or after competition, or ideal on long rides in case the temperature drops (such as when cycling at night or descending mountains).

Rainwear

You are unlikely to ride without ever encountering rain. Of course, some climates are more susceptible to rain than others, and – because of the length of time spent in the saddle – the long-distance rider is more likely to be caught in the rain than most. Although cycling is an activity which generates a great deal of body heat, water is a much better conductor of heat than air so you will chill very quickly when wet – especially since the ambient air temperature also drops during rainfall. Waterproof clothing has to keep you dry and warm without overheating, and be suitably lightweight, compact and streamlined. Fabrics are continually evolving to reduce the weight and bulk of waterproof clothing and improve its waterproof and breathable qualities.

The traditional bell-shaped cycle cape works very well to keep you and your legs dry with good air circulation, but it is a liability in windy conditions. Racing cyclists use the misnamed 'racing cape': a lightweight, close-fitting jacket usually made from PVC or proofed nylon, with a full-length zip or Velcro fastening, a long 'scoop tail' at the back to protect from spray thrown up by the rear wheel, and nylon-mesh side panels for ventilation and to reduce overheating (*see* Figure 8.2, p. 95).

More expensive models are aimed at leisure cyclists seeking a bit more comfort from their wet-weather gear. These are made from waterproof and breathable fabrics like Gore-Tex, often with extra features (e.g. pockets, drawstring fastenings at the neck and hem, adjustable cuffs and reflective trim). Leisure garments are usually a little bulkier and more expensive than the lightweight racing capes.

Waterproof leggings demand either a material that stretches over the knees, or one that is tailored for pedalling. Overtrousers are generally not popular with long-distance riders who find them too hot, too restrictive or too bulky. Until fabric developments change this, most riders accept that they will get wet legs and either ride in shorts (in warm weather) or trust that they will be able to stop and dry their Lycra longs before too long.

Waterproof socks can be very effective at keeping water at bay from your feet, but it is difficult to prevent rain from running down your legs and seeping into your socks from above! Nature invariably wins, eventually.

Shorts

Lycra is ideal for cycling shorts: its stretch and body-hugging properties make it comfortable without any flapping around in a breeze. Genuine cycling shorts have a padded insert for comfort, and a long leg to resist riding-up in use and to keep the thigh muscles warm. They are cut high at the back to accommodate the riding position and keep the kidney area warm. 'Bib shorts' have integral braces to prevent them from slipping down and to ensure that no gaps appear between the shorts and jersey. Avoid buying 'cycling shorts' from high street shops or sports stores if they do not have these features.

Cycling shorts should be worn next to the skin, without underwear, to avoid chafing. The padded insert used to be made of real chamois leather but is now usually a synthetic material. Genuine chamois needs to be treated regularly with lanolin to prevent it from drying out (and acting like sandpaper), but synthetic inserts do not need this attention. For longer rides most riders do still use some sort of cream on the seat insert to prevent soreness occurring (*see* also Chapter 7, pp. 82–3).

Wash your shorts as soon as possible after every ride to avoid bacteria developing. Modern synthetics can be machine-washed and dried very quickly, so most riders can manage their clothing needs quite comfortably with just two or three pairs of shorts.

Touring shorts have more traditional tailoring than the close-cut of Lycra racing shorts, and use other fabrics – although a degree of stretch from a small Lycra content is often welcome. A double seat is a good feature, as are zipped pockets. Some riders wear Lycra cycling shorts or cycling-specific briefs for padding underneath looser shorts to avoid poorly placed seams on regular underwear.

In most cases, women need to find shorts cut specifically for them. Narrower waists, broader hips, shorter leg lengths, a different rise, and redesigned and repositioned seat inserts make a big difference to the comfort factor.

Skinsuits

Really for racing only – and more particularly in time-trialling, track racing, cyclo-cross or short 'criterium' road races – skinsuits may be worn. These are a one-piece Lycra jersey and shorts designed for minimal wind resistance, usually made without pockets to keep the profile smooth (although long-distance racers may wish to have their skinsuits custom-made with a pocket or two).

Socks

Not needing the cushioned soles of most other sports socks, cycling socks are thin and cut very low, to just cover the ankle. Anything longer is superfluous and will merely hold water if wet. Coolmax is a superb material for temperature control and comfort. White socks are 'de rigueur' with road cyclists. Dark or coloured socks are understandably popular with off-road riders coping with mud, but they really don't 'look the part' when worn with shorts – whatever the discipline!

Undervests

These are a vital part of any cyclist's wardrobe. Modern sportsvests 'wick' or transfer moisture from one side of the fabric to the other, moving sweat from your body to the next layer of clothing where it can evaporate. This keeps you drier and prevents you from getting too cold, especially on descents when cold air can rapidly chill you if there is moisture next to the skin.

In the winter a vest keeps you warm by trapping an insulating a layer of air close to your body. Two undervests worn together are surprisingly warm considering their lack of thickness. Avoid cotton – this absorbs moisture and very quickly becomes wet and uncomfortable.

Another good reason for wearing an undervest is in case of an accident. Should you fall your clothing will 'stick' to the road and your skin will slide over the garment, causing skin-burn or 'road-rash'. By having another layer between your skin and the road, it will be the undervest that slides over the stationary garment and not your skin.

Bicycle technology is evolving rapidly. As material technology advances, many desirable concepts previously dismissed on the grounds of cost, weight or complexity can now be investigated and adapted for cycling in all its various forms.

- Mountain-bikes have only been around for just over 20 years, yet they have spawned widespread innovations such as suspension (*see* Figure 5.5) – as well as the rapid development of other ideas like wide-ratio gearing and better braking systems.

- Gear-changing has been revolutionised by 'index' systems and combined gear and brake levers for, literally, fingertip control.

- Cycle computers have become smaller, cheaper and provide more information than ever before.

- 'Clipless' pedal systems are easier to manage than the toe-clips and straps they replaced.

- Aerodynamic studies have profoundly influenced frame and wheel design.

- The relatively new sport of triathlon has introduced a whole new riding position to traditional cycling.

- New fabrics and fashion are changing cycling clothing.

- Clothes are now available that dry quicker; have better thermal properties, sun protection and 'breathability'; transfer moisture; and have less bulk and greater resistance to bacterial build-up.

Perhaps if the Union Cycliste Internationale (UCI) – cycle sport's international governing body – were to be less strict about the design of bicycles used in competition, evolution could be even quicker. Many innovations have been banned by the UCI for the sake of 'equal competition'. Some ideas survive and can be adopted by resourceful leisure riders, but understandably, most manufacturers need the publicity of the racing world to endorse their product before venturing into mass marketing and production.

Figure 5.5 The future: suspension forks on a road bike

Get set

6 Nutrition and hydration

Nutrition

Food is the cyclist's fuel. Many riders spend a fortune on their bicycle equipment but ignore 'fuel' (diet). Truth is, most riders would perform much better if they paid more attention to their 'engines' (bodies) rather than worrying about the merits of one seatpost compared to another.

A healthy diet is a varied one that includes the three principle components of food – carbohydrate, fat and protein – in suitable proportion to one another. Variety is needed to ensure that the essential micronutrients, vitamins, minerals and fibre are provided. Therefore, like everyone else, cyclists should eat a wide selection of food from the five main food groups: most should be cereals and starchy vegetables, with at least five portions of fruit and vegetables per day; then comes dairy products and meat/fish, with the lowest percentage of food coming from oils and fats.

Although there are general guidelines for a healthy diet which can be applied to everyone, the sportsperson's diet needs to be a little different from those of 'the average person'. Matters are marginally more complicated by vegetarian or vegan diets, but there are enough examples to prove that this need not be a hindrance to athletic performance. Indeed, such diets are far more widespread and accepted in mainstream society today, so that it is not difficult to find adequate nutrition in most places.

It is not within the scope of this book to provide detailed information on nutrition and hydration. The following chapter is intended as an overview of the basic principles: for further advice, it's best to refer to an established book on the subject – such as *The Complete Guide to Sports Nutrition* by Anita Bean[1].

Energy systems

There are two major energy systems that power the body's muscles, known as *aerobic* and *anaerobic*. In simple terms, muscles are made up of fast-twitch and slow-twitch fibres; the type of muscle fibre being used determines the energy system required.

The fast-twitch energy system is basically anaerobic: it doesn't require oxygen, but it rapidly produces lactic acid in the muscles as a waste product (causing a painful, burning sensation). This energy form is used for short, intensive efforts such as sprinting, coping with rapid acceleration, or short, steep hill-climbing lasting no more than 1–2 minutes.

[1]Published by A & C Black, October 2000 (3rd Edition).

The slow-twitch system – that most used by long-distance cyclists – is basically aerobic. It requires oxygen and does not produce lactic acid, but is limited by muscular endurance and the amount of fuel supplied to the muscles.

Long-distance cycling is predominantly an aerobic activity. Road races may involve occasional sprints or difficult climbs, close to an anaerobic effort, but for the vast majority of the time the pace is sustainable – in other words, the energy demand is similar to the supply of oxygen to the muscles.

Fuels for exercise

There are four components in food and drink that are capable of producing energy: carbohydrate, protein, fat and alcohol. One gram of each of these produces a different amount of energy, commonly expressed in kilocalories (kcal), or simply as Calories (Cal). More correctly, energy should be expressed in kilojoules (1 kcal = 4.2 kj).

Carbohydrate: 1 g produces 4 kcal
Protein: 1 g produces 4 kcal
Fat: 1 g produces 9 kcal
Alcohol: 1 g produces 7 kcal

Carbohydrate is stored as glycogen in the muscles and liver. Roughly 1600–2000 kcal can be stored in the body – enough to last about one day if you ate nothing. The glycogen is readily accessible for energy use, but unless topped up during exercise, these carbohydrate stores will only last about 2 hours.

Although fat and alcohol provide the most calories per gram they are not the best forms of energy for exercise. Alcohol cannot be used directly by the muscles but is broken down at a fixed rate by the liver. The majority of fat is stored around the organs of the body and under the skin and should be seen as a long-term energy store. Protein forms muscle and organ tissue, primarily as a regenerative material, and only comes into the energy equation in long-distance events when glycogen stores in the muscles become depleted.

At low levels of exercise intensity more fats are metabolised than carbohydrates. As the pace increases, so the amount of fat used diminishes and carbohydrate becomes the main fuel source. In anaerobic activity (such as very high intensity sprinting), carbohydrates are the principal energy source and no energy comes from fat.

Over longer periods of exercise like distance cycling, your body will use more fat stores and less carbohydrate. It will initially use carbohydrate stores, but as these become depleted it will try to conserve the muscle glycogen (some carbohydrate is required in order to metabolise the fat into energy) and will switch to the glycogen in the liver. Muscle proteins will then begin to break down to help meet energy demands.

Such chemical reactions in the body are expensive in terms of energy demands, so it is preferable to:

• begin exercising with properly topped-up glycogen stores, having eaten a meal high in carbohydrates before exercise;

• keep your muscle glycogen stores continually topped up by eating and drinking appropriate, carbohydrate-rich food and drinks.

The fitter you are, the better your muscles become at using fat and sparing the glycogen within the muscles. Less trained riders will use their glycogen faster and so will tire more quickly – but everyone can benefit from high glycogen levels, to ride harder and for longer.

Carbohydrate

Clearly, therefore, carbohydrates are extremely important as a source of fuel and between 60% and 70% of your diet should be made up of them. If you don't have adequate stocks of glycogen in your muscles and liver when you begin a ride, your performance – and your ride – will suffer.

Carbohydrate absorption and energy release – the Glycaemic Index

Carbohydrates are often divided into two categories: simple (sugars) and complex (starches and fibres). It is widely accepted that simple carbohydrates are absorbed more quickly than complex ones. In reality, many foods contain a mixture of the two and the rate at which they are absorbed into the body's energy system actually depends on the Glycaemic Index (GI) of the food (see Table 6.1). The higher the GI of a particular food, the quicker it is digested – with the carbohydrates being more readily converted into glycogen for use by the muscles.

For long-distance cycling at a relatively low intensity, foods with a low GI value (<40) can help to delay fatigue through their slow release of energy. However, they will need to be 'topped up' from time to time by foods with a high GI in order to maintain adequate glycogen levels in the muscles. Shorter distances, covered at higher intensities, can benefit from foods with a higher GI – but you must allow yourself time to digest your food. The usual rule of thumb used by racing cyclists is to eat three hours before racing. Less than three hours before an event (and once the event has started), they will take just small snacks to keep their energy levels suitably topped up.

Protein

Protein is needed for new bone, muscle and skin development and so is essential for young children. Although the requirement is reduced in adults, active people do need higher levels of protein intake than sedentary people to regenerate tissue (muscle) and red blood cells and keep their bones healthy. Protein *can* be used as an energy source for the muscles, but the energy produced from burning protein is relatively small. In extreme cases the body will break down its own muscle protein to be used as a source of energy if there are insufficient carbohydrate and fat sources available (e.g. during intensive riding such as the Tour de France, RAAM or extended touring). Your diet should be approximately 12–15% protein.

Protein-rich foods include:

- chicken, turkey

- fish

Glycaemic Index

This scale of 0–100 measures the immediate effect of food on blood sugar levels – usually compared to glucose – plotted every 15 minutes for a 2-hour period. The higher the blood sugar levels after eating the food, the higher the GI. At present the list of foods which have been tested is somewhat limited (around 600 single foods). The GI of *meals* has to be estimated especially, as mixing foodstuffs alters the GI of a meal. Eating fats or proteins can slow the rate at which the stomach empties, slow digestion, and lower the GI of carbohydrates consumed.

Table 6.1 The GI of different foods

Food	GI	Food	GI
Sugars		**Fruit**	
Glucose	100	Pineapple (slice)	66
Sucrose	65	Raisins	64
Honey (tsp)	58	Apricot	57
		Banana	55
Breakfast cereals		Kiwi	52
Cornflakes	84	Orange	46
Rice crispies	82	Apple	38
Weetabix (2)	69	Pear	38
Sustain	68	Dried apricots (5)	31
Shredded Wheat (2)	67		
Muesli	56	**Pulses**	
All Bran	42	Baked beans	48
Porridge (w/water)	42	Chick peas	33
		Red kidney beans	27
Grains/pasta		Soya beans	18
White rice	87		
Brown rice	76	**Biscuits/cakes**	
Buckwheat	68	Digestive biscuits (1)	59
Couscous	65	Sponge cake (slice)	46
Instant noodles	46		
Macaroni	45	**Snacks/confectionery**	
Spaghetti	41	Mars bar	68
		Ice cream	61
Bread/crispbreads		Muesli bar	61
Rice cakes (1)	85	Crisps	54
White bread (slice)	70	Milk chocolate	49
Wholemeal bread (slice)	69		
		Dairy products	
Vegetables		Yoghurt, fruit (low fat)	33
Baked potato	85	Skimmed milk	32
Carrots	49	Full cream milk	27
Peas	48		
Sweetcorn	55		

Source: Anita Bean (2000), *The Complete Guide to Sports Nutrition*, 3rd ed., (A & C Black), pp. 233–7.

- lean meat

- eggs

- nuts

- beans, lentils, pulses

- yogurt, cheese, milk.

Fats

Fat is a necessary part of the diet and a healthy sports diet is likely to be composed of 15–30% fat[2]. There are three groups of fats, classified by their chemical composition.

- *Saturated* fats are widely believed to be one of the main 'culprits' in heart disease and have no known positive benefits for sports performance or health. Typically, these come from animal products – cheese, butter, lard and meat fat. Processed foods (e.g. cakes, pastry and biscuits) often contain significant quantities of these fats and so are best avoided.

- *Monounsaturated* fats are probably the most beneficial fats for both health and sports performance. Sources include oils – such as olive, rapeseed, groundnut, almond and hazelnut – olives themselves, and nuts and seeds.

- *Polyunsaturated* fats are found in most vegetable oils and oily fish, and can reduce harmful low-density lipoprotein (LDL) cholesterol levels in the blood. They are also important because they include the so-called 'essential fatty acids', which the body cannot manufacture by itself and which therefore have to come from food. However, they may also reduce beneficial high-density (HDL) lipoprotein cholesterol, so need to be supplemented with some monounsaturates.

If you cut down on dietary fat too much, however, it can create skin problems, inhibit the body's control of inflammation, and adversely affect blood pressure and blood clotting. Some research indicates that low fat intake may be linked to heart disease and cancers. Extremely low-fat diets often indicate a very low calorie and nutrient intake, leading to poor energy levels, reduced capacity for exercise, poor recovery and overtraining syndrome. That being said, any excess of dietary fat not required by the body – like an excess of any food component in your diet – will be converted into body fat.

Body fat

Surplus body fat is rarely desirable. For cyclists, this is just extra weight that requires extra effort and energy to be propelled. If you ride in hilly areas you will perhaps already appreciate the difference that a few kilos can make to the ease of riding uphill.

Your body has two types of fat. *Essential fat* provides insulation, protection and cushioning for cell membranes, brain tissue, bone marrow and organs (heart, kidneys, liver). Women have additional sex-specific fat stored mostly in the breasts and around the hips. This is used in oestrogen production and conversion, ensuring normal hormonal balance and menstrual function. For men, essential fat comprises about 3% of their body weight. The essential fat in women comprises around 8–12% of their body weight. *Storage fat* is an energy reserve, stored under the skin and around the organs. This fat is used in aerobic exercise (*see* also pp. 67–8), and even when relaxing or sleeping.

There are different scientific methods of measuring body fat, such as Body Mass Index (BMI) measurements, skinfold callipers, underwater weighing or Bio-

[2]International Conference on Foods, Nutrition and Sports Performance, 1991.

electrical Impedance Analysis. However, these are not always available – or even desirable – for many cyclists. Use how you look and feel as a guide, and if in doubt consult a professional. Unfortunately, it is not possible to spot-reduce fat from a particular area of your body. As you exercise, your body will draw upon the fat it needs, depending your own genetic make-up and hormonal balance. What sports *can* do is help tone your muscles and improve your shape.

Although low body fat levels can help cycling performance, too little fat can cause problems – especially, but not exclusively, for women. There is no ideal figure for total body fat levels: this will vary from one individual to another and be partly dependent on the demands of the activity they do. Extremely lean cyclists will clearly have to pay great attention to their dietary habits to ensure they are adequately fuelled at all times – and even to their clothing, especially in cold conditions. Those who are endowed with greater fat reserves will need to spend more time improving their strength and power if they wish to keep up with the leaner riders, particularly in hilly terrain.

Micronutrients

Micronutrients (vitamins, minerals, enzymes and phytochemicals) are essential for activities within the body such as growth and tissue repair, the regulatory function of the immune and hormonal systems, control of fluid balance, and muscle and nerve function. They are not produced by the body, and so have to be obtained through the diet.

In very simple terms, eating the five portions of fruit and vegetables (excluding potatoes from the vegetable list) per day – as recommended by the government – is sufficient to provide a healthy balance of micronutrients. Choose foods of different colours and textures to give a wider range of nutritional intake.

Many foods quickly lose their nutritional value after picking or preparation. So unless frozen, food should be served quickly after preparation, and fruit and vegetables should be served with the minimum amount of cooking. Meat and fish, though, should be thoroughly cooked.

Cycling food

To avoid running out of energy you will need to consume some sort of 'fuel' on any ride lasting more than an hour or two. Carbohydrate sports drinks such as Maxim, High Five or PSP – often sold by sports shops or pharmacists – are ideal, as they meet both the carbohydrate and the fluid needs of the body (*see* also pp. 74–7). You may find such drinks to be more palatable when mixed at a slightly lower concentration than that recommended by the manufacturers. The speed of absorption of carbohydrate is limited in the body, so there is no benefit in using higher concentrations. Liquid fuels like these are excellent because they are readily digested; however, many riders may want to eat something solid, particularly on longer leisure rides.

For years, the cyclist's staple diet has been a mixture of bananas, raisins, malt loaf and jam sandwiches, topped up at café-stops by baked beans on toast, cakes and rice pudding and washed down with copious quantities of sweet tea. Really, this is not too bad and it could easily be far worse. All these foods are readily digested and contain a good range of simple and complex carbohydrates (with a relatively high GI to ensure that muscle glycogen is kept well supplied – *see* above). The only question mark with this 'on the road diet' is perhaps the quantity of tea, which contains caffeine and is a diuretic. Keep tea and coffee consumption to a minimum, and substitute with fruit juice, squash or an energy drink if necessary (*see* pp. 77–80).

Fatty foods are best avoided, as they contribute little to the immediate energy requirement (many foodstuffs contain some degree of fat anyway) and reduce the GI. An obvious test of a food's fat content is if it feels greasy or leaves a greasy mark on a paper napkin. Pies, pastries, cakes and biscuits often have surprisingly high fat levels.

Foods with a very high simple sugar content (e.g. chocolate and confectionery) can also cause problems if eaten on their own. They can provide an instant boost of energy but may create a 'sugar-rush' that depletes the muscle glycogen stores more rapidly.

Many riders enjoy sandwiches, even in racing. Use white bread or soft rolls (more easily digested than brown or wholemeal bread) and cut them small. Fillings could be tuna, cottage cheese, chicken or lean ham, jam, honey or banana. Dried fruit, fig rolls and cereal bars are nutritious and easily handled on the move. Racing cyclists (and many randonneurs) keep their food in their back pockets or have it handed up to them by roadside helpers – they do not stop to eat!

When to eat, and how much?

The maxim 'little and often' sums up a cyclist's need for food. Obviously, the more intense the activity – or the longer the duration – the greater the need for food. In very cold conditions your body will be using 'fuel' just to keep warm, so you may need to eat more on winter rides.

Food wrappers

Wrap food in aluminium foil, greaseproof paper or paper bags. It's far easier to open up these materials on the move than to try to tear into a polythene bag. Whatever you use, do not drop litter by the roadside but dispose of it in a bin when convenient.

Figure 6.1 Hungry randonneurs tuck into wholesome food supplied at an 'El Supremo' AUK roadside control (photo: Chris Beynon)

On a 2-hour ride, most riders will manage quite happily without extra food, but you need to begin drinking within the first 20–30 minutes. On longer rides, begin eating after the first hour or so – maybe just half an energy bar or half a banana, but enough to keep your energy reserves topped up. If you don't, you may get 'the bonk' or 'hit the wall' – both terms used to describe the depletion of your glycogen stores, so that you feel you have absolutely no energy to continue. Be warned: this is not a pleasant feeling. Your hunger will feel insatiable, your legs will feel weak, and you may even feel dizzy. Most long-distance cyclists will experience it at least once, probably early on in their cycling careers. Prevention, by paying attention to your fuel supply early on in a ride, is better than trying to cope with fuel intake failure and needing a rapid cure in the latter stages.

Hydration

As you exercise you produce heat, and sweat evaporates from the skin to regulate your body temperature. Unless replaced by drinking, these sweat losses will lead to dehydration and to impaired performance.

Many sports drink manufacturers promote *electrolyte* drinks to replace the minerals lost through sweating during exercise. Since sweat is salty to the taste, it must contain some minerals excreted through the skin, leaving the body's mineral content depleted. However, tests have shown that the mineral composition of sweat is far more dilute than that of plasma inside the body, indicating that fluid loss is actually more significant than mineral loss during exercise. *After* exercise and on longer rides, there is a good case for replenishing the body's micronutrients with an electrolyte drink to ensure adequate recovery.[3]

It is vitally important to be properly hydrated before you exercise and to continue drinking throughout the event as much as possible. Thirst is not a good indicator of needing to drink. If you feel thirsty, then you are already beginning to dehydrate. In hot conditions you can easily lose over 2 kg through sweating (approx. 3% body weight) (*see* Table 6.2). This will lead to a loss of around 10% of your capacity to ride (*see* also Figure 6.2), and cause premature fatigue due to:

- reduction in blood volume

- decreased skin blood flow

- decreased sweat rate

- decreased heat dissipation

- increased core body temperature

- increased rate of muscle glycogen depletion.[4]

[3]Gleeson, M. (2000), 'Fluid balance during exercise', *Performance in Cycling* published on the Internet: www.bham.ac.uk/sportex/symposium
[4]Colgan, L. (1990), *Nutrition and Fitness Magazine*, vol. ix, no. 5.

Table 6.2 Fluid loss as sweat during cycling[5]

Exercise intensity (% VO$_2$max)	Ambient temperature (°C)	Relative humidity (%)	Sweat loss (litre/hr)
50	18	50	0.7 (1%)*
60	18	50	1.2
70	18	50	1.4 (2%)*
70	25	40	1.8
70	30	30	2.1 (3%)*
70	30	90	2.8 (4%)*

*% body mass of a 70 kg cyclist

Other consequences may include:

- muscle cramps

- gastric distress

- increased blood viscosity, putting more strain on the heart

- greater risk of heat stroke, organ failure – and, according to Muehling[6], when body fluid losses approach 12–15%, death occurs.

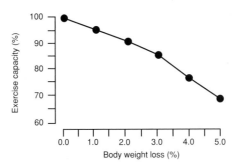

Figure 6.2 Reduction in work capacity with increasing dehydration (body weight loss)[7]

When to drink, and how much

A sedentary person needs between 2 and 2.5 litres of water per day (directly as liquid, and indirectly through foodstuffs), but if you are active in hot conditions your fluid requirement can increase to eight times this figure. The usual rule of thumb is to drink 500 ml of liquid per hour. This figure will increase in hot weather or humid conditions, perhaps even doubling. You still need to drink in cool weather – exercise still produces heat. Keep drinking small amounts, 'little and often', to maintain your fluid balance.

In temperate conditions you can usually manage with two bottles carrying 500–750 ml each, enough for a ride of 2–3 hours. On longer rides you will need to be resupplied along the route either by helpers, at controls or at feed-stations, or by stopping at a store, café or bar to buy drinks and fill up your bottles (*see* Figure 6.3). In hot conditions or in greater humidity, and in more remote regions, you will have to carry more liquid with you either by taking extra bottles on your bike (or at a

[5]Gleeson, op cit.
[6]Muehling, E. (1994), *Pure Water Now*, 2nd ed. (Lincoln, Nebraska), pp. 1–43.
[7]Gleeson, M. et al. (1996), 'Dehydration, rehydration and exercise in the heat', *Insider*, vol. iv, no. 2.

Figure 6.3 Inflight refuelling: long-distance racers don't stop to eat or drink

push, in your pockets) or using a hydration pack like the Camelbak or Platypus (*see* also p. 46).

You may need to experiment with your fluid intake. If you weigh yourself before a ride and then again when you return, and find that you have lost more than 2% of your body weight, you clearly need to drink more when exercising. Another simple test is to check the colour of your urine. A clear or pale yellow colour shows that you are adequately hydrated. If it is a darker yellow (and usually more smelly) then you are under-hydrated.

What to drink

Plain water will keep you hydrated, but for sports purposes research has shown that drinks containing carbohydrate are far better – supplying both the body's fluid needs and the fuel needs of the muscles. Ordinary fruit juices and squash drinks can cause dehydration unless diluted, as they are usually too concentrated for ready absorption and require the body's existing water content to dilute them before they can be used.

Fluid is absorbed into the body through the stomach. Drinks are described as *isotonic, hypotonic* or *hypertonic* depending on how rapidly they move from the stomach into the bloodstream.

- **Isotonic** drinks are 'in balance' with the body's fluid levels and empty easily from the gut into the bloodstream. Typically, isotonic sports drinks contain 5–8% carbohydrate (5–8 g carbohydrate per 100 ml). Sodium helps absorption and these drinks can be consumed at any time without hindering hydration.

- **Hypotonic** drinks empty from the gut even quicker, but they tend to have low levels of minerals or carbohydrate. They are very useful for hydration – especially

Make up your own sports drinks

- Fruit squash diluted with 4 to 5 parts water with 1–1.5 g salt (approx ⅕ teaspoon) per litre
- 60 g glucose (or 100 g glucose polymer powder, sometimes called 'malto-dextrin') in 1 litre diluted, sugar-free or low-calorie squash, plus 1–1.5 g salt
- Pure fruit juice diluted 50:50 with water, with 1–1.5 g salt per litre.

For hypotonic solutions, halve the given quantity of juice, squash or glucose and increase the water content per litre.

in hot conditions. These drinks are usually easy to take; however, as a long-distance cyclist you need to maintain your energy levels, so you must ensure that you consume enough carbohydrate as well as keeping up your liquid intake.

- **Hypertonic** drinks are the slowest to empty from the stomach, typically with a high carbohydrate content (>10%). These drinks can provide plenty of energy but actually hinder hydration. They are best reserved for after-sport use when energy is needed but solid food is perhaps difficult to consume. Be careful of hypertonic solutions marketed as ideal fuel for ultra-distance athletes – they can reverse the normal process of osmosis in the stomach and cause diarrhoea.

Try different commercial sports drinks: some may suit you and your needs far better than others. It is also vital that you test these drinks in training. Competition or a long randonnée is not the ideal place to find that your fuel supply is causing you to dive behind a hedge every hour! The recommended carbohydrate intake is usually 1 g per kg of body weight every hour. In practice you may find this solution too strong, approaching a hypertonic solution, and many riders prefer a more dilute solution closer to 0.5 g carbohydrate per kg of body weight per hour. The ideal drink should:

- be palatable, something that you will not mind drinking

- not cause stomach upsets (you may need to trial different brands and find out which one suits you best)

- contain some carbohydrate (20–80 g/litre) to keep your muscles fuelled

- contain sodium to replace salts lost in sweat

- be isotonic for most rapid absorption

- be cool (10–12°C): cool drinks tend to be easier to drink than warm ones

- not be acidic or gassy.

In summary, for your best performances and to prevent problems of dehydration you should:

- begin each ride well hydrated, and drink as much as you can comfortably consume during the ride to try to match sweat loss

- avoid diuretic drinks such as coffee, tea, cola and alcohol, especially when riding – these will make you want to pee and dehydrate you further

- re-hydrate with plenty of liquid as soon as possible after exercise. You can weigh yourself to see exactly how much fluid you have lost (weight loss in kg = no. of litres to be replaced)

- train yourself to drink regularly during rides.

You can drink too much. Your body can only absorb fluid at a certain rate, depending on whether it is an isotonic, hypertonic or hyptonic solution. Excessive water intake will dilute blood plasma and if you take on more fluid than your stomach can process, you will need to stop and pee more frequently.

> ## Dental alert!
> There is evidence that some commercial sports drinks can be harmful to teeth because of their sugar content. Clean your teeth regularly, especially after training or competition when you have used these drinks.

Ergogenic aids

Ergogenic aids are any substance or group of substances used to improve athletic performance beyond its normal limits. Technically, this may include all perform-ance-enhancing substances, such as steroids, stimulants and other substances illegal for competition or harmful to an athlete's health. However, there are plenty of legal and natural ergogenic aids which are beneficial to an endurance athlete – such as metabolites (micronutrients), trace minerals and some amino acids.

Nutritional supplements

Think of your body as a machine, and the requirement for regular and thorough maintenance seems obvious; lubricate the moving parts, keep the power supply clean and constant, and ensure that nothing is worn or damaged such that output does not fall from the required rate or outside the accepted tolerances.

Maintenance is an ongoing task. It's the same with your body riding a bike all day, or day after day. Invariably some down-time is needed for essential repairs (night-time rest, days off or annual holidays) – but with regular care it's surprising how long a machine, or a body, can continue to run without any problems.

In theory a well-balanced diet should provide all the nutrients you need for athletic performance. A multi-vitamin supplement, perhaps with iron, from a chemist or pharmacy is an ideal and cost-effective 'insurance' for most people. But when extreme endurance activities are involved it becomes difficult to consume adequate calories for performance and so some form of supplementation becomes essential. In normal daily activity an adult male needs about 2000 kcal per day. A more active person may use 3000 kcal or more[8]. A cyclist in the Tour de France or Race Across AMerica will use 6000–10,000 kcal per day[9] and all of these need to be replaced if he is to ride the following day, as well as topping up on the essential micronutrients necessary for proper body function and tissue repair. Actual calorie consumption will vary from one person to another depending on their size, rate of metabolism and the ambient temperature.

Dietary supplements can help to maintain your body's levels of vitamins, micronutrients, amino acids and enzymes for optimum performance, with numerous businesses providing 'health foods' and supplements to a hungry market. The bodybuilding world is an extreme example, where supplements are frequently used to enhance muscle bulk. Cyclists, however, want muscle strength *without* bulk, since big muscles add body weight and reduce flexibility.

The effectiveness of nutritional supplements was evident in the 2000 Race Across AMerica, where the riders using a programme of supplements during the event were noticeably in better shape at the end of the event than those who had not paid such close attention to their diet. These riders showed no signs of salt

[8]Jeukendrup, A. (2000), 'The importance of carbohydrate feeding', *Performance in Cycling*, published on the Internet: www.bham.ac.uk/sportex/symposium
[9]Shermer, M. (1993), *Race Across AMerica* (WRS Publishing), pp. 217–18.

loss during the event, minimal muscle wastage, and were much more mobile than their fellow competitors after 3000 miles of riding and less than 24 hours of sleep in 10 days.

A word of warning, though: more is *not* always better. Too great a dosage of any one mineral, nutrient or vitamin – or combination of them – can have adverse side-effects. Treat all supplements with caution; not all manufacturers' claims have proper scientific evidence to back them up. And whatever they claim, you should *never* exceed the recommended dose.

Drugs

Of course, some athletes will take products with the specific aim of cheating in order to improve their performance. The banned substances and performance-enhancing methods are widely publicised by the various governing bodies and no rider can be excused for falling foul of the regulations. More worryingly, many products designed to improve athletic performance have been found later to have dramatic side-effects adversely affecting the health of the athlete.

Your long-term health is always more valuable than any short-term glory or success. If in doubt about a product, don't take it. You can live without it. Do research manufacturers' claims – apart from their own sponsored literature – and check with your pharmacist if any product appears on the sport's list of banned substances. There are usually suitable alternatives available.

Although leisure cycling is not usually subject to drugs testing procedures, it makes sense to keep close to the guidelines issued by the competitive organisations. For most riders, enjoying the local cuisine of the areas they travel through is one of the joys of travelling. Pills and potions are best left to those involved in heavy training for competition, or perhaps those looking for a performance in an ultra-long randonnée with minimal sleep and recovery time.

The only exception that RAAM makes to the International Olympic Committee (IOC) list of banned substances is that any level of caffeine is permitted, as is the 'topical use of cortisone cream for saddle sores'. If you have any queries about supplements or drugs, make enquiries with the supplier or manufacturer, or one of the sports governing bodies. Alternatively, the doping control unit of UK Sport should be able to help.

Caffeine and other stimulants

Caffeine is a well-known stimulant favoured by many riders, either in the form of coffee, tea, cola and various 'sports' drinks, or as caffeine pills, to stave off tiredness. It can improve fat oxidation and reduce glycogen depletion to help improve endurance, but it is also a diuretic (causing dehydration) and is banned in most competition above 12 micrograms per litre in the urine (equivalent to six cups of instant coffee or nine cans of cola). It can overstimulate some people, causing rapid heartbeat or anxiety – so treat it with some caution.

The following table is useful for those cyclists who need to be aware of their caffeine intake due to IOC restrictions. Some long-distance riders use caffeine to help stay awake and alert.

Table 6.3 Caffeine content of various drinks

Source	mg per cup
Ground coffee	80–90 mg
Instant coffee	60 mg
Decaffeinated coffee	3 mg
Tea	40 mg
Can of cola	40 mg
Caffeine pills	100–200 mg (per pill)

Figure 6.4 Catering for randonneurs' needs, whatever the weather. One of the 'El Supremo' AUK controls (photo: Ivo Miesen)

In summary

The results of a great deal of research have changed the eating habits of sportspeople in recent years. New information is continuing to filter through from various sources about the optimum diet. However, some basic guidelines have been obvious for years and are unlikely to change. Eat a varied and balanced diet with plenty of fresh fruit and vegetables, and make sure that you stay well hydrated. 'A little of what you fancy' – such as an English fried breakfast – won't do you any harm as an *occasional* treat, but some foods and drinks can be more harmful than others to your long-term health (e.g. fatty or processed foods, alcohol). Excess of *anything* should be avoided.

Remember that carbohydrates are the cyclist's staple food, and fat intake should be limited. Protein is the body's building material and so cannot be ignored. If you are worried that your diet may be lacking all the vital vitamins and minerals, take a multivitamin tablet once a day, but this is not an excuse or substitute for a poor diet.

Good hydration is absolutely essential, and you should have a drink with you for any ride lasting over 40 minutes. Carbohydrate drinks are an excellent fuel for cyclists, as they are readily consumable and can satisfy the body's fuel and fluid requirements in one go.

In respect of further information, few sources deal with very long endurance activities like distance cycling (for most sports, anything over two hours really is a marathon). However, Anita Bean's book *The Complete Guide to Sports Nutrition* is regarded by many as the ultimate 'all you'll ever need to know – until we find out more' on diet and exercise. Sports journals and magazines are an excellent source of the latest information – do read them. You can always find a good coach or nutritionist who can tailor-make recommendations for your personal needs.

7 Look after yourself – health and hygiene

All the correct equipment and training is useless if you fail to look after yourself. Health and hygiene are vital ingredients for any sort of sporting performance, whether it is a leisurely ride on a Sunday afternoon, a long-term expedition or a competitive event. On a long ride small irritations, aches or pains can soon become major issues and be enough to bring a ride to a premature halt. Deal with any minor problems before they can get inflamed and out of all proportion. If in doubt, always consult a doctor.

Saddle sores

The most obvious area of concern to cyclists is the crotch. Saddle soreness happens through poor positioning, inappropriate equipment, overuse, or lack of hygiene. (*See* Chapter 2, pp. 17–20 for advice on saddle height and position.) Unfortunately, choosing the correct saddle is partly a matter of trial and error relating to your anatomy, riding style and personal preferences. Remember that comfort should always take priority over fashion. A soft saddle will not provide the necessary support for riding long distances so a firm (but not hard) saddle will be more comfortable.

By gradually increasing the frequency of rides and distances ridden, your skin will become harder and less affected by the pressures of cycling. Surgical spirit (rubbing alcohol) can help toughen up the skin, but never apply it to broken skin. Wearing proper cycling shorts or shorts liners will help enormously (*see* also pp. 61–2). Experienced riders regularly use creams with antiseptic properties (e.g. Sudocrem, Lanacane or A&D, usually sold by pharmacists for bedsores or infants' nappy-rash). Apply this directly on to your skin or rub it on to the padded insert of your shorts to reduce friction. Topical cortisone, and products used to cure acne or fungal infections such as athlete's foot, can also be highly effective in this area. 'Blister rings' can provide padding around any sores and relieve pressure. (If all else fails you may need to butcher your saddle by cutting a hole in it to avoid the sore point!) The new breed of 'cutaway' saddles goes some way to tackling this before it becomes a problem.

Prevention is always better than cure, and hygiene is at all times absolutely paramount. The crotch is a sweaty area of the body – particularly when pressed against a bicycle saddle for hours on end – and bacteria thrive in these warm, moist conditions. Wear clean shorts for every ride. Frequent use of antiseptic 'wet wipes' can be very beneficial on long rides. Change out of your cycling clothes, and wash and dry yourself thoroughly, as soon as possible after a ride. Wash and dry your shorts thoroughly too. 'Street clothes' should not be too tight either, but allow air to circulate. Consult your pharmacist or doctor if infections do not clear up within a week or two. Severe saddle sores may need medical treatment, but this is rare.

Neck and back

Neck and back pains are usually due to muscular strain or overuse, often combined with poor positioning, lack of flexibility, inappropriate technique or poor road surfaces. Sometimes these problems are due to degenerative wear, but they may be non-cycling related (poor posture or muscle tension caused by stress, anxiety, depression or fatigue). Massage may help alleviate the problem, but you need to find and eliminate the cause.

Do not increase your cycling distances too rapidly. Learn to relax on the bike. Avoid overstretching to the handlebars. If necessary raise your handlebars, use a shorter stem, or move the position of your brake levers and use different parts of the handlebars to provide a variety of positions – this can ease the strain on any one set of muscles during a ride. Gentle stretching exercises are a valuable preventative measure – *see* also pp. 148–55.

Poor road surfaces can be countered by using fatter tyres, lower tyre pressures, a suspension seatpost or thicker padding on your gloves, handlebars or saddle. Some muscular pains may be due to trapped nerves, in which case you may need to consult an osteopath or physiotherapist.

Hands and wrists

Your hands and wrists can suffer from aches and pains, tingling, numbness or weakness, usually caused by compression of the nerves in your hands. Many of the solutions suggested for back and neck pains can be used to alleviate the hands and wrists too, e.g. wider, softer tyres. Move your hands to different parts of the handlebar during a ride; check that your position is not too far forwards and that your wrists are not sitting awkwardly. You may need to change the shape or size of your handlebars or change your handlebar stem. Padded gloves and handlebar tape or grips can help, but don't have them too thick (*see* also p. 34). Where permitted, using tri-bars (*see* also pp. 31–3) can solve hand and wrist problems. Every so often, exercise your hands by moving them around, clenching and unclenching your fingers to improve the blood flow and relieve the pressure on the nerves.

Head

Your skull is important! It contains your brain and that is worth protecting. Head injuries can be serious and in any situation where a rider has lost consciousness, feels dizzy or suffers memory loss after a fall – however briefly – an immediate visit to the doctor or local hospital is advised. (Such a visit will also lend weight to any insurance claim.) In most parts of the world, if not in competition, cyclists can still choose whether or not they wear a helmet. However, most accidents happen outside competition. By riding longer and further than most other cyclists the long-distance rider is susceptible to fatigue and will encounter more adverse situations, so it is wise to wear a protective helmet at all times.

Ears

The causes of earache are not always clear. Earaches are more common in cold weather and the simple precaution of using a skier's headband to keep your ears warm, or cotton wool in them, may alleviate the problem. Seek medical advice if problems persist.

Eyes

Airborne hazards are common but avoidance is simple – wear protective glasses (*see* also p. 56). If you get something in your eye, wash it with plain water or a solution such as Visene or Murine. If this doesn't work visit a doctor, hospital or optician.

Feet

Your feet are one of the three contact points with your bike, so treat them with care. Correctly fitting shoes are essential: loose-fitting shoes can cause blisters; tight shoes will constrict your feet. Try on new shoes with your cycling socks – and buy them in the afternoon, when your feet will have expanded relative to the morning. Select your shoes by their fit and not by who rides the same brand, or where the brand sits on the fashion-ladder.

Most cycling foot problems are due to restricted blood flow – caused by shoes that are too narrow, socks that are too thick, or shoe-fastenings or toe-straps that are pulled too tight. Cyclists probably suffer more than most sportspeople from poor circulation in their feet: cycling shoes have rigid soles for better power transfer to the pedals, precluding any running shoe-type cushioning. The use of thin inner soles may help. For more information on cycling shoes, *see* pp. 57–8.

In cycling there is no foot impact to stimulate blood circulation, and the cold can easily penetrate the thin, ventilated uppers of cycling shoes – especially in winter. Prevent this by:

• wearing overshoes

• wearing two pairs of thin socks, if there is room in your shoes (buy shoes a size larger for winter socks)

• spraying anti-perspirant on to your feet before putting socks on (this reduces sweating and thus heat loss)

- rubbing warming embrocation on to your feet

- lining your shoes with aluminium foil to reflect heat losses

- getting off the bike and running up a hill to improve circulation

- using winter bootees with a high-cut ankle.

In the summer, the opposite can be as unbearable – 'hot foot', caused by your feet swelling and their nerve endings being squashed inside the shoe. Avoid this by:

- using well-ventilated shoes

- removing the shoe insoles, or cutting a hole in the insole under the pressure point – the ball of the foot – to give your foot room to expand

- wearing shoes a size larger than normal

- loosening the shoe fastenings (Velcro or ratchet fastenings can be adjusted on the move)

- wearing CoolMax or similar wicking socks

- cutting the toes off a pair of old shoes for those days of extreme heat! (Shimano have even marketed stiff-soled open sandals with SPD fittings – worn by at least one rider in the 1999 Paris–Brest–Paris randonnée).

You may want to remove your shoes from time to time to allow your feet to 'breathe'. But, given the opportunity, your feet will expand and may not return to your shoes so easily! If you require a foot massage on a long event, do this one foot at a time and slip your massaged foot back into your shoe immediately after treatment before it has time to swell.

Very occasionally problems occur as a result of manufacturing defects in the shoe, or from poorly positioned cleats putting pressure on the wrong part of the foot. Check that no bolts or fittings are proud of the sole where they could press into your foot. You may need orthotics to spread the load across the foot.

Athlete's foot is a fungal infection. Although not life-threatening it is unpleasant, causing itching and blisters between the toes and on the soles of the feet. It can easily be treated by powders and ointments but is best prevented by ensuring good hygiene practices at all times. Use only dry, clean towels and socks and wear sandals in places like changing-rooms where the infection can easily be picked up on damp or wet floors.

Knees

Knee problems are usually associated with overuse injuries, although they can be caused by catastrophic (external) trauma such as a fall. There are many possible causes of knee problems and even experts often find it difficult to ascertain a correct diagnosis. Riders who continue to experience such problems should seek the advice of an experienced coach, who should at least be able to tackle the problem by a

Racing cyclists shave their legs. Their reasons are varied (and some really don't know why, but hey, everyone else does it so it must be right!). Vanity may be high on their agenda, but with clean-shaven legs it is:

- **much easier and quicker to get clean and dry than with hairy legs**
- **easier to apply protective oils or warming embrocation**
- **more comfortable when receiving massage – no pulled hairs**
- **easier to apply (and remove) dressings or bandages after a fall.**

However, it is not proven that they are significantly more aerodynamic (sorry).

process of elimination – or better still, a podiatrist who can advise on the use of orthotic inserts in the shoes.

Frequent causes of knee pain are:

- incorrect saddle height or position
- poor cleat adjustment
- using too big a gear
- using bent or damaged equipment (e.g. pedals, cranks, frame)
- anatomical anomalies (e.g. different leg lengths, twisted spine or not using both legs equally).

An early complaint against clipless pedals was that the foot was secured too well so that the lack of lateral movement caused knee injuries. Manufacturers responded with new cleats and pedals that provided a few degrees of sideways movement or 'float'. However, traditional toe-clips and shoe-plates never allowed any lateral foot movement either. The problem actually stems from the clipless systems not permitting any movement in a vertical plane and securing the feet very firmly on a horizontal (pedal) surface. In many cases problems were alleviated with the few degrees of float for the foot, sometimes compensating for poorly adjusted cleats.

Table 7.1 opposite gives some possible indications of the cause of knee pain. Remember that expert advice should always be sought if any problems persist.

Sun care

The sun can be very damaging to your skin. This is especially so in the case of riders from temperate climates, or those with fair skin who may have little resistance to the sun's UV rays (which are present even on hazy or cloudy days). Medical problems can include drying of the skin creating wrinkles or freckles, and more seriously, a very real risk of sunburn and even skin cancer.

Use sunscreen and lip balms with sunscreen, or keep covered up and keep well hydrated. (*See* also Weather conditions, pp. 96–7.)

Bites, stings and infectious diseases

Tetanus jabs are a sensible precaution for everyone. You can easily pick up infections from scratches or 'road rash' in the event of an accident, or from animal bites.

Bites and stings can vary in severity from a minor irritation or inconvenience to life threatening, depending on what inflicted the injury and your reaction to it. If you know that your skin is particularly susceptible to bites or stings, you need to take as many precautions as you can to avoid being stung or bitten in the first place. Cover up as much as you can, especially in the evenings when mosquitoes abound. Insect repellents like Deet or lemon and eucalyptus oil are usually very effective. Cycle-campers may need to use a mosquito net in some areas. It's not just the hot

Table 7.1 Some possible causes and solutions to knee pain

Location	Possible causes	Possible solution(s)
Anterior (front of knee)	Saddle too low	Raise saddle
	Saddle too far fowards	Slide saddle back
	Riding in hilly areas	Choose flatter routes
	Gears too high	Use lower gears
	Cadence too low	Increase cadence
	Cranks too long	Use shorter cranks
Posterior (back of knee)	Saddle too high	Lower saddle
	Saddle too far back	Slide saddle forwards
	Excessive float in pedals	Use pedals with less float
Medial (inside of knee)	Toes point outwards	Adjust cleat to point toes inwards
	Excessive float in pedals	Use pedals with less float
	Clipless pedals too tight for easy exit	Adjust pedal tension
	Feet too wide apart	Adjust cleat position Use shorter bottom bracket axle Use narrower cranks
Lateral (outside of knee)	Toes point inwards	Adjust cleat to point toes outwards Use pedals with more float
	Excessive float in pedals	Use pedals with less float
	Feet too close together	Adjust cleat position Use longer bottom bracket axle Use wider (offset) cranks Fit 1–2 mm spacer between pedal and crank

Adapted from Baker, A. (1998), *Bicycling Medicine* (Simon & Schuster), p. 214.

Figure 7.1 In hot conditions and at high altitude sunscreen is essential. Cassie Lowe applies lip balm on the move

or humid regions of the world that are blighted by mosquitoes; although they may not carry malaria like their tropical counterparts, mosquitoes in the north of Scotland, Scandinavia and North America are remarkably vicious. Still water is always a mosquito magnet and insects are just part of the food chain, so expect other creatures to be nearby too.

Take care when you camp. Insects or snakes may have chosen the same patch for their nest, too. It is always a wise precaution to shake footwear upside-down before putting it on, just in case something has crawled in overnight!

Injections, Foreign Office advice and travel centres

Most booking agents or tour operators can advise you on any vaccinations required for your trip (some countries insist on travellers having valid vaccination certificates before they are allowed to enter the country). Some diseases, such as malaria, can lie dormant in the body for weeks or months and it is essential that preventative treatments are continued as directed even after you have left 'at risk' zones to ensure proper protection.

The Internet is an ideal source of up-to-the-minute information regarding the spread of known infectious diseases. Look up the sites of the relevant tourist offices, the World Health Organisation (www.who.ch), the Foreign Office (www.fco.gov.uk), US Centres for Disease Control and Prevention (www.cdc.gov/travel) or Travellers' Medical and Vaccination Centre (www.tmvc.com.au) for the latest advice.

First aid kit

Some knowledge of first aid, and an awareness of potential problems and how to treat them, is always useful. A basic first aid kit should contain:

- aspirin or paracetamol

- sticking plasters

- sterile dressings

- antiseptic cream

- imodium (for diarrhoea).

Rehydration powders such as Diaralyte are often useful. If you are travelling to less developed countries you may wish to carry an emergency medical kit containing sterile syringes and equipment for use by qualified personnel. Wilderness campers might include a lightweight anti-venom pump too.

RICE

The acronym RICE (Rest, Ice, Compression and Elevation) is a useful aid to deal with most minor injury traumas on soft tissue. Follow these four instructions and many problems should soon be resolved (the sooner this is done after injury, the quicker the healing process will begin):

- *Rest* If you experience pain or soreness, rest may be the cure needed. It's worth checking out possible causes: damaged equipment or poor positioning may need to be addressed. Some injuries occur through overuse, in which case rest, or at least reduced activity, may be required to allow your body to recover.

- *Ice* Many injuries manifest themselves with heat as the body reacts to the injury and pumps more blood to the area. Ice wrapped in a cloth, or a cold compress or even cold water, will reduce bleeding from torn blood vessels and so minimise swelling, bruising and pain.

- *Compression* or bandaging will help to counteract the swelling too.

- *Elevation* by lifting the injured part (preferably above the height of the heart – injured parties may need to lie down!) reduces excessive blood flow to the injury. This helps to reduce the pressure of fluid on the injured part and keeps bruising to a minimum.

Stomach problems

Surprisingly, stomach problems account for more non-finishers of many long-distance events than almost any other cause. In the 1999 Furnace Creek 508-mile race crossing Nevada's Death Valley, over half of the competitors who did not finish cited 'stomach problems' as the reason for their withdrawal.

Most causes can be avoided with some forethought.

- Only race with food that you have tried extensively during your training.

- Regular foodstuffs may not feel so good when being ingested during the more intensive efforts of racing or long-distance riding – have a variety of food available.

- Liquid foods are far more easily absorbed than solid foods, but not all food mixtures are palatable or agree with everyone.

- Do some rides *exclusively* using your race food. If you have a problem with a particular foodstuff, try other alternatives in other training rides.

- Eat in training to prepare your stomach for the demands of eating in an unfamiliar position.

- Eat little and often. This is less demanding on the stomach than trying to ingest large amounts of food at infrequent intervals.

Figure 7.2 Rival crews come to the aid of a suffering RAAM rider – later forced to abandon his race due to severe knee problems

- Top up your reserves before they get too low to ensure that you are always adequately fuelled but never having to cope with too much food. (The same principle can be usefully employed in regular everyday eating habits too.)

- Use your water bottle. Drink frequently. Practise taking your bottle from its cage and replacing it smoothly and automatically so that you do not lose any momentum.

- Infection can also come from other sources (*see* Table 7.2).

Table 7.2 Possible sources of infection causing stomach problems

Source	Prevention
Bottles	• Ensure that bottles are always thoroughly clean • Use disinfectant or sterilising solutions • Do not share bottles or allow anyone to taste drinks from your bottles. Your mouth is a hotbed of germs
Germs spread by hand	• Always wash your hands thoroughly after visiting the toilet or bathroom – taps and door handles are a prime source of germs • Use a hand-sanitising solution • Make sure anyone with you does the same, especially crew handling food or bottles
Bacteria in food and water	• Avoid ice unless you know it is 'safe' • Only eat fruit that you have peeled yourself • Avoid food not kept in ideal conditions • Use distilled water or bottled mineral water, or boil water before use • Be just as careful with water used for cleaning your teeth or washing food

Altitude

It is quite normal to experience a higher heart rate and breathing rate when cycling at higher altitudes until suitably acclimatised. Above about 1800 m the thinner atmosphere makes it difficult to get enough oxygen into the lungs; breathing becomes difficult and feelings of lethargy are common. Fortunately, the body can adapt very quickly, and usually within three or four days riders will be able to tackle most climbs without undue breathlessness.

The change in altitude is more significant than the absolute height. Changes of up to 1500 m shouldn't present too many difficulties, but beyond about 2500 m altitude headaches, nosebleeds, drowsiness, mental tiredness, dizziness, nausea and insomnia are quite common. Above 3500 m, reaction times and mental alertness can be up to 20% below normal.

If you know that you are going to be competing at higher altitudes, there is plenty of evidence to support high-altitude acclimatisation either by living and training at high altitudes or by living at altitude but training at sea-level. There are mixed conclusions about the benefits of altitude training for subsequent competitions at sea-level. If you are changing altitude frequently (e.g. traversing a range of mountains) it is better to sleep at lower elevations.

It is easy to get dehydrated at altitude because your increased breathing rate accelerates fluid losses. The intensity of the sun is also greater at higher elevations, so it is essential that you drink plenty and protect yourself with sunscreen.

Figure 7.3 Cycling at altitude: Kanglung, in eastern Bhutan – a steady, uphill ride all day is rewarded by a spectacular viewpoint and much appreciated seat at 1900 m (photo: Chris Beynon)

8 Safe cycling

You have a duty of care both for your own safety and that of other road users. Be aware of your surroundings at all times and make sure that you are in control. You cannot control variables such as the weather, road surfaces or traffic; but by choosing how, when and where you ride, and through the equipment you use, you can minimise the risks to yourself and to others. Occasionally, some mishaps are unavoidable – but with a sensible approach you can make your own cycling as safe as possible at the same time as ensuring that your activities do not endanger anyone else.

On the road

Bicycle maintenance

Keeping your bike clean and well maintained can avoid potentially dangerous situations. Worn or damaged equipment could break without warning, so wheels, tyres and brakes need frequent checks – either by a bike mechanic, or preferably by yourself. Riding in poor weather or in very hilly areas can accelerate wear, so you need to be especially vigilant in winter and prepared to replace equipment more frequently. Never start any ride with damaged or worn parts thinking, 'That will last' – invariably it will not! Ensure that all components and accessories are fitted securely and check them regularly.

Road surfaces

Slippery, rough or loose road surfaces provide less traction and are less predictable than dry, smooth, firm surfaces, so you need to modify your riding technique accordingly. For example, corners can be taken at speed with a high degree of lean on good roads, but need to be treated with much more respect and care if they are wet, uneven or littered with gravel. Potholes or rough roads can jolt a bike from your grip, damage wheels or even cause a fall. Accessories may rattle loose if not secured properly. If you need to move out into the road to avoid these hazards, look behind and signal your intentions. There is no point in avoiding a drain cover only to get hit by a car!

Riding in a group (*see* also pp. 159–61), even when racing, it is common courtesy to warn following riders of hazards such as broken glass, potholes, loose gravel, dead animals, litter or parked cars – usually by hand signals and a friendly call describing the hazard or its location (e.g. 'Car, left!', 'Hole, on the right!').

Traffic

Traffic is a cyclist's occupational hazard. You share the roads with cars, buses, trucks, motorcyclists and pedestrians whose needs should always be respected. As a cyclist you are more vulnerable than most other road users, so discretion is always wise – even when the other party is blatantly at fault.

Figure 8.1 Landslide in the Crimea: adventurous tourists don't always have tarmac roads (photo: Ivo Miesen)

- Ride positively, about 50–100 cm away from the kerb to allow yourself room to move in should the need arise but still leaving room for motorists to pass you safely. Adjust this distance on busy or narrow roads.

- Do not obstruct other traffic unless you feel that there is not room for the two of you to be on the same spot of road, when sometimes it is better to hold your ground. Get out of the way as quickly as possible afterwards and give a polite 'thank you' wave when the motorist passes you. (Impatient drivers may try to intimidate you with engine revving or by driving very close to you. This is a good sign not to argue with them. Road rage is far too common nowadays and can have serious, even tragic, consequences, particularly for unprotected cyclists. Do not provoke other road users with gestures or by shouting at them.)

- Obey the highway rules – i.e. stop at red lights and do not ride the wrong way along one-way streets. Cyclists' disregard for traffic rules only antagonises other road users who may vent their frustrations on the next rider they encounter!

- Look behind you and give clear and positive indication of your intended movements. On occasions it is better to pull in to the roadside and wait for a gap in the traffic before crossing to the other side of the road.

- Cars and lorries towing trailers or caravans can be the most frightening traffic on the road. Never assume that once a vehicle has passed you, it is safe to resume your position in the road. Trailers may be wider than the vehicle hauling them. Ride steadily and move a little closer to the kerb when vehicles need to pass you.

- Be alert, looking ahead and around you at all times. Pedestrians have an uncanny habit of appearing in the road from behind parked cars. Car doors can swing open unexpectedly, and cars may suddenly pull out into the road without signalling. In particular, watch out for the following: passengers in parked cars;

smoke from an exhaust pipe (indicating that an engine has just been turned on and the car is about to move); pedestrians on the pavement.

Above all, don't ride too close to the kerb or near parked cars, and you will at least give yourself a nano-second or two of grace in which to take evasive action if needed. Expect the worst at all times – you will probably be correct most of the time, and pleasantly surprised when you are wrong.

In some countries the use of cycle paths is compulsory. In the UK this is largely discretionary and many experienced cyclists still use the roads because they encounter fewer obstructions. However, the growth of the National Cycle Route Network should soon allow long distances to be covered with minimal interference from other traffic, though some of the paths may not permit very high-speed usage.

Careful route-planning can help to reduce the chance of meeting traffic and its associated hazards. But in sparsely populated rural areas, the lack of traffic can be just as alarming. The few motorists there may not expect to encounter other road users and may be travelling faster than they ought. Be vigilant and visible at all times. Try to have an 'escape route' to hand (e.g. getting off the bike in a hurry, taking to the pavement or a nearside turn) – anything that avoids impact with a fast-moving, solid vehicle is acceptable and preferable to a collision.

Weather conditions

Extremes of heat, cold, wind, fog, snow or ice can turn any ride into a potentially lethal one. Even in relatively mild climates such as the UK's, conditions can change rapidly and may be life-threatening to the foolhardy or ill-prepared.

Check the local weather forecast using TV or radio broadcasts, newspapers, postings at mountain lodges, or relevant websites (e.g. www.bbc.co.uk/weather). Take into account the length of your ride, time of day and time of year. A mountain route in summer might be relatively simple; in winter it could be a severe challenge with very different weather conditions and shorter daylight hours.

Rain

With proper preparation the rain need not hinder you, but you do need to be prepared for it (*see* Figure 8.2).

- After a dry spell, rain can bring oil, diesel and petrol spill to the road surface. Pay particular attention to this in towns and on corners. Slow down, and avoid taking corners too fast or leaning the bike over dramatically.

- Wet roads are more slippery than dry roads. Some tyre compounds cope better with wet conditions than others. Ask your dealer or cycling colleagues what they recommend for wet or greasy roads. Your own choice based on personal experience may be different. Wider tyres and lower tyre pressures are generally favoured in wet conditions to provide more traction.

- Water between the rim and brake blocks inhibits braking performance. Allow more time and distance to slow down or halt, particularly if riding fast (e.g. down a hill). Braking on steel rims is notoriously poor in the wet; light alloy rims are considerably better. Use the appropriate brake blocks for your rims – rubber or some synthetic compounds are better on aluminium rims and cork is best for carbon-fibre wheels.

- Rain washes debris into the road. Water softens tyre treads, making them more susceptible to flints or broken glass and often leading to punctures. Check your tyres and brake blocks frequently and pick out any grit.

Figure 8.2 Racing rarely stops for the weather: this rider copes with a prolonged shower in the National 24-hour Championship (photo: Paul A. Lawson)

- Avoid painted lines on the road if you can; they can be very slippery in the wet. Cross them at right-angles when possible.

- Avoid puddles – as well as giving you a thorough soaking, they can conceal potholes and other hazards.

Bear in mind, too, that heat moves from warmer to colder conditions, and water conducts heat 25 times better than air. So when you get wet from rain or snow you rapidly lose body heat, especially through your head, hands and feet. Keep dry and you will remain warmer for much longer.

Mudguards go a long way towards protecting you from excess spray from the wheels, but are too much of a hindrance for racing. Instead, try wearing two pairs of shorts with a sheet of polythene between them to keep your backside dry. Carry spare socks, shorts, gloves and undervest for a long ride: changing into dry clothes can be a real boost when it's wet. A peaked cap underneath your helmet will keep rain off your face or eyewear, and reduce heat loss. Knees and exposed skin can be protected by Vaseline or baby oil to help retain some body warmth too. If you wear glasses, wipe them with washing-up liquid or a cut potato (it works!) to prevent them from 'fogging', or use proprietary 'anti-fogging' solutions sold for swimmers' goggles.

Rain pouring over a motorist's windscreen, coupled with road spray, can 'blend' a cyclist into the background. Wear bright colours at all times, and in extreme conditions switch on a rear light – a good reason for permanently carrying a small but bright LED (*see* p. 47).

Sometimes, it's best just to seek some shelter and sit out the worst of the rain. If you are touring, find a café or hotel, do some sightseeing, or use the opportunity to catch up on housekeeping tasks such as laundry or correspondence. Training rides may have to be curtailed, or exchanged for turbo-training or gym work instead (*see* pp. 156–8). Racing is rarely cancelled due to rain, although many riders choose not to start or lack enthusiasm to compete when it's wet – leaving a golden opportunity for the more aggressive rider. For those so inclined, bad weather can be their best friend!

Snow and ice

Treat snow and ice with extreme caution. Dress warmly, ride carefully, and avoid long rides if the weather is so bad. These conditions are the reason indoor turbo-trainers were invented!

Two wheels located one behind another are not particularly stable on icy surfaces, but wider tyres and lower tyre pressures will help. Shaded areas, dips in the road or exposed land can remain frozen long after other areas have thawed. Main roads may be cleared by snow-ploughs or salt, but minor roads are a lower priority and can remain hazardous for days after the snow has been cleared elsewhere. Remember too that salt is used to lower the freezing temperature on roads; this can be very corrosive. Winter riders must clean their bikes frequently to keep them in good condition and avoid deterioration of the components.

Slippery conditions are one of the few areas where tricycles can excel over their two-wheeled counterparts, but even they can be subject to drifting or skating across ice. Fixed-wheel usage is often popular for winter use, too, as braking can be achieved by easing the pressure on the pedals instead of bringing the rim to an abrupt halt with the brakes. The simplicity of the fixed-wheel machine (*see* p. 37) holds great appeal for many riders.

Finally, dealing with the cold demands more energy than riding in warmer temperatures, so you will need to increase your calorie intake. Although you may not feel thirsty in the cold you will still generate heat. As you watch your breath evaporating, this is moisture being lost from your body – so you must drink even on cold rides.

Heat and sun

Heat can have adverse effects on your performance. Your heart rate increases, redistributing blood to the skin to help with the body's cooling mechanisms. Carbohydrate usage accelerates and this can lead to premature fatigue and slower speeds. Your ability to cope with the heat will improve as you improve your aerobic fitness. Riders who fly abroad to hot climates may experience problems initially, before their bodes have adapted to the new environment. In hot conditions, remember the following:

• good hydration is essential – and drink cool fluids

• wear a well-ventilated helmet

- wear lightweight, comfortable clothing that can breathe. Local shops will probably have just what you need! Sleeveless tops are excellent in hot environments, though not permitted in most competitions

- wear light colours to reflect the sun's rays

- ride in the shade when you can

- if possible, avoid riding in the hottest part of the day – usually around 1–4 p.m.

The sun

Suntans may look healthy, but medical evidence tells us otherwise. Skin cancer is a very real problem and the sun can age your skin prematurely. The ideal clothing for riding in hot weather has a high 'sun protection factor' (SPF), but SPF-rated clothing is not yet widespread. In simple terms, the more opaque a garment is, the higher its SPF rating. Lighter colours are more effective at reflecting the sun's rays than dark colours, which absorb light and heat.

Sunscreens are essential, especially if you have paler skin. They are more effective if applied 15 minutes before exposure to the sun begins. Multiply the sunscreen factor by 10 for the number of minutes of effective sun protection (assuming that it is not washed away by sweat). For example, factor 15 sunscreen provides 150 minutes of protection, after which your skin will begin to burn. More suitable for cycling all day are sunscreens with a protection factor in the region of 20+ or 30+ but even these will need to be reapplied during the day. Pay particular attention to the skin at the edge of garments, since your clothes can rub away any sunscreen applied here. Roll garments back when applying the sunscreen to ensure full coverage of exposed skin. Remember to apply sunscreen to your ears, nose and neck, and in the case of the thinner haired, to the top of the head too. Helmet wearers may end up with peculiar suntans – but that is better than skin damage from the sun. Bear in mind that altitude also increases the sun's level of radiation, and 'up' your protection factor accordingly. Do drink plenty of water to combat the effects of the sun.

Riders in hot environments often wisely adopt local headgear as suitable protection from the sun. For the Race Across AMerica, some riders have even had full white Lycra arm and leg covers made for sun protection across the southern deserts. An age-old but highly effective remedy for skin made sore by the sun is to place cabbage leaves on the affected areas!

In very hot conditions the road tarmac can melt, creating uneven and unpredictable surfaces, particularly on corners. Road haze may be confusing and in bright sunlight wear sunglasses to reduce the glare.

Wind

Headwinds are always the bane of any cyclist, but sidewinds can be equally tiring and can actually lift you from the road. Take care in strong winds when passing sheltered areas or when large vehicles pass – you may be leaning against the strength of the wind and you can fall over when that force is no longer there! Holding the bike in a straight

Severe weather

Take note of severe weather warnings. If your journey is not essential, do something else instead.

line may prove difficult, so try to find sheltered roads (but beware of debris blown into the road). Dust can be a problem too, so eye-protection is essential.

Progress will be easier if your clothing and equipment is as sleek as possible – clothing or luggage that flaps around in the wind will only create more drag. Protect your chest with newspaper, polythene or bubblewrap under your jersey to keep the cold wind away. Tuck down on to the handlebar drops or aero-bars, or assume a lower, more aerodynamic position to offer less area to the wind and keep your weight lower for better stability.

Fog

If you have to ride in fog, ensure that you are visible to other road users. A rear light is essential and will provide some warning of your presence to others. Do not ride faster than the conditions allow, especially when descending mountains where hairpin bends, stray animals or vehicles approaching the other way may appear without warning.

Animals

Animals can be highly unpredictable. Dogs, cats, foxes, rabbits or squirrels may run into the road unexpectedly. Sheep have a tendency to move suddenly – not always out of the way. Larger animals like deer or cows can be just as obstructive as brick wall. If you spot an animal on or near the road, slow down and allow it to escape.

In the case of dogs, you have two choices: speed away or confront the animal. An unencumbered rider may well be able to outsprint the dog until away from its territory, but this is not so easy for the laden tourist. Some riders carry devices to ward off aggressive dogs – pepper sprays, airhorns or food to throw for them(!). Others resort to threatening behaviour with a pump (good reason for not using a mini-pump!) or pick up stones to throw. Sometimes it is best to dismount with the bike between you and the dog. Firm talking may appease it. Walk away steadily, keeping an eye on the animal. With luck the owner will soon arrive to end the stand-off. Whatever situation you find yourself in, stay calm.

Horses are large, heavy, strong and easily alarmed. A brightly clothed cyclist speeding past a horse, especially from behind, may be enough to make it rear up or kick with considerable force. Slow down when you see horses on the road: a polite 'Hello' to the riders is usually appreciated to warn them of your approach so they can more easily control the beasts. Pass slowly and widely and continue on your way. Do not attempt to pass if the rider is having problems with the horse. Stop and let the rider bring the animal under control. Displaying a little courtesy is far better than having to deal with a fallen rider, an unmanageable animal or injury sustained from a ton of horsemeat on top of you.

Telephones

Now that mobile telephones are small and light enough to be easily carried in a pocket or seatpack, and for the most part affordable, many riders carry one with them for use in an emergency. However, it is unwise to be totally reliant on a mobile telephone call solving your problem. Some areas have notoriously poor, or even non-existent, signal reception. Your telephone's battery may not hold enough charge for the duration of a long journey and carrying the charger is weighty and impractical. And what if you can't contact anyone to pick you up in the middle of nowhere when your bike has fallen apart? You will need an alternative strategy.

By all means, carry a telephone if you know that you can contact someone during your ride to arrange any assistance required, but a few coins or a telephone card to use in a public telephone might be just as practical to raise help in an emergency. Remember too, that you will need to know *precisely* where you are if help is going to reach you.

Personal safety

Personal identification

Carry some form of identity on you even on the shortest of rides. Accidents do happen. If you are found unconscious by the roadside, the emergency services will need to know who you are.

Take a wallet or purse with your details in it or write your name, address and an emergency contact telephone number on a sticker and put it inside your helmet. Cover it with transparent tape to protect it from rain and sweat. You can hang a pet's identity tag with your details to the zip of your clothing or seatpack – or even round your neck. But do check it from time to time, to ensure that your details are legible and up to date.

Whatever form of identification you carry, make sure that it is readily accessible. An address label under the insole of your shoe or taped around your bottom bracket may be a good idea if you need to prove ownership, but it's unlikely to be the first place that anyone else will look to find out who you are.

Personal security

Apart from safety issues surrounding traffic, road conditions and weather conditions, cyclists need to be aware of their personal security – particularly when travelling in foreign parts where customs may be different and strangers may not always be welcome. A smile and a few words in the local language can go a long way towards breaking down barriers. Lone tourists or a pair of travellers pose less of a threat and are usually more readily received than larger groups.

Do some research before your journey to help you understand the places you will be travelling through. The CTC (*see* Useful addresses, p. 207) has an extensive database of information, compiled from cyclists' experiences of countries all around the world, available to their members.

Travel books like the *Blue Guides, Rough Guides* and *Lonely Planet* guides are excellent sources of information. You may wish to just absorb the feel of an area from these books before you go, copy out notes to take with you, tear out relevant pages or take the whole book. (You might also be able to trade it with another traveller later in your journey.)

The Foreign and Commonwealth Travel and Advice Unit has an excellent website (www.fco.gov.uk) with up-to-date information listing 'hotspots' – crime, combat zones, natural disasters and disease – together with contact details of the local British Consul or Embassy and basic travel protocol. It is well worth checking prior to any foreign journey, or even *en route* using a cyber café.

Talk to other travellers and those who have been to places before you, especially those who share your travelling aims. Ask about places to visit and areas to avoid. If they have the time, local shopkeepers, hoteliers and policemen can be very helpful and are often pleased that you are visiting their part of the world.

Protect your valuables

Be especially on your guard in crowded areas, tourist sites, railway stations and markets where pickpockets make easy prey of the unwary. Make sure that valuables are not on display or near the top of bags where they are easy pickings. Keep your money in several places about you and your bike, and keep some cash readily to hand – you do not want to be rummaging in your luggage for a few coins or banknotes and revealing your 'cash cache' to everyone. Extra cash or travellers cheques can be tucked away in your luggage, in the pockets of spare clothing, or hidden up inside the bike's seatpost or handlebars. (If you have any money remaining after your journey, don't forget to take it out afterwards!) US dollars are always useful and can be used or readily changed almost anywhere in the world.

Travelling abroad

Documents

You need a valid passport to travel abroad. Ideally, ensure that it is valid for at least six months beyond your stay – to ensure that you can continue your journey elsewhere!

You may need visas for some countries, but if you are not sure of your route or exact dates of travel, don't get all you need at once. You may have problems if you arrive at a border earlier than anticipated or worse, if your visa has expired. Instead, carry some spare passport photographs with you and apply for new visas at embassies or through agents as you go, to give yourself maximum flexibility.

Try not to hand over your passport to anyone, especially if you feel uncomfortable with them. (Take an out-of-date one to deposit with dodgy hoteliers.) Carry photocopies of your passport, insurance documents, credit cards, travel tickets and visas, and keep these separate from the originals. Leave another copy of all your important documents with a friend at home: if ever you do need to get replacements, this will ease the process. You can also store this information on the Internet: www.ekno.lonelyplanet.com is a secure site for this purpose.

Travelling companions

Take care who you ride with. Travelling companions can be great but make sure that you can strike out in your own direction when you need or want to. Living in close proximity to another person for a few days usually reveals any fundamental differences or issues pretty quickly!

Cultural differences

In some places cycling garb is just too outlandish and alien, so you may have to modify your clothing. Loose-fitting shirts to cover a large part of your shorts may be in order. Women especially may have to cover their legs – with something other than body-hugging Lycra! Loose cotton trousers gathered at the ankle may be more appropriate. You can usually buy something locally if needed. Respect local customs and your visit will be much more pleasurable.

Stay in touch

By opening up a free web-based e-mail account such as www.hotmail.com or www.yahoo.com it is a simple task to keep in touch with the world at large through the internet and cyber cafés wherever you are. Some travellers actually embark upon their journeys specifically to get away from this, but it can pay to have outside contact sometimes – just for reassurance, to arrange forwarding of funds or spares, or perhaps to check out later parts of your journey.

Locks

A determined thief will stop at nothing to get your bicycle – or even just parts of it – but a few sensible precautions can prevent your prized possession from disappearing. Railway stations, student campuses, outside libraries and shopping centres are thieves' favourite hunting grounds, where they know the owner will be away for a while. Many bicycle thefts are opportunist, but there are bicycle thieves who make an illicit living from stealing and selling bikes.

Your bicycle should be as difficult to steal as is practicable – so lock it. Any lock is better than none and visual deterrents will put off many thieves who are after easier, quicker pickings (see Figure 8.3). However, some locks offer so little protection that they can be cut or picked in less time than it takes the owner to use a key or tumble a combination. These are really only handy for low-risk areas or as secondary security for items like helmets or luggage.

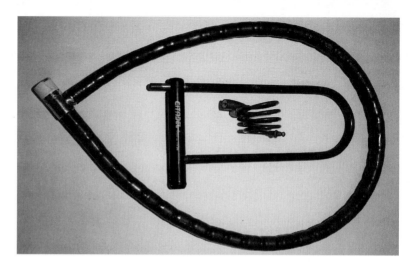

Figure 8.3 Bike locks for different situations: centre) a lightweight cable lock is ideal for day trips and low-security places or for securing luggage to your bike; middle) the D-lock is a popular choice for high-risk locations; outer) the heavy-duty cable lock will provide peace of mind almost anywhere but is not practical to transport around with you

- Lock your bike to a secure and immovable object where it cannot be lifted off (e.g. cycle racks, benches, lampposts or railings). Do not lock your bike to objects such as parking meters, where it may be lifted off, or to small trees or wire fences which are easily cut.

- If you are travelling in a group, lock the bikes together (making sure that breaking one lock will not expose all the bikes to theft).

- U-shaped or D-locks are usually better than cable locks, but the gap in the D must be filled by the bike and whatever it is secured to. Heavy-duty, flexible chain locks overcome this problem but they are heavy.

- Lock your bike up even at home in the shed or garage – and especially if you keep it in the hallway of shared accommodation.

- In the street, lock your bike in open view. Side alleyways out of sight give the thief an unhindered opportunity to attack your lock at his leisure. Do not lock your bike where it will obstruct entrances, fire exits or pavements – the fire brigade or council will remove it!

Choosing your lock

Better locks cost more money. Consider how much your bicycle cost and how much you want to keep it. Stronger locks are also heavier locks – so you need to decide which of the factors of security, cost, weight and portability is the most important to you, bearing in mind your type of riding and where you are likely to leave your bicycle.

- If your bike has quick-release wheels, secure them by removing the front wheel and locking it next to the frame and rear wheel. Better still, use a second, separate lock. Two or three locks are a better deterrent than one, and keeping the wheel in the frame prevents the fork ends from being damaged.

- If the bike is being left for a while, remove any accessories (pump, seatpack, lights, computer, etc.) and take these with you.

- Use a barbag or *musette* to carry your valuables and paperwork when stopping for meals or playing tourists. Rain-covers over your panniers can inhibit stray hands from delving inside your bags.

- On tour, find accommodation (or a friendly shop or garage) to store your bike while you go sightseeing by foot and public transport.

Fortunately, bikes loaded with luggage are less attractive for the thief's quick getaway, but this is no reason for tourists to be complacent. Take every precaution you can to prevent your bike going missing. It's worth it. Never leave your bike unlocked – even if you are only popping into a shop for just two minutes. In that time your bike could be over a kilometre away!

Some riders try to make their bike look unattractive – even preferring not to have the maker's name on it, since certain marques can attract the wrong sort of admirers. For the day-rider this is unnecessary, but commuters and long-distance tourists might consider a subdued paint finish rather than something flashy and bright. Dirt on a bike may disguise its true pedigree, but be aware of the problems that a dirty bike can hide: there is no excuse for poor maintenance.

Record your bike's frame number (usually stamped underneath the bottom bracket shell or on one of the rear dropouts). In the event of theft you will need to report it to the local police and obtain a crime report number for the insurance company.

Unfortunately, relatively few stolen bikes ever get returned to their rightful owners. To improve the chances of the return of your bike you can have your postcode and house number stamped into the frame. This can be done by most local bike shops or by the police. A more high-tech approach is electronic data-tagging but this is not yet widespread. Advances in electronics and GPS technology could make bicycle-tracking devices a more viable security measure in the future.

Further deterrents

Many cyclists use a very basic bike for commuting purposes just so that the bike is of less value, less attractive to steal and more easily replaced if it does get stolen. If you use your bike for commuting you may also prefer to use lock nuts on your wheels instead of quick-release hubs. Quick-release seatbolts should definitely be replaced with regular ones.

Insurance

Insurance can cover personal injury or illness, damage or loss of equipment, and third party cover where a claim may be made against you. For bikes and equipment the most cost-effective insurance is usually to include them under a household policy. These usually allow for use away from home and even abroad for a number of weeks during a year. As a precaution, send the insurance company a valuation note each year so that they cannot deny the value of your cover should a claim be made. Note any conditions of use: usually that the bicycle is locked, or in a locked garage, and check that your cover includes accessories such as lights, pump, tools, carrier etc.

Few regular insurances cover for racing use or extended periods abroad. In these cases, seek advice from one of the sport's governing bodies, membership organisations or specialist travel insurance companies.

Third party insurance cover is relatively cheap and is included as part of the membership package for organisations like the Cyclists' Touring Club and the British Cycling Federation (see p. 207). These bodies also employ specialist legal departments and can chase claims on behalf of members involved in accidents.

UK citizens can benefit from healthcare arrangements in EU countries by completing a simple E111 form (available from post offices). Elsewhere, however, healthcare costs can be very high and there are numerous cases reported from both developed and less developed countries of extremely expensive hospitalisation. Treatment may even be refused until payment can be guaranteed. Check that your insurance does cover you comprehensively for your cycling activities.

Safety at night

Night riding can be a very rewarding experience: tranquillity and quiet roads, glimpses of wildlife, a different taste to the air… but it's not without its problems. You must make yourself visible at night. Your lights must work efficiently, with the lenses clean and not obscured by poor positioning on the bike, clothing or luggage.

Stay bright

Reflective products – Sam Browne belts, ankle bands, or stickers – are extremely effective at highlighting a rider's presence (*see* Figure 8.4). Sign-makers can supply off-cuts of adhesive reflective sheet in all sorts of colours to match your frame or accessories so that they do not look hideous in daylight. This is particularly effective on moving parts like cranks, hubs, rims, pedals and the backs of your shoes. (Some riders swear that blue reflective tape has a surprisingly calming effect on motorists who associate the 'flashing' colour with the presence of the police!) Reflective fabric can be bought from outdoor fabric suppliers and sewn on to clothing or luggage. Position it low down near the rear hem of jackets, high on the shoulders at the front, or around sleeve cuffs, making sure that it is not obscured when in use.

Always ride in bright colours. Road repairers' vests combine fluorescent colours and reflective materials and can be used to good effect by riders and anyone involved in roadside assistance. Some clothes manufacturers now use reflective inks that are unobtrusive in daylight but reflect brilliantly at night when a light is shone upon them.

Helpers and marshals often need to identify individual riders in the dark. Help them by attaching an extra light to your bike in a distinctive manner – for example, fit one lamp above another, use a head-torch, or fix small, distinctive LEDs to the

Figure 8.4 Night-time at the start of Paris–Brest–Paris, 1999: note the use of compulsory reflective vests or belts, and the useful head torch (photo: Liz Creese)

forks or handlebars. It can save you valuable time if your support crew or race officials can recognise you at a distance and prepare for your arrival at a particular point.

Stay warm

Night-time heralds a drop in temperature. Even in summer, temperatures can drop to close to zero. Gloves and hats are essential luggage for the night-cyclist. Cover your legs to keep the muscles warm and wear an extra top to ward off the chill. Wear your extra clothing until the day has properly warmed up – this may not be until some hours after sunrise. At night you may quickly lose body heat, so put on another layer of clothing if you are stopping for five minutes or more. You may need to keep this extra layer on for a short distance until you get properly warmed up again.

Many randonneurs carry a Space Blanket. This ultra-light (60 g) sheet reflects up to 90% of radiant body heat and is excellent for emergency situations or where roadside sleep is a priority. Find a sheltered spot out of the wind and wrap the blanket all around you – large amounts of body heat can be lost to the ground as well as to the air (park benches are ideal beds!). Tarmac or pavement is usually warmer than lying on grass and doesn't attract the morning dew – but don't ever lie in the road, that's asking for trouble!

Ride with care

Many riders forget that safety is a bigger issue in the dark. Visibility is reduced, you have less time to notice obstacles such as potholes or obstructions in the road. Motorists may not expect to see cyclists at night and can erroneously take advantage of apparently clear roads to travel faster. Animals can be startled by the silent approach of a cyclist in the dark. Distances can be deceptive and tiredness can take over. As a night-rider you must be alert at all times, both for your own safety and that of others. Sometimes it is best to get off the road if traffic cannot see you properly, and especially if you are feeling tired and are falling asleep on the move. Take action before you have an accident!

Invariably, you travel more slowly because of the dark and so should adjust your expectations of distance travelled at night. Allow for this when calculating 'time of arrival', or for food and drink purposes.

Sleep – before, during and after events

Sleep is vital to proper functioning of the body. All the time that you are awake you are using up energy, more so when you are active and riding a bike. Your body needs time to repair itself and this is best done when the brain, muscles and other vital organs are at rest. Without sleep your body will fatigue and deteriorate both mentally and physically.

Driving home safely

Driving home safely

It is alarming after an endurance event when tired riders or helpers get into their cars to drive home. The adrenaline rush and concentration of the event is gone and fatigue can easily take over in the warmth of your car, especially on tedious sections of road or motorways. If this happens:

- take a 'power nap' before embarking on any further travel
- use the car's cold-air blower or loud music to maintain alertness
- stop to stretch or run about
- if you feel any signs of sleep (heavy eyelids, watery vision, etc.), stop immediately – while you are still in control of the vehicle
- stop and go to sleep
- eat
- drink coffee or plain water
- have a wash
- make safety your priority.

Repeat as necessary all the way home. Time spent doing this is better than falling asleep at the wheel and having an accident.

Poor sleep or lack of sleep is a recognised medical condition causing poor performance at work, memory difficulties, concentration problems, less resistance to illness, increased accident rates and drowsy driving as compared to good sleepers.[1]

Ultra-distance cyclists, whether racing or on a long randonnée, need methods of legally and safely maintaining performance with significantly reduced sleep. Although this is possible, adequate consideration must be given to proper recuperation afterwards and you must carefully consider your calendar to make sure that you are not subjecting yourself to more stress than necessary by losing excessive hours of sleep. Prior rest and adequate food intake will help. You can trick your body into thinking that sufficient sleep has been taken by having shorter sleep breaks consisting of full sleep cycles.

The stages of sleep combine for varying lengths of time. Most complete cycles of sleep are about 90 minutes (+/– 30 minutes) according to the individual and the circumstances. To maximise the benefits of your sleep in the shortest possible time, you need one or more complete sleep cycles, so you should wake either when REM begins (*see* Table 8.1) or in the stage immediately following REM. If you wake in the middle of a sleep cycle, especially during Stages 3 or 4, your metabolic rate is at its lowest and it will take time to recover from this. It's better to stay asleep (actively recuperating) through the complete cycle rather than trying to take a shorter sleep break.

Figure 8.5 Sleeping where you fall, Paris–Brest–Paris, 1999: when fatigue takes over, you don't need a bed, but you do need to sleep (photo: Ivo Miesen)

[1]Gallup Studies (1991 and 1995).

Table 8.1 The stages of sleep

Sleep stage	Body activity	Depth of sleep	Thought process	Miscellaneous
0 (awake)	Slows down, relaxes, decreased muscle tension	Drowsy	Relaxation, mind wanders, vague awareness	▼ Heart rate ▼ Blood pressure ▼ Temperature
1	Body movements slowed, eyes gradually move less	Light sleep, easily awakened	Drifting thoughts, feeling of weight loss or floating	▼ Heart rate ▼ Temperature
2	Little movement, eyes quiet, snoring common	Light to moderate sleep	Thought fragments but memory process diminishes. If woken, may recall parts of dream	▼ Heart rate ▼ Metabolic rates ▼ Temperature Regular breathing
3	Eyes quiet, occasional muscle movement	Deep sleep, may be difficult to awaken	Vaguely formed dreams, rarely recollected	Continued ▼ in heart rates, etc. ▲ Secretion of growth hormone
4	Eyes quiet, occasional muscle movement	Deepest sleep, difficult to awaken	Very poor recall of sleeping thoughts	Further ▼ in hear rates etc. and ▲ secretion of growth hormone (regeneration process)
REM	Snoring usually ceases, large muscles paralysed; fingers, toes and facial muscles twitch	Variable, but can be difficult to awaken if sound is incorporated into dream	80% dreaming with good recall	▲ Heart rate ▲ Metabolic rates ▲ Blood pressure and ▲ Blood flow to brain ▲ Temperature Irregular breathing Best time to wake

Adapted from King, R. (1989), 'The Combat Nap', *Approach* (US Navy) and *UltraCycling* (May 2000).

9 What to take

One rider's essentials may be another's unnecessary luxuries, but a lighter load is always easier to manage than a heavy one. You can minimise your load by having items do double duties: a battery cycle-lamp can also be your camping torch; a penknife your eating knife; dental floss for sewing repairs; or use your maps between your clothing layers as a protective wind-block. Think laterally whenever possible.

A week's tour needs little more luggage than a weekend awheel. Clothes can be washed overnight – modern synthetic fabrics dry very quickly in most conditions (*see* also pp. 58–63) – so you need not carry more than one spare set and some washing powder.

Experience will soon tell you what is necessary and what is not. If you do not use an item on tour, don't take it with you next time (with exceptions for repair tools, wet weather clothing, first aid kit, etc., which ought to be carried on all but the shortest of rides).

How light can you go?

Ardent proponents of minimalist luggage, cousins Nick and Richard Crane, cycled 5300 km on their 'Journey to the Centre of the Earth' (the point on the earth's surface most remote from the sea) – from Bangladesh, over the Himalayas and into the Gobi desert. Their bikes weighed just 10 kg and their luggage weighed a fraction over 8 kg (including the clothes they wore). Most of that was recording equipment to document their adventure for the BBC!

The Crane cousins' journey is not one that every cycle-tourist would want to repeat. Their intention was to ride almost commando-style, foregoing luxuries to complete their mission as quickly as possible. It illustrates well the methods of weight-saving which enabled them to travel faster and more easily despite the arduous nature of their two-month expedition. They travelled with few spares and relied upon finding food and shelter as they went. They removed all excess material: their maps were cut to size, they even shortened their T-shirts and their contact lenses shared a pared-down case. They shared between them: one pump, one compass (base-plate detached), one watch (strap removed) and the smallest possible Swiss Army knife (two blades). The few tools they consented to carrying were cut or drilled for lightness.

Audax

Randonneurs could do well to adopt an approach similar to, if not quite as extreme as, the Cranes'. On randonnées, controls are usually spaced every 50–100 km – which most riders will manage within a few hours – and at places where a meal or

Table 9.1 The ideal load – items and location – for a randonneur or tourist

	Handlebars	Bar bag	Jersey pocket	Neck pouch	Under saddle	Seatpack	Rackpk/S'bag	Panniers
Route sheet or maps	●	●	○	○			○	○
Brevet card	●	●	●	●		○	●	○
Cash and credit card		●	●	●				
Lightweight racing cape		●	○		●	●	●	○
Two spare inner tubes		○	○		●	●	●	●
Basic tools		○			●	●	●	●
Bonk rations		●	●			●	●	○
Extra clothing		●	○		○	●	●	●

Key: ● Recommended location   ○ Satisfactory/possible (but not ideal)

supplies can be obtained, so you need not worry too much about surviving the next stage. On longer rides you can usually find a corner at a control or by the roadside for some sleep or shelter if the weather is particularly inclement, and on bigger rides there may even be some mechanical assistance available.

In addition to the items shown in Table 9.1, you might also call upon lip balm, sun lotion, antiseptic cream and wipes, together with other minor medical items such as paracetamol or aspirin, digestion tablets and a toothbrush to freshen your mouth.

The randonneur's load (tools, spares, spare food, clothing and bag to put them in – excluding lights and fluid) need not exceed 3–4 kg. The weekend to two-week cycle tourist staying in B&B or hostel accommodation will probably carry about 5–10 kg.

Touring

The two-week or even transcontinental cyclist needs to be ruthless with his luggage. The popular rule when packing for any expedition is to lay out everything you think you need, and then halve it! Where you will be sleeping and eating will dictate much of your load. By staying in hotels or B&B you can carry minimal luggage. You will need to carry a towel if staying in hostels ('travel towels' are not bulky and do the job of drying you very well but are not quite as comforting as big, fluffy, cotton bath towels) and you may wish to take your own sheet sleeping bag.

You do not need a change of clothing for every day. One spare set of clothing should be sufficient for most rides. Street clothes can be kept to a minimum; a lightweight pair of trousers, T-shirt or polo shirt and perhaps a thin fleece or sweater for the evenings. If you are moving on each day, no one will care that you've worn the same shirt for seven evenings in a row – and if you are travelling with others, they will be in the same situation as you, so they won't mind either! Manufacturers such as Rohan, Lowe Alpine, Sprayway and Columbia produce

Figure 9.1 A loaded touring bike: note the tri-bars fitted for comfort, and the rider's well-used leather saddle

travel clothing with the specific qualities of light weight, low bulk and ease of care, often with other technical features in the fabrics, making them perfect for touring cyclists' needs.

You can walk around in most touring shoes but it can be a relief for your feet to be in a different pair of shoes after a day's riding. If your cycling shoes become soaked during a ride, it is good to let them dry out naturally while you wear a dry pair. But shoes can be bulky and heavy. Sandals are an option for hotter climates; 'summer shoes' with very lightweight soles are ideal for the cycle tourist's pannier. Carrying a second pair of shoes depends on your personal priorities.

Figure 9.2 All you need to carry for a weekend away or a two-week tour: street clothes, spare riding kit, waterproofs and cool weather gear, toiletries, maps and reading matter. You could fit everything here into a large rackpack (or saddlebag) and bar bag. Don't forget your roadside repair kit!

Racing

Racing cyclists should not be carrying any excess luggage. However, unless you have close support or the race HQ is nearby it is wise to carry a spare tyre and pump.

Cycle-camping

As a cycle-camper your load will be considerably more. It is worth considering a tent for one more person than is actually doing the journey – not so much to offer another lonely soul some shelter for the night, but so that you have space to sit up, move around a little and store your kit away from the elements or from prying eyes. Except in adventure races, the little extra weight is worth the trade-off for the added comfort factor. A two- to three-man tent will weigh approximately 2–4 kg, depending on how much 'weather' it needs to withstand.

Down sleeping bags are lighter (<1–1.5 kg), warmer, and usually pack smaller than synthetic ones, but down is difficult to wash and loses its thermal properties if it gets wet. Synthetic fillings are easy and quick to clean, though constant compression will damage the fibres so they do not last as long as down bags. However, modern synthetics do perform very well and their ease of use often makes them a better choice.

Sleeping mats are a wise investment. The ubiquitous, closed-cell foam 'Karrimat' is cheap, lightweight and impervious to water but it is bulky and offers limited comfort. Lightweight, inflatable camping mats provide better insulation from heat losses to the ground and improved comfort. Shorter, three-quarter-length mats are quite sufficient for covering your body and hips and they roll up into lighter, more compact packages for stowage.

There is no agreement amongst cycle-campers on the best cooking-stove and fuel. Multi-fuel stoves are a good choice if you intend to travel widely, since not all fuels are universally available. Think about your likely needs: what you want to heat (e.g. just water for tea, dehydrated meals or 'real' food), how often you will use the stove (once or twice a day, weekends, every day for a week, a month or a year); and where you will be (in terms of fuel supply, altitude and weather conditions, availability of spare parts, etc.). Specialist camping stores or magazines can help you decide which stove and fuel is best for your requirements.

10 Maintenance and problem-solving

There are many books and publications covering bicycle maintenance and repair in great detail. Read and practise as much as possible in order to understand how your bicycle works, so that you can cope with, or prevent, any mishaps on the road. Some dealers hold bicycle repair clinics for customers to learn and understand how their machines work. This chapter provides some basic advice, together with some ideas for problem-solving and emergency repairs which may not be covered in other literature.

Maintenance and repairs

Clean your bike

'Prevention is better than cure' is an old but very pertinent cliché. If you can spot wear or damage early, and take steps to repair or rectify it, you will save yourself a great deal of trouble when on the road. To this end, keep your bicycle clean. Dirt hides wear and tear, but if you clean your bike on a regular basis you will notice any problems and be able to deal with them before they become a disaster on a subsequent ride.

For cleaning, a bike-stand can hold your bike with the wheels removed – but it is not essential. You can lean the complete bike against a wall or suspend it by the saddle from a beam or strong washing-line. Do not turn the bike upside-down. This can damage the saddle and handlebars or brake levers, and makes it almost impossible to check the gears, brakes or headset.

Use warm, soapy water – car shampoo is excellent and less aggressive than regular detergents – and a couple of large sponges or soft brushes to clean inside all the curves and corners of the bike. For your chain, buy degreaser from bike shops or car accessory suppliers. Rinse the bike with clean water and rub it down with a clean rag. Chrome, steel or aluminium parts can be buffed up with a polish like Solvol Autosol, and furniture polish is excellent for bringing a shine to the frame's paintwork.

Check for damage

A quick check over the frame, wheels, tyres and components should reveal any trouble. Typical findings are:

- flints embedded in the tyres (pick them out carefully before they penetrate to the inner tube)

Figure 10.1 A quick check of the bike will reveal any damage

- small cuts in the tyre (these can usually be repaired with Super Glue)

- deeper tears in the tyres (these may need a strong fabric patch – boot – fixed inside the tyre, but discard tyres with extensive cuts)

- grit in the brake blocks, which will score the rims unless removed.

Look carefully at other components for any cracks – usually dirt accumulates, showing hairline fractures – and replace any damaged item straight away. Cleaning the bike is a good opportunity to spot any loose nuts or bolts. A light touch with an Allen key or spanner should reveal any fittings that are not tight. Do not overtighten threaded parts; this stresses them and makes them more liable to break. Before any ride lift the bike's handlebars up about 5 cm and let them drop, or knock the frame with your fingers. Any significantly loose components will rattle.

Annual overhaul

It is worth stripping your bike down for a full clean and overhaul once a year. This may be a job for your local bike shop if you do not have the time or knowledge to do it yourself. Some modern components such as brake-shift levers are sealed units and should be left that way!

- Components should be re-fitted with grease. This is *essential* for the seatpost, the handlebar stem, the bottom bracket unit and the pedals – otherwise they can 'fuse' into the frame or cranks, making later removal impossible without damaging one or other item. Grease prevents the threads from binding and allows the component to be tightened fully. It also lubricates it so that it can be easily removed later.

Do it at home

The best place to do any maintenance is at home – where it is warm, dry and light, and you have the appropriate tools and spare parts to hand – not out on the road in the middle of a ride.

- Grease the cables where they run through outer casing.

- Finish the cable ends with solder or special caps to prevent them from fraying and being a hazard.

- Items such as mudguard and bottle cage bolts are best fitted with a locking compound.

- Materials such as titanium (*see* also p. 7) may require special grease compounds like Copperease, which contains fine metal particles to prevent fusion of the two metal surfaces.

Roadside tools and spares

Even with the best maintenance, accidents do happen. You may need to be resourceful to cope with such instances in order to get back to civilisation.

If your bicycle is well looked after, you should not need to carry many tools with you. The following table shows those items recommended for a day ride, longer rides and extended tours.

Cable ties and adhesive tape (insulating tape, duct tape or 'gaffer' tape) can be used for all sorts of temporary repairs, such as replacing lost bolts or even holding shoes together. A couple of spare safety pins might be just what's needed to temporarily hold an item of clothing together or replace a broken zip on a bag. If your bicycle does not have any Allen bolts, don't bother to carry the tools, but do make sure that you do have the right tools to fix your own bike. The versatility of a simple penknife is always useful. Even if you don't know how to use a tool properly, it is worth carrying it. You may be able to flag down another cyclist who will be able to help you with a repair and get you on your way again.

Table 10.1 Recommended roadside tools and spares

Day rides	Longer rides	Extended tours
• 2 spare inner tubes, dusted with talc and wrapped in strong polythene bags • Inner tube repair patches, glue and emery paper or self-adhesive repair patches and emery paper • 2 tyre levers • 10 cm section of old tyre (bead and tread removed) to use as tyre repair patch • Allen keys to fit bike (usually 4, 5 and 6 cm) • Small adjustable spanner • Small pocket penknife with screwdriver blade • Selection of cable ties ('zip ties')	*As for day rides, plus:* • Spoke nipple key • Chain tool • Spare spokes (taped to carrier or seat-stay) • Roll of adhesive tape • Spare lamp bulbs and batteries if riding at night	*As for longer rides, plus:* • Crank tool • Brake blocks • Rear brake cable • Rear gear cable • Spare tyre

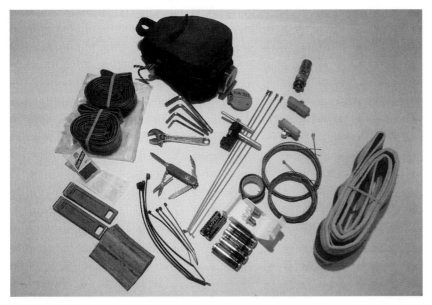

Figure 10.2 You can carry all you need for roadside repairs in a seatpack: far left column) two spare inner tubes, repair patches, tyre levers and tyre patch; centre left) allen keys, small adjustable spanner, penknife and cable ties; centre right – for longer trips) spoke key, chain tool, spokes (usually taped to chainstay), adhesive tape, spare bulbs and batteries; right – for extended tours) crank tool, brake-blocks, brake and gear cable and spare tyre (often secured under seat-stays or under carrier). Note the emergency LED on the seatpack

Multi-tools

Small 'multi-tools' need to be chosen with care. Some weigh more than the tools they are replacing, and not all of the tools on them can be used in all situations. Their design may not allow the tool to be turned in awkward spaces (such as under the saddle), or they may lack the leverage to tighten, say, a 6 mm handlebar bolt. If your bicycle has any particularly esoteric equipment then you will need to be equipped for that too.

Punctures

It's much easier to replace an inner tube by the roadside than to fix a puncture – but even on short rides you can experience multiple punctures. Hence, you should always carry repair patches as well as two spare tubes. Unless you have a support crew nearby, *always* take your pump!

Problem-solving

Lateral thinking

The key to fixing problems at the roadside is to think laterally (*see* Figure 10.3). What is at hand to fix the problem? For example, a woman who once broke a saddle managed to fashion a new seat by wrapping clothing over the seat-pillar. It wasn't very comfortable but it was sufficient to enable her to get back to base some 100 km away! A detour to a larger town or out-of-town retail park may prove useful, especially as so many shops now keep longer opening hours. Sports or motoring shops and DIY or department stores may have a bike department where spares can be purchased to help you on your way.

Figure 10.3 Emergency repair in Russia: here a rider has borrowed a local farmer's hammer – instead of using a handy rock – to insert a steel tube into the cracked subframe of his recumbent (photo: Axel Belinfante)

Split tyre

Wrap strong paper or polythene around the tube *inside* the tyre. Brochures, maps, socks (and even banknotes) have been used in such situations. Adhesive tape around the tyre may help. If you wrap tape or a section of old inner tube over the tyre and rim, remember that you will not be able to use the brake (you may need to remove the brake blocks to allow the wheel to rotate). Do check what caused the tyre to split in the first place – if the brake blocks were misaligned they may have chafed through the tyre wall and will do so again unless corrected.

No spare tubes

In desperate situations, if you have run out of spare inner tubes, it may be possible to tie a knot in the old inner tube tight enough that it will hold air, or stuff the tyre with grass. (Remember, these are desperate solutions!) It takes a long time to get the tyre packed with enough grass and get it sufficiently hard, and you may decide that your time is better spent walking to the nearest source of assistance instead.

Damaged cranks

The square, tapered hole in an aluminium crank can wear extremely quickly if it is not properly tightened on to the bottom bracket axle. If ridden when loose the crank may become so misshapen in a ride that it can never be tightened adequately again. Using a shim cut or torn from an aluminium drinks-can between the axle and the crank, a worn crank may be fitted on to a regular, square-taper bottom bracket axle such that it can be ridden home – although the crank will still need replacing. It is worth checking the tightness of cranks after the first 100–200 km of fitting as the relatively soft aluminium will 'bed in' and the axle bolts will require tightening to keep them secure.

Broken gears

If you break the rear gear mechanism, shorten the chain and remove, or by-pass, the gear mechanism altogether. You will have a single-speed bike, but riding that will be much quicker than walking.

Snapped gear cable

Screw down the 'high' adjuster screw on the gear mechanism so that the chain is kept on one of the middle sprockets and you should be able to manage to keep going – especially if you still have your front changer working. If the front changer cable breaks, adjust the screws on the mechanism to remain in the middle chainring as a good compromise.

Freewheel failure

Zip-tie the sprockets to the spokes in the back wheel. Take care because you will now be unable to freewheel. Judicious use of the brakes will be necessary. It's unlikely that the repair will stand much pressure, but if treated gingerly it should be sufficient to get you home in all but the most severe terrain.

Bent rims

Severely bent rims can often be straightened to a reasonable extent by using drain covers for leverage or even by standing on them. The rim will need to be replaced after such damage and treatment, and it may not be possible to use the brakes, but this may just be enough to get you mobile.

Broken seatpost

Remove all excess weight (seatpack or saddlebag) and then wedge a piece of wood into the two halves. Brace the saddle by straps to the top-tube and seat-stays, or lower the saddle so that enough seatpost is fitted into the frame.

Damaged frame or fork

Bent frames may be straightened to a large degree with some brute force. After all, if the item is already damaged then there is little to be lost by being brutal if it will help you out of trouble. Aluminium, however, does not like to be bent and may fracture if an attempt is made to straighten it.

Cracked frames have been temporarily held together by bracing tools or wood along the frame tubes and securing them with toe-straps or zip-ties. Be very cautious with this repair, especially when cornering or descending!

Be careful!

Don't expect bodged repairs to last long. These are just suggested, temporary solutions to help get you home, to the nearest railway station or suitable safe haven. With all of these repairs, extreme care should be taken when riding the bike – and even during the attempted repair, as parts may fail without warning.

11 Logistics and navigation

Getting to the start

Getting to wherever you want to go with your bike is much simpler than many people imagine. Bicycles are relatively easy to transport by other means of travel. You can get to new, more interesting or different places in a short time – perhaps to maximise holiday time, or to avoid tedious, or even dangerous areas.

Cars

It's often handy to use a car to reach a cycling area further from home, either for a specific event or maybe just to explore somewhere different.

For reasons of fuel economy, care of the bike and security, the bike is best carried inside the car. This is easy in most cars, especially if the bicycle is not fitted with mudguards. Put the chain on to the biggest chainring. Remove the bicycle's wheels and use an old axle or proper chain-hanger to keep the chain in place. Lay a blanket over the car-seats first and wrap a large piece of cloth over the transmission to prevent oil from damaging the upholstery. Then place the bike upside-down on the rear seats of the car. In a hatchback or estate, it be may possible to lower the rear seats and fit the bike in the car by just removing the front wheel and sliding the bike into the luggage compartment.

Car-racks

On cars used by racing teams, car-racks exist to transport up to eight bikes plus spare wheels. Most secure for the bike are roof-racks that clamp the front forks and rear wheel (*see* Figure 11.1). However, roof-racks add to the fuel consumption and can be awkward to fit, so some people prefer racks on the back of the car: either a simple pair of hooks, or a more secure gutter-style attachment fixed to a tow-ball.

It is a legal requirement that boot-mounted loads must not obscure the vehicle's lights or number plate. You may need to fit a lighting board on the back of the load. Make sure, too, that the load is secure and the bikes are not near the exhaust output as the heat can cause serious damage.

Bikes on car racks can be a target for thieves, especially at motorway service stations, and even at road junctions. Do make sure that they are securely fastened and, if the vehicle is left for any time, ensure that the bikes are locked too.

Don't forget it's there!

When travelling with bicycles outside the car, remember that they are there! Fix a note to the steering wheel to remind the driver not to drive under a car-park barrier with a roofload of expensive machinery, or reverse into a short parking place with bikes on a boot-rack.

Figure 11.1 Transport assistance: this car roof-rack secures the bike by the front forks and rear wheel; others can take whole bikes upright or upside down, or fitted to the rear of the vehicle

Trains

Train operators' rules on travelling with bikes vary considerably from one region to another. Usually a nominal fee is charged for any length of journey – but this may be multiplied if the journey crosses different rail companies' territories. In some cases, pre-booking is required. If you can, make enquiries with the rail company before you travel. Dismantling of the bike is not usually required but it is sensible to affix a label to your machine showing ownership, itinerary and final destination. In some countries bikes need to be bagged for rail travel.

In France, for example, bikes are not permitted on all trains, so it is best to find out which trains will take your bicycle and then ensure that you travel on the same train as your bike. Most operators do not like bikes being locked to the carriage – they may have to be moved depending on other goods being carried during the journey. Lock your bike to itself and attach an

Figure 11.2 Bicycles by train: a touring party off-loads their bikes from a train in Ryazan, Russia (photo: Ivo Miesen)

elastic bungee cord to any convenient handrail to hold the bike upright and prevent it from falling over or disappearing.

Air travel

Most airlines carry bicycles provided that they are suitably protected. There are numerous 'bike bags' and 'bike boxes' on the market. Space is restricted on aircraft so the bike needs to be as compact as possible (*see* Figure 11.3). Usually, you will need to:

- remove the pedals (RH pedal has a RH thread, LH pedal has a LH thread)
- move chain on to biggest chainring
- remove accessories
- remove wheels (and mudguards if fitted)
- move rear gear inboard to lowest gear position
- fit axles or old hubs between the rear dropouts and front forks (prevents frame dropouts from being squashed together and takes up some chain slack)
- turn handlebars through 90° (in line with top-tube) and rotate dropped handlebars to fit the hook underneath the top-tube
- wrap all tubes with plumbers' pipe insulation or bubble wrap

Figure 11.3 Air travel: cheaper than a bike box, bicycles can be taken apart, covered with pipe lagging and tied into a neat bundle – although some parts are still exposed to knocks and damage

- for extra protection, place tape underneath any bare wire cable runs to stop them from rubbing against the bike's paintwork

- remove wheel skewers

- if the bike is being transported in a box or bag, it may be necessary to remove the saddle and seatpost. Wrap tape around the seatpost to indicate its insertion point

- strap wheels to side of frame, ensuring that they cannot move and that both frame and wheels are suitably protected from one another. (An old margarine pot or similar can be taped or strapped over the freewheel cassette to prevent the sprockets from damaging other items)

- if you are using mudguards, secure these over the tyres

- put pedals, accessories and wheel skewers in a bag, inside the box or bike bag, together with some clean rag and tools for re-assembly at the destination

- have ownership and destination identification both inside and outside the package.

Bike boxes and bags usually have some spare corners which can be used for packing other items – dirty washing is a favourite for the return journey!

Airlines may require you to let some of the air out of your bicycle tyres for air travel, fearing that the low pressures experienced at 30,000 ft will cause bicycle tyres to expand and explode off the rims. In practice, most aircraft holds are pressurised so this is unlikely. However, the airline may insist on it, so you will need a good pump to get your tyres back up to working pressure upon arrival.

Rigid boxes offer more protection than soft bags, but they can be very expensive, heavy and cumbersome. A good compromise is a cardboard bike box which can usually be obtained free of charge from a local bike shop. Dealers receive new bikes in boxes, so they are the correct size and shape for a bike, and most are happy to give them away to save on their own disposal costs. Pack some parcel tape and a marker pen for the return journey packaging.

This kind of packaging is ideal for fixed-centre travel, but if you are flying into one place and out from another you will either have to abandon it at your point of arrival, arrange for your bike packing to be sent on to your journey's end, or take it with you. Some bike bags are made with this in mind. However, they do little in the way of protection other than keep dirt on your bike away from other people's luggage. Most airlines can provide enormous polythene bags to engulf a bike (and even tandems) that will do the same job. It is still wise to protect the bike as best you can. Find newspaper, bubble wrap or pipe insulation locally and use that to protect the frame tubes from damage.

Bus

In many rural and remote areas, buses are the only form of mechanised transport for the local population. It is therefore very simple to carry your bike by bus should the need arise.

Navigation

Maps

Riding a bike on the road, you can easily cover more than three times the distance as someone walking. In the UK, the Ordnance Survey 1:50,000 Landranger maps are ideal for walkers or off-road riders who need this amount of detail, or for those wishing to explore a region in depth. However, the long-distance rider needs very little of this information and – since each map covers only 40 × 40 km – you may need to carry more than six maps just for one day! A smaller scale such as 1:100,000 is excellent for most cycling purposes. Michelin maps cover Continental Europe and are readily available. These usually show all the minor roads which are of interest to the cyclist, but do not detail smaller features like footpaths or the names of farms.

Some maps are merely road diagrams and do not feature the lay of the land, or all the smaller, less busy roads which are ideal for cycling. These are fine for motorists, but as a cyclist you will usually want to know what sort of country you will be traversing. Relief can be shown by any combination of contour lines or shading, or by spot height markers – but on road diagrams you have to get some clue about the topography by studying other features such as railways, rivers or even names of places.

Road atlases

For the price of two good maps you can purchase an atlas covering the whole country (making it viable to upgrade the atlas every season or two). Scales of 1:200,000 or 1:250,000 (roughly 1" to 3 or 4 miles) are ideal for the kilometre-eating rider. Tear out the relevant pages of the atlas (they are double-sided) and few rides will ever require more than three sheets to cover the whole route. Fold the pages into 3 × 3 sections and they will easily fit in your jersey pocket or under a map-holder on the handlebars.

Map holders

For precise navigation you need to follow the map at all times. Keep it on your handlebars either on a bar bag or on a special map-holder. You can buy commercial map-holders or you can make your own (*see* Figure 11.4). Use a 10 × 12 cm off-cut of Correx or similar (the plasticised corrugated material used for grocery boxes and lightweight signs) and two cable-ties to secure it to the handlebars and stem. The map itself can be secured with a bulldog clip or rubber bands. Do not be afraid to re-fold your map to a more convenient shape or size to keep your current location 'face out'.

Map protection

A wet map is very soon a useless map, so it needs to be protected from rain, water splash and sweat. If you do not use a bar bag with a waterproof map-holder, use a clear polythene bag – especially if you carry your maps in your jersey pocket.

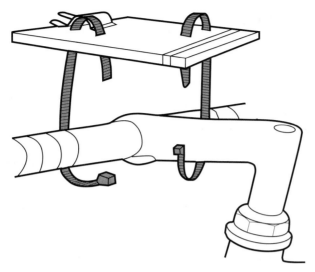

Figure 11.4 DIY map-holder using 10 x 12 cm Correx and two zip-ties: the map can be held in place with rubber bands or a bulldog clip

Walkers' map-holders tend to be too cumbersome for cycling. Transparent adhesive film (from good stationery stores) is excellent for covering individual atlas pages, or you can protect them with Nikwax Map Proof Spray. You can buy some maps ready-laminated.

Route sheets

Some organised rides will have direction signs at the roadside, marshals or directions painted on the road. But this is not universal. On randonnées or similar events you are issued with a route sheet. There is no uniform notation but Audax UK does have a very good 'recommended standard' (though individual organisers may choose their own layout and type-faces). Some riders re-write their route sheets or enlarge the print for easier use on the road. It is worth protecting route sheets from the elements or sweat in the same fashion as maps (*see* above). An illegible or *pâpier maché* route sheet is not much use.

Route sheets issued to randonneurs can be carried in the same fashion as a map. Usually, route sheets detail all the road junctions and turns – so there is less need to refer to a map, which can be tucked away into a pocket for reference only if needed. However, mistakes do happen and it is always useful to have a map handy. If in doubt, trust the cartographer. Road signs can be damaged, missing or turned around 'for a laugh'.

On larger or foreign randonnées, directions are often painted on the road or provided via signs at the roadside. Many riders like this as it does not tax them mentally on a long ride, but it does require that you stay alert so that you don't miss any turnings.

Where there is no map

When touring in wilder parts of the world you may not find suitably detailed maps readily available. Most mapping began because of military interests and some

Don't always follow the pack

Be wary of blindly following other riders. They may not be on the same route as you, or they may not be paying attention. Should you get dropped from a group, you'll need to know where you are in readiness for the next turn. Stay aware of your position on the route at all times, even when riding with others who appear to know where they are going.

nations still withhold mapping information because of its strategic value. In many remote lands there is little call for commercial maps, either because of the limited numbers travelling through the area or because the vast majority of travellers follow regular trade routes. In regions such as the Sahara dunes or the interior of Iceland, the topography changes too rapidly for detailed mapping to be worthwhile. There you either have to accept whatever is available knowing that it will not be entirely accurate, follow the directions of local people, or just guess and hope!

In the latter cases it also helps to have some compass skills too. General direction can often be gauged by the sun, but this is unreliable – as the earth moves in relation to the sun during the course of the day, the sun is not always visible and a twisting route can soon have you disoriented.

GPS

GPS (Global Positioning Systems) have significantly changed many navigation techniques. A small handset receives signals from a series of satellites orbiting the globe and can pinpoint any location on the earth's surface to less than 10 m. These devices are universally used for sea and air navigation but are arguably less useful where narrowly defined paths are followed. In addition, they only indicate direction, not topography (sometimes suggesting impossible routes over cliffs or through water). Some GPS handsets can be programmed for changes in direction, but this is not always feasible for a long-distance ride. In future, no doubt devices will carry more detailed mapping for more immediate use by cyclists. The big drawbacks at present are:

- cost (not prohibitive but not cheap either)

- size (similar to mobile telephones – although Casio has already produced a wristwatch GPS receiver)

- reliance on batteries.

GPS users are always advised to have a regular compass to hand as a back-up.

'Get set' – summary of key points

- Good nutrition is absolutely vital to sustain your long-distance cycling activities. Pay careful attention to your diet and you will be able to ride more strongly and for longer. Ensure that you get a healthy, balanced diet with plenty of fresh fruit and vegetables. A multivitamin supplement can provide good dietary insurance, but this is not a substitute for good practice.

- Carbohydrate is the single most important element of your diet. Aim to obtain at least 60% of your diet from carbohydrate-rich foods. Keep your fat intake to a minimum (15–30%), especially saturated fats.

- Eat little and often when riding, and begin eating within two hours after exercise in order to replenish your muscle glycogen stores as quickly as possible. If you postpone eating, your body will absorb the nutrients more slowly and this will delay your recovery.

- Make sure that you drink enough before, during and after exercise. Expect to drink about 500 ml per hour (although this will vary according to your size, the ambient temperature and the intensity of your exercise). A carbohydrate drink will supply both your liquid needs and much of your nutritional needs.

- Your own health and hygiene are just as important as the smooth running of your bicycle. Develop good habits and attend to any minor ailments or injuries before they become major traumas. Do check the cause of the problem to avoid recurrence (e.g. position on the bike).

- Keep safety in mind at all times. Ride sensibly and be aware of how you might need to adapt your riding to your environment.

  Riding at night is good fun, but be aware of the problems. A good lighting system is essential to ensure that you are visible to other road users and so that you can see where you are going. You must remain alert at all times too, so respect your need for rest and sleep – and that's just as important after your ride.

  Always pay attention to where you are going – though your navigational needs will vary according to what type of riding you are doing. Racing cyclists are far less concerned about route-finding on a marshalled road than are wilderness cyclists, or even randonneurs trying to follow a route sheet.

- There will never be complete consensus as to the right equipment to take when cycling, but there are some basics which you should never be without – repair kit, spare inner tubes and pump. Beyond that, try to keep your luggage to a minimum. Invest in good-quality equipment which will not let you down.

It pays to have some knowledge about how your bike and equipment work. Keep your bike clean and you will be able to spot wear or damage and take preventative measures to avoid most problems on the road. Occasionally you might have to think of a unique solution to a problem.

Go!

12 Training principles

Training and preparation

The basic training principles outlined in this chapter can be applied by anyone embarking upon cycling over a long distance. If your aim is a pleasurable day out on a charity ride, or an easy touring holiday, you need not concern yourself unduly with the details. The principles still apply, but the methodology needs to be diluted according to your aims, your chosen activity and your current level of fitness. As you get fitter you will be able to ride more often, at greater intensity and for longer; but to begin with, you need to take exercise gently and gradually build up to greater levels of activity.

At the root of all fitness is the genetic code determining how your muscles can develop. This can make the difference between some cyclists being potential Tour de France winners, and the rest of the world's cycling population who will never achieve the level of power and fitness required to ride at an average of 40 kph for 200 km every day for three weeks. Despite this, almost anyone can ride a bike over long distances if they prepare for it – albeit at their own pace.

The scope of this book cannot cover the physiology of training any great detail. However, the following section should provide you with a good foundation – to help you understand the basic principles, and perhaps solve some fitness issues that may have eluded you in the past – putting you on the right road for longer distance cycling.

For more detailed explanations of some of the terms used in this section, the following are recommended:

Body In Action (1999), Introductory Study Pack 2 (rev. ed.), (National Coaching Foundation)

Friel, J. (1999), *The Cyclist's Training Bible* (A & C Black)

Training (2000), Course Resource Level 2, Club Coach Award (British Cycling Federation)

Sleamaker, R. and Browning, R. (1996), *SERIOUS Training for Endurance Athletes* (2nd ed.) (Human Kinetics)

General principles of training

You need to prepare or *train* to ride your bike over longer distances. Training allows your body to adapt to the demands that are going to be placed on it in the future – though it doesn't have to be hard or intense to achieve this.

There are a number of principles that govern the effectiveness of training or *conditioning*. These are shown in Table 12.1. (Bear in mind that to a large extent, your genetic make-up dictates how you will react to any training. For example, some riders adapt better than others to riding long distances or making a quick recovery.)

Table 12.1 Some general principles governing training effectiveness (conditioning)

Principle	Explanation
Adaptation	Your ultimate goal might be quite daunting initially. But through a process of *adaptation* and getting used to both the physical and mental aspects of your task you will be better able to cope with the stresses involved.
Specificity	As a cyclist, the vast majority of your preparation must be cycling *specific* – *see* also below.
Progression	You will need to have a steady *progression* of activity if you wish to improve your fitness or cycling ability.
Variation	Your workload has to be *varied*. Repeating the same type of exercise and intensity can lead to boredom and staleness; without variation, you will plateau and reach a stage of diminishing returns. Nor will you have the variety of fitness to cope with all the situations you are likely to encounter.
Overload	To improve, you have to stress your body to a greater level than you usually experience – a process known as *overload*. This must be closely linked with *progression*, *adaptation* and adequate *recovery*.
Reversibility	If you do not maintain your levels of activity, you will lose the training effects you have gained.
Recovery	After any stress, your body needs to recover and recuperate to build to a higher and stronger position. As the training load increases, recovery becomes more and more vital.

Components of fitness

The principal components of fitness are strength, speed and stamina, with flexibility, skill, mental approach and rest playing an important part in being 'fit for purpose' too. All sporting activities include these ingredients in varying combinations, and some athletes are better predisposed to some of these elements than others. However, training and exercise – its duration, frequency and intensity – can influence and improve all the components of fitness.

Specificity and 'fitness for purpose'

To ride a bicycle efficiently you need to develop specific muscles to power the pedals, and have the cardiovascular 'plumbing' to cope with your body's oxygen needs. You cannot expect to be a good cyclist without riding a bike. The vast majority of your training time needs to be spent on a bicycle, developing particular muscle movements and strength (plus handling skills and riding technique). This is 'specificity' and it applies to any sport.

Cross-training

Using different sporting activities to help train for another sport can improve your muscular strength and cardiovascular output, but these benefits diminish at higher levels of fitness where sport-specific fitness is much more important. Arguably, elite athletes should concentrate solely on their sport – cyclists should simply ride a bike, runners should run and rowers should row – to improve their abilities.

While it is true that your main focus should be on cycling, there is room for another training avenue known as cross-training. For example, by using weights you can improve your strength more easily than by just training on a bike. Improving flexibility and suppleness almost certainly has to be done away from the bike. Other activities may help to balance muscle usage and prevent overuse injuries. Sometimes it just helps to have a mental break from the same year-round activity by doing something quite different, or when cycling is impractical such as in icy conditions or if you are away on business without a bike to ride. However, any alternative activities need to use muscles in a similar fashion to cycling if the benefits are going to be transferable. You gain what you train. Too much activity away from your target one (e.g. speed or distance) will have an adverse effect on it.

The training effect

As a long-distance cyclist the principal element of fitness you require is stamina or endurance. There is only one way to improve this, and that's by increasing the duration of your rides. However, after a while, fatigue will begin to set in and this will limit the duration of any ride. As you exercise, your muscles actually get damaged. If you continue cycling for a long time your muscles may become so damaged that you will be literally worn out and unable to carry on. With more intense activities (such as racing at speed, frequent climbing or sprinting), the fatigue may be induced by a build-up of lactic acid in the muscles (*see* p. 140), and pain will stop you.

Remarkably, the human body is capable of self-repair. Muscles damaged by exercise in training or racing rebuild when you are asleep (aided by appropriate protein nutrition – *see* p. 69–70). But better than that, your muscles get repaired to a higher specification in order to cope with the demands just experienced. The key to improved fitness lies in balancing the amount of exertion (intensity and duration) and the amount of rest (frequency) in order to maximise the beneficial training effect. If the activity is too intense, more muscle damage will occur and your body will need more time to effect repairs. If another training session begins before you have properly recovered and rebuilt the muscle tissue to the improved specification, this will exacerbate the muscle damage and lead to excessive fatigue (*see* Figure 12.1).

Your body wants to be 'fit for purpose' and will not carry muscle if it is not being used. If you leave long intervals between training sessions your body will not keep the improved muscles, but will let them 'atrophy' (waste away) instead, leaving you under-trained for your next ride.

Progression

Your muscles, heart and lungs (and backside!) need to be introduced to the demands of long-distance cycling over a period of time. If you do too much too soon, you will feel over-tired. If you do the same training every week, every year, you will plateau at a particular level and not get any fitter. This is typical of amateur racers who repeat their training patterns year after year but do not improve their performances. You need to vary your riding, so that your body is pushed a little harder if you wish to become fitter. You can do this by riding more often (frequency), for longer (duration), or by riding faster (intensity). Sometimes it is beneficial to reduce the frequency and duration of your riding to avoid becoming overtrained.

Overtraining, rest and recovery

More is not always better. If you exercise without enough time to rest and recover you will become fatigued, leading to poor performances (*see* Figure 12.1). Overtraining is characterised by:

- chronic injury or infection
- greater incidence of infection
- fatigue and unexpected sense of effort during training

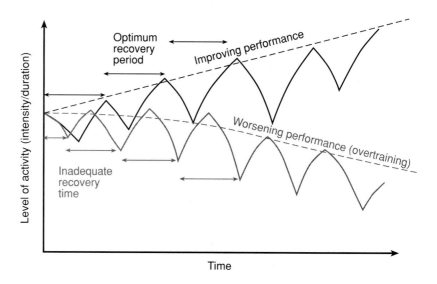

Figure 12.1 The effects of optimal and inadequate recovery times

- unexplained loss of performance

- heavy, stiff or sore muscles

- slow recovery

- disturbed sleep

- mood swings or irritability

- loss of energy/drive/libido/appetite.

Recovery from infections like glandular fever or Chronic Fatigue Syndrome can take months or even years. It is vital that recovery is absolutely complete before resuming full training, or the condition may re-occur more severely and be even more difficult to overcome. Figure 12.2 shows how training periods and adequate recovery achieve optimum results.

The sooner you begin eating after exercise, the quicker you can replenish muscle glycogen and be ready for the next activity. Aim to eat within the first two hours after exercise, as carbohydrate is absorbed at a quicker rate then than at other times.

Overload

Overload is necessary for building your body up to cope with the stresses and demands you are going to put on it. When Chris Boardman set the world hour record distance in 1996, his overload training was riding the gruelling three-week Tour de France. He then came 'up to speed' with a brief recovery period and six weeks of fast, short-distance training to bring him to the level needed.

Your overload training could be one or two weeks of high-mileage cycling holiday or a training camp, 3–6 weeks before a big stage race or 12-hour time-trial. You must allow time to recover from the overload to avoid being tired when you begin your target event.

Avoiding overtraining

- **Ensure adequate carbohydrate intake before and during exercise**
- **Vary training intensities, activities and locations**
- **Reduce psychological stress**
- **Reduce exposure to over-heating**
- **Eat a balanced diet**
- **Avoid excessive training volumes**
- **Control the rate of training progression**
- **Allow adequate recovery between sessions**
- **Include rest and low-intensity/low-volume work in the training programme**

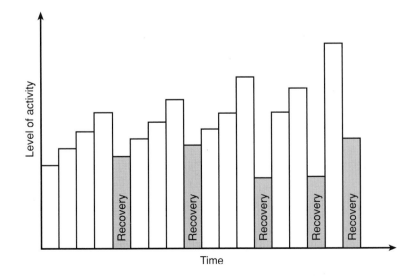

Figure 12.2 The progression of activity (training) achieved with recovery periods

Adaptation

As you progress through the months of cycling, you are adapting your fitness (muscular and cardiovascular) to suit your needs. This is essential in the development of 'fitness for purpose' (*see* above). If your goal is to be a faster long-distance racing cyclist, then your training will have to include some faster, shorter rides instead of just riding long distances at a steady pace.

Periodisation

Coaching parlance organises time into three different periods, fitting specific aims into each unit. The novice or leisure cyclist need not concern themselves unduly with these terms, but understanding the reasoning behind them can help in organising a more effective training programme.

- **Macro-cycle** – this is usually a period of a complete season or year, although it could be four or five years – e.g. from one Olympic event, or Paris–Brest–Paris randonnée, to the next.

- **Micro-cycles** – these usually last 7–14 days and help hone specific skills or qualities such as speed (maybe used as a tapering process prior to a big event, to ensure that a rider is adequately rested and not fatigued prior to competition or a major target of the season).

- **Meso-cycles** – lasting 2–6 weeks, these are the building blocks of training and competition. For competitive cyclists, these blocks are: foundation or preparation; pre-competition or transition phase; competition and recovery.

The year-planner given in Table 12.2 indicates how you might divide your year (macro-cycle) if you were aiming to compete in an event like a 24-hour time-trial at the end of July – or perhaps a big randonnée such as PBP at the end of August. By dividing the periods into manageable meso-cycles, you can aim to bring yourself to peak condition at the end of each period. The end of each period (or beginning of the subsequent period) is a good opportunity for a brief rest to help you to recuperate fully before embarking on the next phase approaching your goal.

Notice that this rider's year does not begin on 1 January! Preparation has to begin much earlier than that for the successful cyclist – especially one wishing to do well at a true endurance level.

Tapering and peaking

It is simply not possible to continue improving your strength, speed and general fitness at a steady rate. Initially you can make great gains, but your *rate* of improvement will diminish as you become fitter – and if you train too much you will become tired and overtrained. In order to *peak* (be at your best possible form) for an important event, you need to *taper* (gradually reduce) your training. The greater the demands of the forthcoming event, the more tapering you will need to do, but the usual period is around 5–21 days.

Table 12.2 Training calendar showing suggested training activities for racing or randonnées

	Oct	Nov	Dec	Jan	Feb	Mar	Apr	May	Jun	Jul	Aug	Sep
RACING meso-cycle	Recovery meso-cycle	Preparation meso-cycle #1	Preparation meso-cycle #2	Preparation meso-cycle #3	Transition meso-cycle prior to racing		Racing meso-cycle #1		Racing meso-cycle #2	Racing meso-cycle #3		Recovery meso-cycle
	Easy rides	Progressive build-up of long, steady distance rides. Progressive work on strength and areas of weakness			Speed training (anaerobic)		Racing – progressively longer distances, interspersed with short-distance speed work and rest					Rest
	Zones 1–2	Mainly Zones 1–2, occasionally Zone 3			Mostly training Zones 3–6		Racing in Zones 4–5 Training in Zones 3–6 Tapering to peak for specific goals					Rest Zone 1
	Recovery	Preparation			Pre-competition		Competition					Recovery
RANDONNEES	80–150 km	100–150 km			100–200 km		200–400 km	200–600 km		200–1200 km		<200 km
	Recovery	Preparation			Transition		Randonnées					Recovery
	Easy rides	Progressive build-up of long, steady distance rides. Progressive work on strength and areas of weakness			Short-distance Audax		Randonnées – progressively longer and hillier distances, interspersed with shorter distances covered at slightly higher speed + rest					Easy rides
meso-cycle	Recovery meso-cycle	Preparation meso-cycle #1	Preparation meso-cycle #2		Transition meso-cycle prior to audax rides		Audax meso-cycle #1	Audax meso-cycle #2		Audax meso-cycle #3		Recovery meso-cycle

Note: for an explanation of training zones, see pp. 136–7.

Monitoring your resting heart rate

Ideally you should measure your resting heart rate when you wake up first thing in the morning, every day. But most people do not have time to lie in bed calmly for an extra few minutes taking a pulse reading. You can take your pulse at any time of day, provided that you are consistent.

For example, in the three weekends prior to a 12-hour time-trial you might race 100 miles, 50 miles and 25 miles. This will ensure that you are not too fatigued before the 12-hour race, and the shorter events will help to develop some extra speed. Exactly the same principle can be employed by the randonneur preparing for long events of 400 km or more.

Measuring training intensity

Your heart rate is a good marker of both your basic level of aerobic fitness, and the intensity of effort during exercise. As a general rule, the lower your heart rate, the fitter you are.

As you get fitter:

· your heart becomes stronger

· it pumps more blood (and oxygen) with each heart beat

· you produce more power for a given heart rate

· your speed of recovery after effort will improve

· your resting heart rate becomes lower

· you will be less fatigued.

Small fluctuations in your resting heart rate are quite normal due to variations in training and rest, or the influences of illness or heat. However, if your resting heart rate is 10% above its normal level for three days or more, this could be an indication of overtraining or illness. Ease back on your training for 7–14 days to help your recovery.

Training zones

How many levels?

In the UK in the mid-1980s, cycling sports scientist Peter Keen identified four distinct levels of training, or 'zones'. He later divided his Level 2 into two . . . and then revised the whole idea in the late 1990s, renaming the (now five) levels as six zones of training plus a recovery zone. The French cycling academy has used eight levels of training since the early 1980s, and the Americans use five – with three sections for the fifth level. There is no one definitive answer!

Many formulae have been proposed to help calculate training or racing efforts – but all should be used cautiously and only as a guide. The human body doesn't necessarily conform to the neat, mathematical figures given by sports scientists.

Essentially, these formulae use a maximum heart rate (MHR) figure found by an exhaustive test on an ergometer or by sprinting up a long hill. Various levels or 'zones' for training are then calculated beneath this – each with a different physiological response (*see* below). However, since you do not usually ride until you drop with exhaustion (MHR), there is some doubt as to the value of these methods. Even worse are formulae that use a HR calculation of a random figure minus your age, sometimes with a statistical twist. These are simply too general to be of any use and can easily be 20 beats out – the difference between training in Zone 2 or Zone 4! In simple terms, the accepted training zones are as follows.

Recovery

Non-training rides carried out at a very low intensity and for relatively short duration. Active recovery in this manner aids blood flow to the muscles and helps more rapid recovery after a long or arduous training session or event than just passively resting.

Basic level – Zones 1 and 2

These are low stress zones of activity. Cycling at this low intensity will allow you to develop a smooth, economic pedalling action. You should be able to breathe and talk easily when riding.

Very long rides at Zone 1 aid the utilisation of fats. High-volume rides at the slightly higher intensity of Zone 2 provide a greater overload on the cardiovascular system – fundamental for building a good foundation of aerobic endurance ability. Riding at this intensity develops the highest rate of fat burning. Provided that proper attention is given to avoiding carbohydrate and fluid loss, rides at this intensity can continue for many hours and are typical of close-season training rides and most randonnées.

Intensive level – Zones 3 and 4

Characterised by deeper and faster breathing, especially when riding uphill – conversation may stop altogether. Riding in Zone 3 develops aerobic power and endurance, largely through improved cardiovascular efficiency. Long rides at this intensity place high demands on muscle glycogen, so sufficient carbohydrate intake is essential.

Zone 4 is often described as typical race-pace for events that last around two hours or more. The concentration required to *train* at this level means that such sessions will probably only last 30–60 minutes. Blood lactate levels rise, close to the threshold (or maximum sustainable) level. The muscles are under significant stress, as they switch fuel sources from fat to carbohydrate.

Maximal level – Zones 5 and 6

This is racing 'on the limit': as fast as you can ride for 20–40 minute, short distance racing. Naturally, this places extreme demands on the cardiovascular system and the ability of the muscles to deal with the build-up of lactate, heat and carbon dioxide.

Zone 6 is anaerobic – e.g. sprinting, very rapid acceleration or putting a great deal of effort into climbing a short, steep hill at speed. Riding at this very high intensity develops maximum muscle power, but this is not sustainable for more than a minute.

Your HR can change over time, so it is worth checking every three to four months where your zones lie. The figures given in Table 12.3 are not rigid, but rather should be viewed as a continuum: your zones may be quite different from those of another rider.

In Figure 12.3, the three riders have the same resting and maximum heart rates, but they have very different characteristics (and zones). The 'elbow' or 'Conconi point' on each of these graphs is a characteristic found in most HR testing procedures, and indicates the threshold between aerobic and anaerobic activities (*see* also pp. 67–9) – the cut-off point between Levels 3 and 4 (Zones 5 and 6).

Rider 1's HR increases very quickly as power demands are increased – indicative of a rider who is not particularly fit. For any given HR, his power output is less than that of riders 2 and 3 who have shallower power outputs. As you get fitter, your power to HR graph will shift to the right and take the desired shallower profile.

Table 12.3 Description of training zones

Training band or zone	Recovery	Basic		Intensive		Maximal	
		Zone 1 Level 1	Zone 2 Lower level 2	Zone 3 Upper level 2	Zone 4	Zone 5 Level 3	Zone 6 Level 4
% MHR	<60	60–65	65–75	75–82	82–89	89–94	94+
% VO$_2$max*	<42	42–49	49–63	63–72	72–83	83–92	92–100
Blood lactate mm	<1.0	1–1.5	1.5–2.0	2.0–2.5	2.5–3.5	3.5–6.0	>6.0
RPE	1 Vv light	2 Light	3 Moderate	5 Heavy	6	7 V heavy	10 Vv heavy
Duration of a continuous training session	<60 mins	1.5–6.0 hours	1 to 4 hours	45 mins to 2 hours	30–60 mins	15–40 mins	4–10 mins OR intervals
Sensation	Easy, apparently effortless	Easy breathing. Able to hold conversation when riding	Breathing generally easy, a little deeper on hills	More concentration. Breathing heavier. Conversation reduced to simple sentences	Deep breathing. Brief words only		Lung-busting. Can utter no more than a weight-lifter's grunt!
Effects and applications of training zones		Weight loss (fat burning)		Carbohydrate usage	Cardiovascular development	VO$_2$max. development* / Lactate threshold development** / Incr. in max. muscle power	Anaerobic energy sources
Pace	V easy	Easy	Brisk	Fast		Racing	
Fitness component developed	Recovery		Endurance Strength		Intervals, speed, race pace, sprints		Sprinting

Source: British Cycling Federation (2000), *Training*, Level 2 Coach Resource.
*VO$_2$max – the peak rate at which somebody can take in and use oxygen.
**Lactate threshold – the exercise intensity that results in an abrupt increase in blood lactate concentraiton. Continued exercise beyond this point ultimately leads to rapid muscle fatigue.

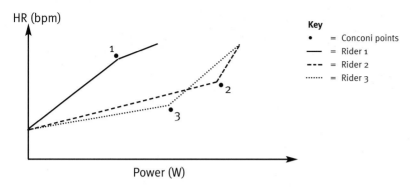

HR (bpm)

Key
- • = Conconi points
- —— = Rider 1
- - - - = Rider 2
- ······· = Rider 3

Power (W)

Figure 12.3 **Different heart rate (HR) responses and power outputs for three cyclists with the same MHR**

Rider 2 might typically be a time-triallist, able to cycle very close to his anaerobic threshold. But if such riders get into Level 4 (or Zone 6) they are very quickly exhausted and cannot repeat the effort. Rider 3 is characteristic of road racers and mountain-bikers who need to reproduce efforts of very high intensity in a race – to cope with repeated hills, or sprinting out of corners – and still have something 'left in the tank' for a fast finish.

Heart rate monitors

Heart rate monitors (HRMs) are extremely useful tools if used correctly. A chest strap with a transmitter sends a signal of the heart beat to a wristwatch for immediate display. More expensive HRMs can record data and even download it into a computer in graph form for later analysis.

HRMs provide an objective figure to quantify your training intensity. Speed alone can be deceptive. You could easily ride at 40 kph or 50 kph – downhill, with a tailwind, or in a bunch behind other riders – but you have not ridden hard to achieve that speed. Conversely, covering 30 km in two hours may not look impressive, but if you do it up a mountain or into the teeth of a gale you will have worked much harder than the figures suggest.

Problems with HRMs

Your heart does not respond immediately to exercise demands. It takes a while for it to 'get up to speed' to cope with extra effort, and your heart rate may actually increase for a few seconds *after* you have stopped riding. In a very short sprint your HRM cannot respond fast enough; you have to use *feel* for the effort to know that you are giving everything to it (*see* also RPE below).

Under stress (e.g. in competition) your body releases adrenaline which stimulates the heart to beat faster for any given effort. In other words, muscular effort in racing does not exactly replicate the same muscular effort for that heart rate in training. Riders have lost races by watching their HRMs and worrying that they were too close to their threshold in competition! Be wary of using a HRM to dictate your race strategy. Know your body. If you want to know how much effort you have put into to a race, wear your HRM for downloading later, but do not let it distract you.

A useful HRM tip

Wrap the HRM around your handlebars for easier viewing – a short piece of plumber's pipe insulation is ideal for padding out the handlebar to a suitable size.

Calculating training load using RPE

You can train very efficiently without any figures – after all, that's how cyclists always rode before the invention of convenient HRMs, using basic notations like 'easy', 'moderate', 'brisk', 'hard', 'very hard' and 'exhausting'. You can fine-tune these zones with a + or a –, use any adjective to help define them, or mark them with a figure.

Therefore, if you do not have access to a HRM you can still gauge your efforts for training purposes by judging how hard a ride feels. One simple method of calculating your intensity of effort is to use a Rating of Perceived Exertion (RPE). A simplified model of the Borg Scale (sometimes shown from 6–20) is reproduced in Figure 12.4 below.

You can also correlate your RPE to your zone of training. It is subjective, but the numbers you use are just to compare one ride or training session with another. Smaller increments, for example 6.5 or 8.2, can be introduced to fine-tune the description of effort if necessary. Calculate your training load by multiplying the RPE by the duration of your ride, as follows:

RPE 5 (heavy) × 80 mins = 400
RPE 7 (very hard) × 60 minutes = 420

You can draw up your daily figures on a graph so that you clearly see any periods of excessive exercise which will require greater rest.

Very, very light	Light	Moderate	Somehwat heavy	Heavy or hard	Heavy +	Very heavy	Very heavy +	Very heavy ++	Very, very heavy
1	2	3	4	5	6	7	8	9	10

Figure 12.4 Rate of Perceived Exertion (RPE) – The Borg scale

Lactate threshold

As effort increases lactic acid builds up in the muscles. This is a metabolic waste product produced by prolonged high-intensity (anaerobic) activity. Characteristically, anaerobic activity is a short-duration effort which cannot be sustained for long because the lactic acid becomes concentrated to such an extent that it causes muscle fatigue, laboured breathing, discomfort (usually a burning sensation in the muscles) and distress.

By training, you can raise your lactate threshold level – the point at which lactate levels begin to rise abruptly in the blood. Thus you can ride at a greater intensity before fatigue limits your efforts. Lactate readings – measured in millimoles (mM) – are more accurate than heart rate readings as a physiological response to exercise – but to get them you need blood samples taken every few minutes. Clearly this is not practical in most circumstances, and for all except those striving to perform at the highest elite level such a degree of accuracy is not essential.

'Feel' is a reasonable indicator of effort. When your legs are 'screaming' going up a long steep climb, you don't need someone in a white coat to tell you that lactic acid is building up inside your muscles. By using RPE in conjunction with HR information you can make quite accurate assessments of how your fitness is improving over time. If you can establish how you feel say, on a brisk 2-hour ride and how that compares with racing a 1.5-hour event, then you have some notion of Zones 3 and 4 (*see* also p. 137 above). A very fast or hard race or a very steep climb is likely to be within zone 5. Cross-check that with your HRM figures and you are now compiling your own personal HR chart.

Diary records

Training records are important to assess your performances, so that action can be taken either to reproduce good results again or to avoid disappointing ones in the future. By recording the duration, intensity and frequency of cycling activities, you can monitor your progress. Distance covered is less important – though some riders may still wish to record this information for their own purposes.

Competitive cyclists should record the daily values of your resting heart rate (RHR), hours and quality of sleep, and subjective 'feel good' ratings both generally and in training or racing. Check your weight every 1–4 weeks too. Like HR, your weight needs to be recorded at a regular time of day, i.e. first thing in the morning or last thing at night. If you are aiming to lose weight, you should not lose more than 2–3 kg per month. More dramatic weight losses may indicate a problem.

Use a graph coloured for the various intensities of riding, showing how long a ride took, how hard you rode and the frequency of such rides (*see* Figures 12.5 and 12.6). Plot this on loose-leaf sheets and place the sheets side-by-side. Any trends in overtraining or undertraining will be much more apparent than if written as text in a diary. You don't need any more information than this but you can annotate your records with simple details of where you rode, weather conditions, new equipment or changes to position etc. if you wish.

Remember
- The harder you train, the more recovery time you will need
- Monitor your training to ensure that you vary your training activities and reduce the chances of overtraining
- If you spend all your time in one zone, this will have a detrimental effect in other zones

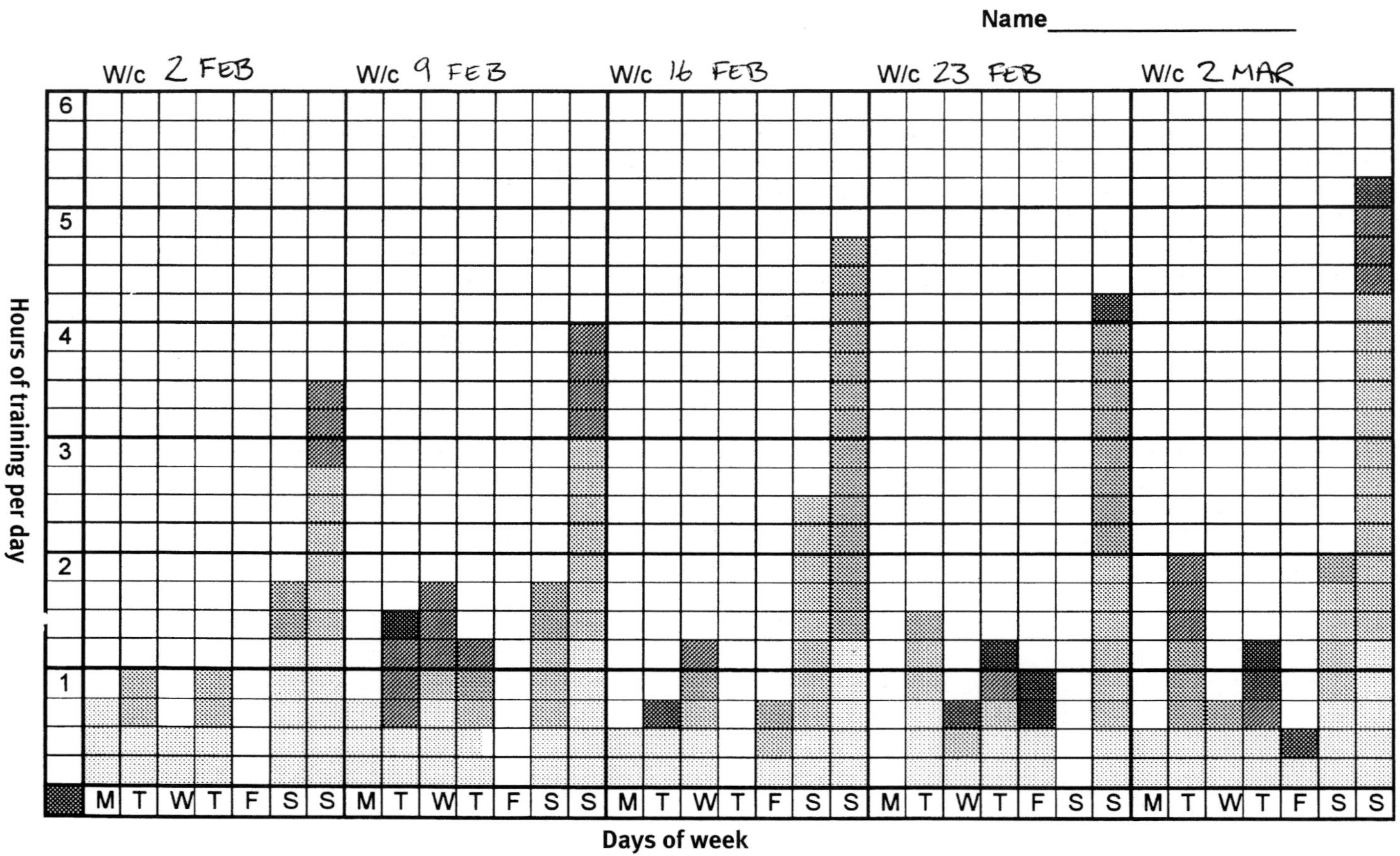

Name _____

Days of week

Hours of training per day

ZONES	
Blk	Zone 6
	Zone 5
	Zone 4
Org	Zone 3
Blu	Zone 2
Grn	Zone 1
Yell	Recovery

LEVELS	
Blk	Level 4
	Level 3
Blu	Upper L2
Grn	Level 2
Yell	Level 1

Figure 12.5 Weekly training log

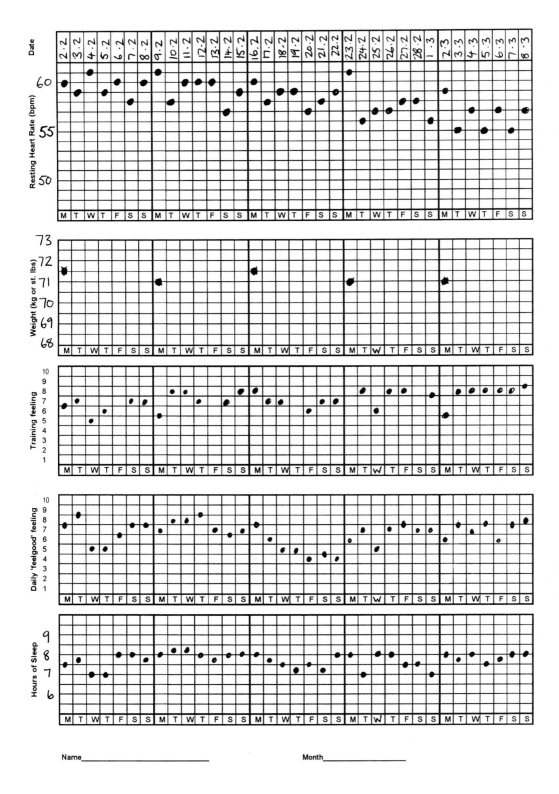

Figure 12.6 Daily records

Name_____   Month_____

Goal-setting

You cannot expect to hold top form throughout the season, but you can *peak* for two or three specific events, races or particularly long or difficult randonnées. First, however, you need to decide upon your goals.

Goal-setting helps you to focus on particular targets and split a daunting task into manageable stepping stones. It is equally applicable to racing cyclists and long-distance tourists – to help you to justify the time spent training, riding in the rain, sticking to a particular diet or making personal sacrifices either preparing for or actually executing your personal mission.

The popular acronym for goal-setting is SMARTER, standing for Specific, Measurable, Agreed, Realistic, Time-phased, Exciting and Recorded.

- **Specific** – you need to focus on a particular target, event, time or achievement, not just aim to 'do better'.

- **Measurable** – goals need to be measurable, such as a particular time for riding a certain distance. Alternatively, have a target distance or adventure to aim for, with a definite end so that you know when you have reached your objective.

- **Agreed** – share your goal with someone else. Family members will understand why you spend time on your bike or abstain from certain foods if you tell them what you are doing. You're more likely to get help and support if people know what you are going to do. Agreeing your goals with a coach will allow him to tailor your training programme, working on your strengths and weaknesses and ensuring that you reach peak fitness at the right time. Plus, it is more difficult to back away from your goal if you have shared it with other people!

- **Realistic** – be sensible. Set yourself a challenge, but if you are over 40 you are unlikely to get a professional contract to compete in the Tour de France . . . or if your time is limited by work or family commitments you are not going to be able to spend six months touring around South America (at least, not for a while).

- **Time-phased** – decide when you are going to achieve your goal. This year, next year, within the next five years? Without a definite timescale it is too easy to put the goal off time and time again and never actually do it.

- **Exciting** – if your goal does not excite you, then it will be extremely difficult to motivate yourself to achieve it. Goals should be challenging, not too easy, but something that will really stretch you and give you satisfaction when completed. You have to decide on your goal. It is not something that can be decided for you.

- **Recorded** – write down your goal. Use a diary, or leave a note by the bathroom mirror or next to your bike to remind you what you are aiming for.

Start with your goal and work backwards. In that way you can look at the time available and calculate the rate of progression you will need to accomplish the task. You can then break this down into manageable steps to get from where you are now to where you want to be in say, nine months or two years' time. Think of it as looking at a map of where you want to go and deciding the route and speed of your journey.

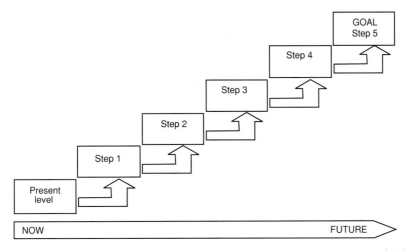

Figure 12.7 Goal-setting breaks down challenging targets into a manageable series of stepping stones of achievement

Setting such steps helps you to check your advancement and confirm that you are on target to reach your goal within your timescale. Goal-setting can be applied to any cycling activities, whether the target is beating 4 hours for a 100-mile time-trial, completing your first season of Super Randonneur rides, or getting fit enough to ride across a continent.

Once you have achieved your goal, or are perhaps even on the way to it, set yourself a new target. This will help to keep you motivated and prevent you from feeling stale or finding everything a big anti-climax after your achievement.

Do not try to over-achieve. You may feel disillusioned if you don't manage to reach your goal. Remember, R is for 'realistic'. The positive encouragement from achieving a series of progressive, small successes is much greater than reaching for a bigger target and falling short of it. However, by setting yourself a target you will achieve far more than if you did not have a goal to focus on.

Sample goal-setting exercise for a 200 km randonnée

Your chosen goal could be to ride a 200 km randonnée. Check that this goal meets the SMARTER criteria above. Say that it is measurable, could be agreed, is realistic, exciting and – if you have written it down – recorded. But as it stands it is neither time-phased nor very specific. If you specify a particular event or date – say, in six months' time – and give yourself a target time in which to complete the event (10 hours, for example), then your goal is much more focused.

Now you can look at both your starting point and your finish point and calculate the necessary steps in order to achieve your goal. If your longest ride to date has been 100 km covered in 6 hours, you will need to embark upon a series of shorter, faster rides to increase your speed from your current average of 16.66 kph to 20 kph to accomplish your task. You now have two aspects of your riding to address in the next six months: your endurance and your speed. You have to increase your endurance by 100% and your speed by around 20%.

By keeping the task in simple terms you can see what you need to achieve and divide both aspects by the six months (or 26 weeks) – creating six (or 26) much more manageable, incremental 'stepping-stones' to aim for. You can also use these to check your progress towards your goal (*see* Table 12.4).

Table 12.4 Goal-setting for a 200 km randonnée in six months' time

Month	Longest ride	Time taken	Average speed (kph)
Now	100 km	6 hr 00 min	16.66
Month 1	117 km	6 hr 40 min	17.56
Month 2	132 km	7 hr 20 min	18.00
Month 3	149 km	8 hr 00 min	18.63
Month 4	166 km	8 hr 40 min	19.17
Month 5	183 km	9 hr 20 min	19.89
Month 6	200 km	10 hr 00 min	20.00

13 Training session basics

Warming up

If you going to embark on strenuous cycling it is a good idea to warm up before-hand. Warming up:

- prepares your muscles and related systems for the demands and stresses they are about to receive
- reduces the likelihood of injury by raising deep muscle temperature and by stretching the muscles, ligaments and connective tissue (improving mobility and range of movement)
- increases performance levels, especially in the early stages of an activity
- can improve your body's efficiency by raising heart, metabolic and respiratory rates
- should be done gradually, so that there is little or no discomfort
- needs to combine intensity and duration without inducing undue fatigue.

The shorter the event, the more important a good warm-up becomes. For long rides, easy pedalling for the first 20 minutes or so will be sufficient to raise muscle temperature and stretch the muscles and connective tissues before you begin to use bigger gears or tackle any hills. For racing, a progressive warm-up routine – starting gently and lasting 15–30 minutes – is beneficial to bring your heart and breathing rate close to the level needed in competition in readiness for a rapid start. Ideally, this warm-up should finish no more than 5–10 minutes before your start time. Wear a track top to avoid cooling down too rapidly. (You can usually leave it at the start with a helper or official and collect it when you have finished your event.)

Cooling down

After a training session or hard ride it is equally important to cool down gradually. Your body needs to make a number of adaptations; if you stop quickly, your muscles – which have been working hard and processing a large quantity of fluid (blood, lactic acid) – will not be able to disperse the excess fluid, and this can cause you to feel stiff and sore later. Continuing with gentle exercise will help to disperse this fluid out of your muscles, as your heart rate returns closer to its normal, slower rate. If you have been working very hard it is a good idea to put on some extra clothing when you finish exercising as you may continue to lose heat (through sweating) too rapidly.

Many club runs involve a mid-ride sprint for a café stop. It is unwise to exert yourself in this manner – raising your heart rate, pumping up muscles and then immediately climbing off your bike and sitting down for 30 minutes. Getting going again afterwards can often prove quite difficult! If your club ride is going to have a pre-café sprint, make it 1 or 2 km before the stop to allow your body to cool down and recover before coming to a halt. The ride home will then be much easier.

Stretching

Flexibility is a key component of fitness, and sports science has proved the benefits of stretching. During activity, muscles contract and get shorter. This may be particularly noticeable after a period of prolonged, intense effort, when just straightening out the limbs can be an extremely uncomfortable sensation. However, your posture may be adversely affected if you do not stretch your muscles on a regular basis.

You should incorporate an element of stretching into your daily routine with particular emphasis on the muscles used when cycling and those muscles that oppose the active ones. Many overuse injuries are the result of excessive stress or tension on a tendon or ligament. Stretching the muscles and connective tissue and increases their length and allows them to absorb more strain without injury.

Different types of stretches

Static stretches
In these you first hold the muscle stretch for 10–30 seconds – working from an easy position, where there is just mild tension (this should subside after a few seconds) – and then progress a little further into the developmental part of the stretch for an additional 10–30 seconds. Static stretches are best done after exercise, or a hot bath or shower, but do ensure that you will not get too cold when actually performing them.

Ballistic stretches
Generally, these are best avoided. If you stretch a muscle beyond its comfortable limits a nerve reflex will respond, sending a signal to the muscle to contract – as a protective mechanism. Holding a stretch beyond its natural extension, or bouncing or jerking your limbs in an uncontrolled manner, will activate this *stretch reflex* and actually tighten the very muscles you are trying to stretch!

By forcing the stretch beyond its limit and against the stretch reflex, you may damage the microscopic muscle fibres. At the very least your muscles will become tight, sore and lose their elasticity – and at worst you can catastrophically tear the muscle or tendon.

The benefits of stretching
- Reduces muscle tension
- Helps relaxation
- Increases range of motion (flexibility)
- Ensures that muscles are at optimal working length
- Reduces the likelihood of injury
- Improves circulation
- Develops body awareness

Dynamic stretches

Many people use stretching as part of their warm-up in order to ensure that their muscles are at full working length at the start of their training session or event. However, stopping exercise in order to stretch can actually have the reverse of the desired effect, as the muscles cool down and become less flexible. Indeed, more recent research indicates that 'loose' muscles may lack the necessary 'snap' required in many competitive activities.

Instead, dynamic stretches are now recommended and can be incorporated into a progressive warm-up routine. These involve movement throughout the exercise, with only a very brief 'hold' (2–5 seconds) in the maximum reach position and minimal time between each stretch.

General stretching guidelines

- Stretch only when your muscles are warm – i.e. after some exercise or perhaps after a hot bath or shower – and keep warm while stretching.

- Stretch gradually. Do not 'bounce': this activates a neurological reflex which contracts the muscle (*see* also Ballistic stretches, above). Slow stretching bypasses this reflex.

- Stretch limbs individually to ensure that all muscles are stretched appropriately – this is not necessarily equal on the right and left sides.

- Stretch the centre of the muscle by keeping limbs 'in line'.

- Hold each static stretch for 20–60 seconds, to allow the muscle to return to – and even exceed – its normal length.

- Stretch to the point of tightness, not pain.

- Stretching is an individual activity. Do not try to compete with somebody else's flexibility.

- Develop a basic routine and add other stretches as and when you can.

- Stretch the most important muscles first (*see* below). If you do not have time to complete your routine, at least you will have covered the key muscle groups.

- Do not cheat when stretching. Concentrate on the movement and feel of the stretch rather than the range of movement.

- Be careful if you are stretching to regain range of movement after injury. If in doubt, always consult an appropriate specialist.

A good stretching routine will take 10–30 minutes, but many of these stretches can be done while doing other things like watching TV at home, talking on the telephone or sitting at a desk at work (careful!). Competent riders can even stretch while cycling (*see* pp. 153–5). Do this whenever you need to on a ride, especially if you feel that your muscles are tightening – but don't do it in the middle of a bunch! If you are not confident about stretching on the move, wait until you next stop and get off your bike – or pull over specifically for a stretch or two.

Stretches for the main muscle groups used in cycling

There are many different stretches that can benefit the cyclist: the following is a brief selection. For simplicity, just the right-side stretch is described – remember that all stretches need to be done on both sides.

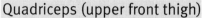

Quadriceps (upper front thigh)

This stretch can be done standing up (you may need to steady yourself by putting your other hand against a wall or table), or lying down on your side. Hold your right ankle and gently bring it back towards your buttocks, keeping your knees close together. You should feel the stretch in the big quadriceps muscle down the front of your leg. Extend the stretch by moving your hips forward and pulling your ankle (and knee) further back. Hold for 10–30 seconds and then gently return to the starting position. Repeat on the other side.

Hamstrings (back of thigh)

Sit down with your right leg straight out in front of you and your toes pointing straight up. Bend your left leg so that you can place the sole of your left foot against the inside of your right thigh. Hold your head up, your back straight and your arms straight out to your right leg. Now reach forwards from the hips with your fingertips (do not curve your back), trying to stretch them beyond your right foot. Hold this position for 10–30 seconds. Extend this stretch by bringing your toes back towards your head. Relax and repeat with the left leg.

Gluteals (buttocks)

Lying on the floor with the left leg extended, bend the right knee and gently ease it upwards and across your body using your left hand for support. Hold for 10–30 seconds and repeat on the other side.

Calf (back of lower leg)

Stand about 50 cm away from a wall and lean against it using your arms to support you. Bend your right leg and – keeping your left foot pointing straight towards the wall – move your left leg behind you. Keep your left heel flat on the ground, and gently move your hips forwards. Bend your right knee a bit more to lower your hips and stretch your calf muscles (sastrocnemius). Hold this position for 10–30 seconds. Then gently bend the left knee – still keeping the heel on the ground – so that you feel the stretch lower down the calf (soleus muscle).

Back extension

Lie face down, bring your hands next to your shoulders and push up with your arms while arching backwards and looking up straight ahead.

Neck

Stand upright and slowly move your chin down towards the top of your chest. Hold this position for 10–30 seconds then lift your chin up and forwards. Keep your back straight and hold in this position for 10–30 seconds.

Shoulders, arms and upper back

Place your hands shoulder-width apart against a wall. Keeping your hands in place, drop your upper body, bend your knees and bring your hips over your knees. You can repeat this with your hands in a different position to alter the stretch.

Hip flexors and groin stretch

Stand and, moving your right foot back and bending your left knee, slowly lower your right knee towards the floor. Push your hips forward, and extend this stretch by moving your feet further apart.

Stretching on the bike

You need good balance to do these exercises on the move – and preferably quiet, safe roads too.

Calves and hamstrings

Stand out of the saddle and drop your right leg down, bringing your right ankle lower than the pedal. Extend the stretch by leaning forwards. Hold for 10–30 seconds and repeat with your left leg.

Quadriceps

Sitting in the saddle, take your right foot off the pedal and grasp your ankle. Pull your right foot up towards the saddle. Bring your right knee back and push your hips forwards. Hold for 10–30 seconds and repeat with your left leg.

Shoulders, chest and arms

If you can ride 'no hands', sit up, clasp your hands behind your back, turn your elbows inwards and straighten your arms

If you cannot ride 'no hands', hold the handlebars close to the centre with your left hand. Sit upright, straightening your left arm, bring your right shoulder back so that your shoulders and left arm are in line (keep looking forwards) and push your chest out. Repeat with the other arm.

Neck

Sit upright, holding the tops of the handlebars. Bring your shoulders forwards and drop your chin towards your chest – keep looking forwards. Hold for a few seconds. Lift your head up with your chin forwards and bring your shoulders back. Hold for a few seconds again and then relax.

Back

Holding either the drops of the handlebars or the hoods of the brake levers, bring your body forwards, off the saddle. Push your hips forwards and straighten your back, pushing your shoulders back. Then, with the pedals horizontal, drop your head down and arch your back upwards so that you feel a stretch along the length of your back.

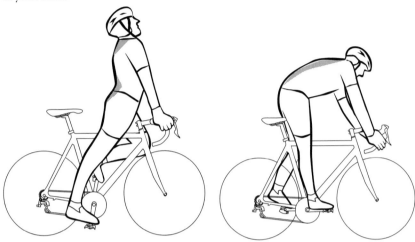

Massage

Few leisure riders use massage, but racing cyclists find it invaluable to help them recover and prepare for their next race or hard training session. If you are riding ultra-distances you may well benefit from massage to ease aches and pains in tired, stiff or sore muscles too. There is some debate about the scientific merits of massage – how it works and what it achieves – but clearly it does speed up the recovery process.

You can do self-massage (always working *towards* your heart) but received massage is better. A masseur will be able to work more deeply on your muscles and attend to areas of your body that you cannot access (e.g. shoulders, back). Ideally, a whole body massage is best. However, this may not be practical, so work on the larger muscles first – particularly the muscles of the leg (quadriceps, gluteus maximus, soleus) as these are some of the most hard-worked muscles during cycling. Obviously, if you are experiencing any stiffness or soreness in other areas (such as your back, arms or shoulders) ask the masseur to attend to these areas too. It might be worth checking your riding position if these problems persist (*see* also pp. 17–22).

Winter training

Cycling is predominantly a summertime activity (March–September), with a 'close season' between October and February. The winter, though, is the ideal time to begin developing fitness and improving technique for any summertime ambition – whether that is a 12-hour time-trial, 600 km randonnée or long-distance tour.

Long, steady distances ridden at low intensity are the foundation for all cycling activities. This builds up your 'engine' by developing the body's energy and oxygen transport systems, and this is absolutely vital for the long-distance rider. Because of reduced daylight hours and less clement weather, most winter rides will be shorter (approx. 3–7 hours) than the long summer rides. This is, after all, the close season and a time for preparation rather than trying to prove yourself. Later, as the summer season approaches, racing cyclists will also need to develop strength and speed. Leisure cyclists will be less concerned about top-end speed, but will still benefit from having greater strength, particularly for hill-climbing.

Sometimes it is clearly not advisable, or even possible, to ride in winter conditions. Fog, icy roads, or short daylight hours can make winter riding hazardous. In these circumstances you need to improvise in order to maintain or build your fitness in readiness for the following summer season.

You can maintain much of your cardiovascular fitness by circuit-training, using rowing machines, running or swimming. Using weights at a gym will help your strength (*see* also Developing your strength, p. 158). However, not all the benefits gained from these alternative activities are fully transferable to cycling. If you are concentrating on cycling then you will have to find alternative cycling-style activities – made harder by the fact that very few sports use similar muscles in a similar fashion (speed-skating and, to a lesser extent, cross-country skiing are probably the only ones). Off-road mountain-biking during the winter is a good way to have some cycling fun whilst developing your bike-handling skills, strength and fitness away from the hazards of the roads. However, this is best left to the weekends when more daylight is available (although night-time off-road rides can be extremely exhilarating!).

Turbo-training and spinning classes

More suitable for many riders who may get home from work or college after dark are 'spinning' classes at a local gym, or using a turbo-trainer at home. The great benefit of a turbo-trainer is the ability to get a good workout from a relatively brief session. Do not attempt to replicate a long ride on a turbo-trainer: you will become very numb and very bored. Use your turbo-trainer for a quick workout (20–60 minutes), raising your heart rate to higher levels for fitness gains and to develop cycling-specific muscles.

The turbo-trainer or 'home trainer' (*see* Figure 13.1) is an apparatus which accepts a regular bicycle for static cycling. It is usually of an A-frame design, with an adjustable roller providing friction (resistance) on the bicycle's rear wheel. There are various models, ranging from the cheap and cheerful (but often noisy) using fans (turbos) to provide resistance, to more sophisticated models using magnets or fluids. Some models have variable resistance and others even incorporate computer read-outs showing your speed and power output. One big advantage of the turbo-trainer is that most will accept any regular bicycle, enabling you to train with the equipment and position you would use on the road.

Figure 13.1 Turbo-trainer: an excellent training tool for dark winter evenings. A large fan would help keep this rider cool (photo: Paul A. Lawson)

Tips on turbo-training sessions

- Make sure that the bike is secure on the turbo-trainer on a flat, safe surface
- Have a plan for each session and make these progressive
- Some turbos are very noisy, so choose your training time or location so that it does not disturb other people
- Meet with friends for a group turbo session to keep everyone motivated
- Be aware of the ambient temperature where you train. Wear a track top to begin with, but discard it when you heat up with exercise. Use a large fan to create a cooling breeze while you exercise. However, if you train in your shed or garage, you may need to wear leg-warmers if it is very cold
- Allow at least 10 minutes to warm up using low gears
- Take plenty of fluid during the session
- A heart-rate monitor (*see* also p. 139) and stopwatch are very useful on the turbo-trainer
- A towel over the handlebars and top-tube will protect your bike from sweat
- Vary your sessions: include short sprints, long sprints, sustained efforts, progressive exercises, one-legged pedalling, intervals, etc. Raise your front wheel for some sessions to replicate muscle usage during hill-climbs
- Music may help you tolerate a turbo session
- Allow 5–10 minutes to cool down after the exercises, using very low gears
- Do not spend more than 40–60 minutes on the turbo-trainer at any one session
- Clean your bike thoroughly and regularly: sweat is very corrosive
- Turbo sessions are good for strength, speed and power training, but of little use for endurance. Most turbo exercises will be conducted at Zones 3–6 (*see* also p. 137)
- Do not be a slave to the turbo-trainer. Ride outdoors when you can

'Spinning' machines rarely replicate the equipment or the position you might have on your own bicycle. However, these machines are very useful to exercise your cycling muscles, and even hardened club cyclists can often find a spinning class – perhaps best described as 'bicycle aerobics' – much to their liking. It provides a variation on their normal regime; and working with others in a warm, dry, bright and up-beat environment on a cold, winter evening can be a good mental boost – especially if the alternative is either turbo-training alone in a cold garage or a wet ride in the dark.

Developing your strength

The principal muscle groups you need to develop as a cyclist are naturally the muscles of the leg. The hip, knee and ankle are involved in the pedalling action – involving nine major muscle groups. But your back, neck and arms can all feel tired after a long ride, clearly indicating that riding a bike involves many more muscle groups than just those in the lower body. You may notice this especially after a hilly ride, a ride over poor surfaces, or if you have held an uncomfortable, aerodynamic position for any length of time.

It is best to work on the larger muscle groups before the smaller ones. By doing this your training will not be limited by smaller muscle-group fatigue. If working on weights in a gym, it will pay you to start on the larger muscles of the leg and finish with the upper body (arms, shoulders).

Refer to *Weight Training for Cyclists* by Eric Schmitz and Ken Doyle (Velo Press, 1998) and *The Cyclist's Training Bible* by Joe Friel (A & C Black, 1999) for further reading on improving strength for cycling.

Riding techniques

This section deals with some of the techniques that can make your riding more efficient – and, if you ride with a group, gives you some tips on how to ride economically to ensure that you can stay with the pack.

Whatever kind of cycling you are doing, a good riding position will help you be energy-efficient and safe, and ensure that you have control of your bike at all times. Remember, select your gears to maintain a pedalling rate (cadence) of around 90 rpm, or even a little higher. Lower cadences show a poorer oxygen uptake and more rapid muscle fatigue as the energy waste products are not dissipated quickly enough[1]. Bear in mind the distance or time that you will be riding, so that you can pace yourself for the whole ride. The fun of a rapid outward journey will soon wear off if you are too exhausted and struggle to ride home.

[1]Coast, J. R. (1996), 'Optimal pedalling cadence', *High Tech Cycling*, Edmund R. Burke (ed.), (Human Kinetics), pp. 101–16.

Solo riding

When riding alone you can travel at your own speed, stop or move on as and when you wish. You will not be pressured to ride at an uncomfortable pace, or get frustrated by having to wait for anyone. You are free to follow the wind and even to end up somewhere totally different from your original plan if that holds more appeal once your journey has started. The downsides, of course, are that you cannot share equipment; you must fix your own problems; and there is no one to share the moment with – good or bad!

Group riding

Cycling can be a very sociable activity. You will find that time passes more quickly in the company of others, as you can keep one another going through mutual encouragement. You may even find that your mind is totally distracted from the exercise of cycling by conversation on the road. You can also use the opportunity to learn from more experienced riders, by watching their example and by talking to them, and you will discover some of their favourite cycling routes too.

By riding in a group you can also divide the workload of pacemaking and facing the wind, allowing the riders behind to rest slightly. On tour, items like tools, tents, cooking equipment and food can be distributed among the party to lessen the load of each individual.

Riders of different abilities will probably not ride together for very long. On randonnées, small groups often form in the early stages as riders sort themselves out by their different speeds. Similarly in road races, strong riders will climb better than weaker riders and gaps will appear in the peloton. In a touring party, unequal cyclists can ride together if the slower ones start their day earlier than the faster ones, or the stronger ones detour along a longer route, meeting up at one or two points along the way. All riders can meet up at intervals during the day and arrive at their destination at similar times.

Figure 13.2 By riding in a group you're sure to find a helping hand along the way! (photo: Ivo Miesen)

To ride in a group the pace needs to be reasonably steady (not necessarily a constant *speed*, but an even *effort*). Speed is likely to decrease up hills and some riders may get dropped. For social riding the leading riders need to control the pace and perhaps slow down or wait for the tail-enders. When racing such mercy is rarely given – unless a weaker rider can be 'used'. If two or three riders have escaped from the main bunch but still have a way to go to the finish, then it might be useful to have an extra rider to share the work with them and avoid being caught by the rest of the pack.

Slipstreaming or drafting

A rider uses approximately 25% less energy by sitting behind another rider. 'Drafting' behind two or three riders increases the energy savings a little more, and it allows more 'rest time'. Sitting in the middle of a moving pack provides an energy saving of nearly 40%[2]. By sharing the lead of a group for 20–60 seconds at a time, it is possible to ride faster than an individual. A group working together like this can swiftly sweep up breakaway riders in a race's closing stages.

Less strong riders can conserve their energy by spending less time at the front of a group. You can even control the speed of a group by sitting at the front and discouraging others from taking your place. However, if the pace is too slow the stronger riders are likely to take over and the less strong will still get dropped!

On a social ride, training ride or randonnée where riders are in-line – either singly or two abreast – there are two accepted forms of changing the leading rider(s). If the road is clear, they can pull off to the side(s) of the group and rejoin at the back. Effectively, all except the original leader(s) then advance(s) by one place. The second method, associated with faster speed, is known as the 'chaingang'.

Chaingangs

In the chaingang one line is the 'up-line' and the other is the 'down-line' (*see* Figure 13.3). The direction of change depends on the wind direction. The down-line is on the sheltered side, allowing these riders to recover ready for their next turn at the front of the group. When the leading rider A begins to slow or tire, he pulls over to the front of the second line and allows the rest of the up-line to come past him. As he does so, the new leading rider B pulls off in front of him and also drifts to the back of the up-line. This pattern continues until the rider A sees C, who was originally in front of him in the up-line, again. At this point A moves back into the up-line and the chain continues its progress.

When the speed is really high, or the wind very strong and directly against the riders, the group will single out into just one line of riders for maximum shelter. In this case the pattern is the same as that described above, but the lead rider will endeavour to get back on to the rear of the group as quickly as possible, rather than battling into the wind by himself for too long.

Direction of
travel

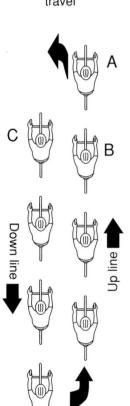

Down line

Up line

A

C   B

Figure 13.3 The chaingang: the sheltered 'downline' allows riders to recover

[2]McCole, S. D. et al (1990), 'Energy expenditure during bicycling', *Journal of Applied Physiology*, vol. 68, pp. 748–53.

Echelons

Where there is a crosswind, echelons will form (*see* Figure 13.4). Riders shelter in staggered formation behind one another in order to gain maximum protection from the wind. The principle is the same as in the chaingang (*see* above). The rider closest to the wind is providing shelter to the others. He will do his turn in that position for a few seconds before easing off just slightly, drifting behind the group and taking up his new sheltered position on the other side of the echelon. The next rider gets buffeted for a few seconds before the group rotates completely and the first rider's turn comes round again.

If the road is not wide enough for all the riders to find shelter, second, third and fourth echelons have to form. When the road changes direction the riders must quickly recognise the corresponding change in wind direction and alter their formation and direction of change accordingly – otherwise they are likely to lose their place and will be battling against the wind by themselves. European randonneurs with a background in road racing, or simply more exposure to professional cycling, often ride 'in echelon'. Any riders who upset their pattern and rhythm are soon dumped into the wind without protection.

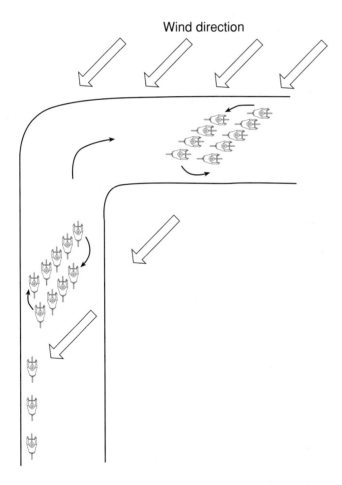

Wind direction

Figure 13.4 Echelons: riders must change formation to remain in echelon and sheltered from the wind; some riders may be forced out of the echelon

Hills

Gravity sucks! Riding up an incline requires more work. Smaller or lighter riders are usually better climbers than heavier, stronger ones because of their better power-to-weight ratio.

A good racing bike weighs between 7.0 and 8.5 kg[3], but riders' weights may vary by anything from 55 kg to over 100 kg. Tourists and randonneurs will have an even greater spread of weight through their different bikes, luggage and body types. It's no wonder that some riders climb better than others. Without doubt, however, the biggest area for weight savings lies in the riders themselves. Remember, though, you need both muscle and fat to ride – severe diets can be harmful to your health as well as reducing your muscle mass (*see* also Chapter 6, pp. 71–2).

Some riders have muscles better suited to climbing than others. Good climbers usually have more fast-twitch fibres than the time-triallists, but not as many as sprinters, and their bulk is much less. Nevertheless, all riders can improve their hill-climbing ability with practice and attention to their technique.

Short, sharp hills as are often found in Britain can frequently be tackled with an explosive effort of a few minutes. Nothing in the UK can rival the climbs of the Pyrenees, Alps or Rockies, where the ascents may be 40 km or more and are often affected by extreme weather conditions. Such climbs cannot be overcome with brute force; instead, a steadier approach is required, to eke out your energy over the whole climb. Novices may benefit from adopting this approach in all their riding.

In a group, poor climbers are well advised to begin each climb near the front. Although others may pass you, at least on shorter climbs you may still be in close contact with the tail-enders and be able to regain some lost ground on the descent.

Tips for climbing

- Count *1-2-3* with each downward pedal stroke, increasing the force of each third stroke. This will alternate the power from one leg to the other – left-right-*left*, right-left-*right* – helping you to maintain your power with a good, strong rhythm. If this becomes too tiring, increase the count to *1-2-3-4-5* or *1-2-3-4-5-6-7*, etc.

- Stay seated for as long as possible. Although you can harness more power when standing on the pedals, aerobically this is less efficient.

- Sit back on the saddle, to increase the leverage of the big muscles in the back of the thigh.

- Hold the top of the handlebars for easier breathing.

- When standing, hold the brake hoods for better bike control and breathing.

- Move the bike slightly from side to side with relaxed arms to help your pedal stroke when standing, but don't swing the bike excessively.

---

[3]UCI regulations demand a minimum weight of 6.8 kg for road-racing bikes.

- When you stand on the pedals, move into a higher gear to compensate for your lower cadence and to maintain your power output. Return to a lower gear when you sit down again.

- Maintain your momentum. Don't ease off at the summit but aim for a point 50–100 m over the top of the climb before you relax.

- On long climbs, gear down and keep your pedalling cadence high, close to your usual level.

- Maintain an even power output without dramatic changes in pace.

- Move on to the smaller chainring before your cadence becomes too slow (otherwise the mechanism may have difficulty moving the chain).

- Climb at your own pace, not that of others. On a long climb, riders who start too fast may 'blow themselves out'.

- Take advantage of flatter sections or tailwinds, and move up a gear or two to increase your speed.

- Weight training for your arms and back will help your climbing ability.

- Remember to eat and drink, even on a climb.

- Unzip or remove extra clothing when climbing to help keep cool (but wrap up warmly for the descent).

- On hairpin bends, ride wide for a smoother, easier gradient.

- You can zig-zag up the road (if it is clear) to reduce the gradient – though this usually means that you are over-geared.

- Don't try to emulate the professionals and their bikes. If you have difficulty on the climbs, change your gears to lower ratios.

- Practise climbing hills. There is no short cut to being a better climber.

- Lose weight – either from your bike or from yourself.

14 Training for specific events

50–100 miles

If you are new to cycling and desire to ride further than your immediate horizon, 50 miles or 100 miles in a day is a manageable goal. The annual London–Brighton charity ride is 55 miles long, with a sting in the tail, climbing over the South Downs at Ditchling Beacon. A fit racing cyclist could cover this distance in around 2 hours, but that's not the point. You have a day to cover the distance and enjoy the experience.

For many people, sponsored rides or charity events have been an excellent catalyst to cycling longer distances. They may not have realised it at the time, but such events are often a good example of goal-setting (*see* also pp. 144–6) – providing a target to aim for, and requiring an improvement in their current level of fitness or cycling ability. Sometimes there are other benefits too, such as improved health, perhaps less dependence on motor transport and economic savings – especially if you use a bicycle for local errands or for commuting.

You don't need to give yourself the 9-month preparation time of the racing cyclist aiming to peak at a major event, but 9 weeks from a zero-cycling base is a good idea, largely to help you get used to sitting on a saddle for the 4–8 hours that this journey may take. If you are going to invest in some cycling gear, shorts and a helmet are the wisest purchases (*see* also Chapter 5, *Cycling Clothing*). Have your bike checked over by a specialist bike shop where staff

Figure 14.1 Charity rides: the 55-mile London–Brighton regularly attracts over 30,000 participants – seen here tackling Ditchling Beacon on the South Downs (photo: Chris Beynon)

Table 14.1 Sample programme to prepare for a 55-mile day ride

Rides (minutes)	Rest	Rest	90	120	Rest	150	180	60	**TARGET**
	45	45	60	90	90	90	120	120	Rest
	30	45	60	60	90	60	60	60	60
	30	30	45	45	60	45	45	60	45
Week	1	2	3	4	5	6	7	8	9
Phase	Preparation				Recovery	Overload		Tapering and peak	

can advise on appropriate equipment – such as fitting 'slick' tyres to a mountain-bike instead of off-road 'knobblies' – suitable tyre pressures, and using the gears on your bike.

Start training. Don't worry about distance at first – 20–60 minutes pedalling may be more than enough initially. You need to pace yourself. If you feel that you are struggling for breath, slow down. Use a lower gear so that you're pedalling a little faster, but more easily. Racing cyclists' cadence is around 90–100 rpm; yours should be similar but using lower gears (expect this to drop when climbing).

Aim to ride your bike between two and four times each week. Every second ride, increase the duration by about 10–20 minutes. After the third week, you should be able to ride for 60–120 minutes without too much difficulty. You may find it easier to schedule midweek rides as reasonably short distances, but increase the distance on one weekend day. Vary the duration of your rides and try to ride a little faster over the shorter distances. You'll soon be getting fitter, faster and have greater endurance.

Table 14.1 shows a sample training programme to prepare for a 55-mile ride. Notice how this programme tapers in Week 8, before the target ride, so that you are not too exhausted for your goal. Also, note the easier Week 5 to recover from the initial foundation rides, prior to longer rides and then a less intense period before the event itself.

For a 100-mile ride, your goal might be to complete the distance in 8 hours. The same principles apply but you will need to allow yourself a longer preparatory period and you will have to ride progressively even longer distances.

2 0 0 k m r a n d o n n é e

This is the basic standard distance for audax events. The speed limits are usually 15–30 kph (equating to a finish time of between 6 hr 40 min. and 13 hr 20 min.). Unless you are a regular or experienced cyclist, it is worth targeting an event in the summer months. This will give you time to train and prepare yourself in better weather conditions and more hours of daylight than if you try to tackle an event in February or March.

The lower speed limit of 15 kph is quite generous – unless you have chosen a particularly hilly area for your ride (in which case even some veteran campaigners can struggle to finish with much time to spare). However, it is worth training to ride at a higher speed than this. Remember that this is the average speed limit, and does not allow for any time spent at stops, mechanical mishaps or navigational errors. For these reasons it's always comforting to have a little time in hand.

Points to remember

- Take a drink with you, especially on any ride of 40 minutes or more. Carbohydrate solutions are best, especially on longer rides (see also pp. 76–7). You may also need to eat some food on rides of over 60 minutes.
- Vary your routes, both for interest and to train over different terrains.
- Find some hills to practise on – there might be some in the event.
- Avoid busy roads. B-roads and unclassified roads are usually much quieter, safer and more interesting for cycling. Use the opportunity to explore your local area.
- On longer rides (>90 min.) you may want to rest for a while. Don't stop for too long or your muscles will cool and you'll have difficulty starting off again. 5–15 minutes should be sufficient. Use this time to eat and drink, and stretch your muscles.
- Pace yourself. Do not set out too fast. If you begin by using an 'out and back' route and find that your return journey takes 10 minutes longer than the outward passage, this means that you are tiring on the return leg (or your outward journey was downhill or with a tailwind). Aim to ride at a consistent pace throughout the ride.

- On longer rides especially, make sure that you have some food with you and that you eat during your ride.
- Practise some 'audax pit stops' on your longer preparation rides. Stop at a café – eat, drink and get on your way as quickly as possible.
- Practise eating on the move. That's what cycling jersey pockets (or bar bags) are for!
- Practise riding with your audax load. You might want to jettison some items, or add something for the ride itself.
- See if you can persuade a friend to ride the event with you. Persuade your friend to train with you too!
- Finding a small group to cycle with can prove an invaluable aid for an easier (and more enjoyable) ride.

See also Points to remember, 55-mile day ride, p. 165.

Keep in mind that in 200 km you are likely to encounter a variety of terrain, so it's worth training over varied roads. If you train in hilly or windy areas you will be stronger, and more prepared for any difficult conditions you may encounter on your randonnée.

Most 200 km events begin around 8.00 a.m., leaving you the whole day to complete them. If you build up your cycling with some half-day rides, and manage to maintain an average speed of 20 kph or more, then you should have no problem in tackling most 200 km events, given reasonable weather conditions.

Your preparation may look something like this:

Table 14.2 Sample programme to prepare for a 200 km randonnée

Rides (km)	Week					TARGET
	4	70	90	120	140	TARGET
	3	50	70	90	100	80
	2	60	60	100	100	120
	1	50	60	70	100	80
Month		1	2	3	4	5
		Preparation	Recovery and continued preparation		Overload	Tapering and peak

Table 14.2 shows the longest ride that you might tackle in any one week. By riding your bike on two or three other occasions during the week (roughly totalling the longest ride distance) you will soon build up the base fitness to deal with these distances.

Figure 14.2 Randonnées attract all sorts of riders: the start of this 200 km ride is led by a tandem and a recumbent (photo: Chris Beynon)

300 km randonnée

After a few 200 km events you may want to tackle a 300 km randonnée. Three or four 200s are usually sufficient for most randonneurs to know if they have what it takes to move up to the next distance. You may prefer to stick to events of no more than 200 km in your first season, and only progress the following year. That's not a bad plan. Even experienced riders tend to start their season with a few 200s before riding the 300.

Experience is especially useful as you may have to start or finish by riding in the dark. You don't actually need to train in the dark but you certainly need to check that you are happy with your lighting system(s), that you can see the road with your lights, and that other road users can see you. You may also want to have some means of reading your route sheet in the dark.

Look at the equipment being used by experienced randonneurs on 300 km events, talk to these riders and you'll soon get a good idea of what is required and what equipment best tackles the job.

Points to remember

See **Points to remember, before,** plus:

- **Check your lighting system. You may be riding in areas of complete darkness.**
- **Have extra clothing available for cold (before sunrise or after sunset) or poor weather – and somewhere to stow it when conditions improve.**
- **Use reflective materials to improve your visibility.**
- **Pay great attention to the route sheet, especially in the dark.**

400 km randonnée

The watershed distance. It is only a very few riders who can complete this distance in daylight. Most have to ride through the night, which for many is a whole new experience (*see* also Night riding, pp. 104–7).

The best preparation for a 400 km event is … other randonnées. 400s are held over the summer months, usually May–late August for best use of daylight, better weather conditions, and allowing riders to progressively prepare for this distance in the earlier months.

Figure 14.2 This randonneur is prepared for 400 km. Note his lights, two waterbottles, waterproofs on his saddlebag and the handlebar mounted route sheet (photo: Chris Beynon)

Points to remember
See **Points to remember, before,** **plus:**

- Plenty of rest and sleep in the week before a big event is essential.
- Pace yourself and allow yourself extra time to stop, rest and eat.
- Starting early on, eat and drink little and often during the ride – even at times when you would not normally eat (e.g. in the middle of the night).
- You will travel more slowly when tired.
- You will travel more slowly in the dark (whether tired or not).
- Keep rest periods short.
- If you feel sleepy, stop immediately and sleep – even if only for 20 minutes.
- Riding with others, especially in the dark, will help you.

A good diet of 200s and occasional 300s is ideal preparation, but do ensure that you are well rested before the event. Take your cycling easy in the six or seven days before a marathon event like this, and make sure that you get plenty of sleep (early nights). Riding a bike for 24 hours or so will certainly make you tired. There's no point in being tired before you begin!

It is definitely a good idea to be riding well above the minimum speed limit in a long event. This will give you time in hand to rest, eat and even sleep along the way so that you can recommence your journey refreshed and alert.

Your experience gained from riding 200 km and 300 km events will help to prepare you for the night rides. It is always reassuring to ride with others in the dark; together, your lights will provide better illumination and safety in numbers. Multiple heads for navigation can be useful at times, and riding in company can help to keep you awake. However, it is important that you can ride safely in a group – skills learned in daylight are essential for safe night-time riding.

Your plan for approaching a 400 km event could be something like this, as before showing the longest ride you might do in each week:

Table 14.3 Sample programme to prepare for a 400 km randonnée

Ride (km) Week	Jan.	Feb.	March	April	May	June
4	90	120	120	90	200	**TARGET**
3	80	150	200	300	120	100
2	80	Rest	100	150	Rest	150
1	70	100	200	200	300	200
Month	Jan.	Feb.	March	April	May	June
Phase	Preparation		Continued preparation, 'pre-comp' with recovery			Tapering and peak

600 km randonnée

This is the longest standard distance in the audax calendar. The time limits are 20–40 hours. Of course, it pays to have built up to this length of ride by completing plenty of 200 km, 300 km and one or two 400 km events before you embark on a journey of this length.

Many randonneurs wisely spend a season riding events of no more than 200 km before they tackle an overnight ride. Events beyond 300 km are usually held between the end of April and the end of August for reasons of daylight and better weather, and to allow riders to get physically prepared for these marathon rides.

Table 14.4 Sample programme to prepare for a 600 km randonnée

Rides (km) Week	1	2	3	4	5	6	7	8	9
4	80	90	100	90	120	300	300	Rest	**TARGET**
3	80	80	90	100	200	Rest	200	200	Rest
2	60	70	80	100	200	200	100	400	200
1	60	Rest	70	120	120	200	400	200	300
Month	1	2	3	4	5	6	7	8	9
Phase	Progressive preparation including recovery periods				'Pre-comp' with recovery periods		Overload		Tapering and peak

Good preparatory distances are vital. If you begin your campaign with 200 km rides in February or March, that will prepare you for the more demanding events later. It is not necessary to push yourself to ride the longest event available every weekend. In fact your performances will soon decline if you do attempt that. Do give yourself time to recover from the longer rides. Your preparation via weekend rides should be along the lines shown in Table 14.4.

Time-trials – 'the race of truth'

Time-trialling is often referred to as 'the race of truth'. It's one rider, tackling a course against the clock. In the UK, time-trials are governed by the Road Time Trials Council (RTTC), and events are organised by local racing clubs. The standard distances for races are 10, 25, 50 and 100 miles. Riders are set off at one-minute intervals – you are not allowed to pace each other or slipstream (draft) behind another rider – and the cyclist who covers the course in the quickest time is the winner. For events held over 12- and 24-hours (*see* below), the winner is the rider who rides the furthest distance in that time. Although the majority of riders know that they are unlikely to be event winners, the goal and attraction for them is always seeking to beat their own time or *personal best*.

Figure 14.3 Long-distance time-trialling: ride up hills steadily and within yourself – there's no point in being fastest up the hill if you collapse at the top! (photo: Paul A. Lawson)

100-mile time-trial

The '100' is a big test for many club riders. The top riders can race at close to 30 mph for this distance, but for most riders, being fit enough to complete the distance and finishing within 4–5 hours is often the goal. The big difference between a race like this and a randonnée (which may be a longer distance and so require more stamina) is the greater effort required when racing.

Because of the effects of fatigue, you can legitimately calculate your '100' speed to be somewhat slower than your speed for shorter distances over 25 or 50 miles (although the differences are less marked for fitter riders). To ride a 100 successfully, you need to prepare both speed and stamina.

Just like a randonneur's build-up to a 400 km event in the warmer months of the season, so most 100-mile time-trials are held after the beginning of May, to allow riders time to progress and develop their speed and stamina in the earlier months.

As always, stamina needs to be developed first of all. This is best begun in the winter months with some long, steady rides to develop your aerobic base level. Early season races over 25- and 50-mile distances can be used to improve your speed. Road races can also be used very successfully, as the variable speed demands will certainly aid the development of power.

It is possible to ride a 100-mile time-trial without support, but you will need to be well prepared. Most time-trials start early in the morning (6.00 a.m. is common) so it is rare that the temperature will rise too high during the event and make excessive demands on your hydration needs. Ensure that you are well hydrated before the event, carry two large bottles (750 ml each) containing a carbohydrate drink, and take advantage of any drinks or feeds offered along the route by the organising club. Begin taking a few sips of your drink within the first 20–30 minutes of the event and continue this every 15 minutes or so. This way you should manage to complete the distance without any unnecessary stress caused by dehydration. It's a good idea to carry some solid food too, just in case of emergency. Eat before you feel hungry! Choose a small selection from this list: energy bars or cereal bars, a small banana or two, some dried fruit or thin malt loaf sandwiches (buttered thinly with jam). This should be sufficient to supplement your energy drink. Once the event is over, do drink and eat to begin replenishing your glycogen supplies as soon as possible afterwards. (*See* also Chapter 6.)

If you can persuade a club-mate, friend or partner to provide you with support during the race, you need not worry too much about carrying supplies with you. You do, however, need to ensure that your support crew is well briefed about the rules concerning assistance to riders, and that they know how to feed you, and the appropriate times and places.

Training rides and shorter races are the ideal (and essential) opportunity to try out your feeding strategy. It is worth doing a few training rides purely on your race foods to check that you like the food you have chosen, that it is palatable, and that it is doing the job required – keeping you supplied with energy – without causing you stomach upsets. Food can taste very different 'on the move' compared to eating it at regular mealtimes.

Just like the randonneurs for their big events, you need to be properly rested in the week prior to your 100. The early-morning starts of a time-trial will mean getting up very early, so plenty of sleep 'in the bank' is essential. The final week before a 100 should be quite low-volume and not too strenuous. You do not want to arrive at the starting line feeling tired: that feeling is for the finish.

Table 14.5 provides a sample training programme for a 100. As intensity is increased from March onwards, the volume (duration) of training is decreased. Most riders will probably have one or two short-distance, high-intensity training sessions or races during the week and one or two easy, recovery rides in addition to racing once at the weekend.

Table 14.5 Sample programme to prepare for a 100-mile time-trial (in hours)

Week							
4	10	14	12	9/45 RR	10/25 TT	8/50 TT	6/TARGET
3	12	13	15	9/40 RR	9/50 RR	7/Rest	9/25 TT
2	11	13	13	10/25 TT	9/55 RR	6/70 RR	60 RR
1	10	12	12	10/10 TT	10/25 TT	8/50 TT	50 TT
Month	Dec.	Jan.	Feb.	March	April	May	June
Phase	Preparation		Pre-comp		Competition		Tapering and peak

Key: TT = time-trial; RR = road race (both shown in miles)

12-hour time-trial

The 12-hour season is from early August to mid-September, to ensure that you have had every opportunity to 'get the miles in' and prepare for this event – the longest that most club riders ever tackle. You do not actually have to ride for 12 hours non-stop in training to prepare for this event. Indeed, it is better if you train for shorter periods at a higher speed than you expect to ride the half-day event. The same principles as for a 100-mile time-trial apply, but your foundation mileage is even more important. Many riders can 'hang on' for 4–5 hours in a 100, but a full half-day ride is much more taxing, especially after 6–7 hours.

Some early season audax riding can be a great benefit, just to help you get used to the necessary hours in the saddle. As it is a race, you will need to develop some speed by riding other races – although the endurance factor does warrant more emphasis in the longer events, and perhaps even a few 200 km randonnées mid-season.

A support crew is essential if you are out to do a performance, but with some careful planning, and reliance upon the organiser's feeding points – perhaps dropping off some of your own supplies at these – it is possible to ride a '12' unsupported.

The effort of *racing* for 12 hours can be much more painful than merely *riding* for the same time. You need to be comfortable on your bike. Many riders raise their handlebars by 2–5 cm for a 12-hour. This may not be quite as aerodynamic as the position they use for 10- or 25-mile time-trials, but it is far more manageable and puts less strain on the neck, arms and back, thus enabling them to ride further and faster for the duration of the event.

Points to remember

- Include some training sessions using the food and equipment you intend to use in the event.
- You need have a good base of 'foundation hours/miles', best achieved during the winter pre-season months. (Long club rides and early season randonnées are ideal for this.)
- Have plenty of rest in the week before the event.
- Some of your training must be above your racing speed (the road races, 25- and 50-mile time-trials are ideal for this).

Table 14.6 Sample programme to prepare for a 12-hour event at the end of August

Dec.	Jan.	Feb.	March	April	May	June	July	Aug.		Month
Progressive build-up of long, steady rides, easy pace		Long, steady, rides, some increase in pace. Occasional short, fast training sessions		Shorter, faster training rides. Some short-/medium-distance races		Occasional long distance ride (200 km). Short, intense training rides. Races of 10–100 miles		TARGET	4	Week
								25 TT	3	
								50 TT or RR	2	
								100-mile race	1	

24-hour time-trial

There are very few '24s' left in the racing calendar. Riders have switched to faster, short-distance events. 10-mile (16 km) and 25-mile (40 km) events used to be regarded as distances only for juniors and women, but now they carry more prestige than most RTTC championships. It is a truism that the longer events are ridden at a slower speed, and many randonneurs are in their element where racing cyclists, more used to riding events of 2–4 hours, are floundering in unknown territory.

For a 'performance', riders need a mixture of racing speed and longer distances in their preparation. A randonneur could complete the time with a very respectable distance if he undertook a programme similar to the one outlined for the 600 km randonnée (*see* above). Add in some short-distance speed work, especially in months 7, 8 and 9, and that plan would work for many riders.

For greater speed (and distance covered in the event) more racing is required. As always, the foundation months are crucial. Long, steady miles during the winter, perhaps mixed with some strength and power training on a turbo trainer will prepare you for a season of racing and randonnées. Road racing is an ideal way to develop speed, as the pace changes frequently, forcing you to work hard and helping to develop stronger muscles and cardiovascular system.

Table 14.7 Sample programme to prepare for a 24-hour race

Ride (km) Week										
4	120	110	160	120	80 RR	400 rand.	80 TT	Rest	**TARGET**
3	120	130	140	200 rand.	200 rand.	80 TT	300 rand.	80 TT	80 TT
2	100	130	130	120	200 rand.	40 TT	100 RR	120 RR	110 RR
1	100	100	120	150	Rest	200 rand.	160 TT	160 TT	160 TT
Month	**Nov.**	**Dec.**	**Jan.**	**Feb.**	**March**	**April**	**May**	**June**	**July**
Phase	Progressive preparation				'Pre-comp' with recovery periods		Overload		Tapering and peak

Key: RR= road race; TT = time-trial; rand. = randonnée

The above programme again shows the principal rides each week. However, the dedicated racing cyclist would also need to supplement these with midweek racing and training too, and adjust the balance of these extra rides to fit in with his weekend events and the recovery required.

15 Staying the distance

Everybody can understand and appreciate the need to prepare both themselves and their equipment for a particular activity – but many overlook the importance of the psychological aspect of what they are embarking on.

You may not be aiming for Olympic success but perhaps you want to tackle 100 miles in a day, achieve a personal best time for a 12-hour time-trial, complete a randonnée within a certain time, cycle the length of the Pyrenees or compete in the Race Across AMerica. Any one of these challenges may be bigger than anything you have ever attempted before – physically and mentally. Sitting on a bicycle for hours on end, what will you think about? Will your mind play games with you and try to convince you that you are too tired, or not capable of this task, or just not interested enough in it? How can you overcome these intangible hurdles? They exist for everyone, and are even more prevalent on longer runs as your brain undergoes an emotional roller-coaster ride in and out of fatigue (not necessarily in tandem with your body). However, by progressively working up to longer distances and riding more frequently, long distances will not feel so daunting. Instead they will be the next natural step or, at worst, achievable challenges.

Randonnées, for example, pose different psychological problems for different riders. Some worry about the distance, others concern themselves with sections of night riding, and others are paranoid about mechanical failure, navigational errors or weather conditions. Simple measures can deal with each of these issues: the key, as always, is preparation.

Some general guidelines

Relax

It's only a bike ride and this is your hobby, not your livelihood. Consider what you can control and what you cannot control. There is little point in wasting energy in worrying about matters out of your hands – like the weather – but you can prepare for most eventualities. Have appropriate clothing with you: wet weather gear, gloves and a hat if there is any possibility of the temperature dropping. Make sure that you are drinking enough liquid on your ride; carry and use sunscreen if appropriate. On most rides you will pass through small towns and villages, so provided that you have some cash on you, you can usually pick up anything you need on the way.

Figure 15.1 The rider who looks untroubled has a psychological edge over his rivals

Think positively

Always think positively and reflect on your successes. An Olympic athlete might have his sights set on the gold medal but may not achieve it. It's a hard blow to take if you think that you have failed after perhaps four years of hard work: but if the athlete considers what he *has* achieved in that period – perhaps setting records on the way, and almost definitely setting personal bests – then it is much easier to re-focus and work towards the next target.

Practise and prepare

If you ride regularly then you will encounter most weather conditions and know how to handle them. So it will not be a problem for you to deal with anything thrown at you in the course of a ride lasting between one and four days. This is a good reason for being a year-round cyclist. Even in June or July a holiday in the Alps can encounter snow!

Night riding (*see* pp. 104–7) is a challenge for many riders. However, there are now so many good lighting systems on the market that there is little reason why cyclists cannot see and be seen adequately at night. On longer rides in the summer, randonnée time limits are quite generous and the hours of darkness are short. On a 600 km ride it is possible to find a B&B stop or use a control to bed down for the night, taking to the road again just before dawn to limit riding in the dark. (Do check that you have sufficient time to do this and still finish in time!)

If your bike is well maintained, checked regularly and any worn parts replaced as soon as they are spotted, there is very little reason to worry about mechanical failure.

Pay attention

Keep a watchful eye on the route sheet at all times – especially when riding in a group – and randonnée navigation should not be a problem. If in doubt, slow down or stop and check the route against a map. It is better to spend 10 minutes checking your position and direction than 5 minutes travelling the wrong way. A properly calibrated computer is a very useful aid where route sheets give intermediate distances between places or turnings.

Split stages

Do not consider a ride in its entirety. Instead, break it up into stages. Randonnées already divide the ride into sections, usually of around 50–80 km between controls. Any long place-to-place ride can be separated like this into manageable distances between towns or overnight stops. Focus on the next target – a control point in a randonnée, somewhere to stop for a drink or meal, or a town for a bed. You can then embark on the next section satisfied and confident that you are chipping away at your overall distance. Stage racers do the same, concentrating on one day at a time with just a nominal consideration of the full race.

Treat yourself

For the long-term tourist, one of the most difficult aspects to manage is not the physical part of the journey at all – living out of pannier bags, sleeping in a tent, and pedalling for hours every day – but the psychological side of it. It's worth stopping from time to time to give yourself a rest day or two. This not only helps your body to recover from the depredation of daily cycling and get stronger for the next 'stage', but it provides great mental relief too. You might choose to stay in a hostel or cheap hotel and enjoy the luxury of a shower, bed and roof over your head instead of the confines of a tent and sleeping bag. Such stops are useful for catching up on household chores such as laundry or bike maintenance, contacting home, or looking around a place of interest and meeting local people or fellow travellers – after all, isn't that why you're doing the ride?

Treats such as spending some money on a decent hotel room or proper meal once in a while, or even something as simple as a packet of chocolate biscuits, can be a tremendous mental boost. Use them as a reward to encourage you to reach a particular destination, or more simply just to provide some relief from the nomadic lifestyle of pitching tent, cooking noodles and sleeping in a bag every night.

A few small 'home comforts' can be very useful in coping with the loneliness of the long road. For years travellers have carried letters and photographs as homely reminders. Many travellers knowingly add weight to their load with non-essential luxuries – talismans from home or collected *en route* are common – for the psychological benefits of having the company of a radio, Walkman or books with them. Riders have been known to carry anything from solar panels to power music-players and provide light, to make-up, binoculars for wildlife spotting and even copious amounts of alcohol to ward off the isolation.

Be flexible

Being on your own for weeks or months can be difficult, but by the same token, spending every minute of every day in close proximity with one or two others can prove extremely taxing too. There are no simple answers, as everyone is an individual. Some people relish solitude where others seek companionship. Some people are better at integrating into the cultures they encounter on their journeys. The most successful cycle-tourists seem to be those who have a flexible attitude, absorb the local way of life and are not too hurried. Most of them have a plan – somewhere to aim for, usually with a time scale attached (e.g. Jerusalem for Christmas, Katmandu before the rainy season, or home in a year) – but they do not stick to a rigid itinerary of daily distances. Instead they follow their instincts and advice from locals or fellow travellers to add interest to their journey or to avoid difficult sections.

Have confidence in your crew

A racing cyclist tackling a 12-hour or 24-hour time-trial needs to have the confidence that he can complete the distance and that his crew is suitably prepared for him (*see* also pp. 192–7). He needs to calculate his preparatory training back from the date of the race to ensure that he has a suitable mix of long training rides and races, perhaps mixed with randonnées, so he has no need to fear the distance and is confident of his abilities. Plenty of sleep in the week preceding the event will ensure that he is not starting the event already fatigued. He can check his feeding and drinking arrangements in training. He will have ensured that his crew is well briefed, so they know when to provide support and what sort of timely assistance they need to give. During the event the rider should not have to think about anything other than riding his bike. Marshals or race signs will direct him around

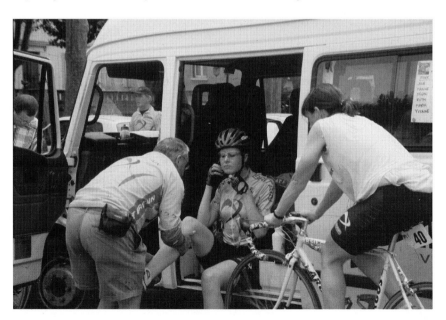

Figure 15.2 Warming up on a turbo-trainer and pre-event massage can help to prepare and focus your mind and body on the task ahead

the course – though it is sensible to check the route on a map for some peace of mind prior to the event. His crew will just 'appear' at the right time to hand up food or drinks and anticipate his every need without him even realising that he wanted another bottle or bite to eat. They will be ready with a change of clothing if required, wet sponges for him to wipe sweat from his face, neck and hands and always be 'just around the corner' should mechanical disaster strike.

A well-turned-out and efficient crew can boost any rider, and impart negative thoughts to his rivals. If a rider is not concentrating on the event he is losing time and distance. Keeping support vehicles clean in a long race is a good indication of well-organised and ordered crew, and provides extra confidence for the supported rider.

Pace yourself

Long races are usually won in the final stages, rarely at the beginning. No one is interested in who is leading at half-distance; the finish line is the point of reckoning. A good distance rider will pace himself. He may be passed by other riders early on in the event, but 12 or 24 hours is a long time to race, and many riders will fade after five or six hours when the 'stayer' will begin to come into his element and start to catch up the fast-starters. The riders who can finish the strongest will usually have the best results. That approach is very much a psychological one. Riders used to racing for an hour or two at close to 50 kph may feel that riding at 35 kph is far too easy and so will press on at 38 kph or 40 kph instead. However, many of these riders will pay for their efforts later in the day and may finish the event at no more than 25 kph, losing valuable distance to the steadier riders, who also get a psychological boost from catching and passing them. The opposite – being caught by those whom you passed earlier – is demoralising too.

Maintain a psychological advantage

The rider who looks untroubled has a psychological edge over his rivals. A useful move is to take a drink just before you catch another rider. Everyone needs to take fuel on board, but not being seen to do it adds an air of mystery to a rider.

Pyschology of stage races

Stage races are just that: races divided into a series of separate stages – anything from two or more races held on one day to those lasting up to three weeks. The winner is the rider who completes all the stages in the shortest aggregate time, although it is possible that the overall winner may not have won any of the individual stages. There are other prizes to be gained in most stage races – as well as the individual stage wins, there are usually other competitions for climbing, sprinting or consistency throughout the race. Some riders are good 'all-rounders' and can make an effort to take the overall honours. Other riders have their strengths and weaknesses, so they may focus on a just a small number of stages which suit their abilities, such as hilly or mountainous stages for the good hill-climbers. Flat stages may favour those with a

Figure 15.3 Almost cocooned from the outside world, stage races bring their own share of psychological pressures upon riders and support. The Great Britain women's team prepares for a mid-race time-trial in the 10-day Tour de L'Aude, France, oblivious to onlookers

strong sprint, or there may be a time-trial to suit the specialists against the stopwatch. These specialist riders will virtually use the other stages as training (although in top-level racing all riders will always have a team role to play). By taking this attitude they remove much of the pressure from themselves to perform at their maximum for day after day, and so make the race manageable and maximise the chances of success when 'their day' comes.

For many riders, one of the more difficult aspects of stage racing is the itinerant lifestyle. Each night is spent in a different hotel room. The rider's worldly possessions are a bike and suitcase. The food is often monotonous, either too bland or too rich. Contact with the outside world is almost forgotten as the race convoy is a cocooned world all by itself. This is a shock to many young riders and new race-staff. Sean Yates – a highly respected, top continental professional rider for 15 years – said that 'one of the best attributes a stage-race rider can have is a strong constitution'. In other words, riders have to cope with the demands placed upon them not only by the racing, but also by their nomadic existence. Food and water not always of the highest standard; extremes of temperature and altitude; minimal time to rest; and living and working so closely with other team personnel for nine months of the year – all this can be extremely taxing on an individual's mental and physical health.

As with any event, a clean bike is always a good psychological boost, providing the rider with confidence that it is working efficiently, that the mechanic has done his job and checked that nothing is worn or damaged, and that the rider is not carrying any excess weight in the form of dirt. If this can be minimised, then the rider will perform better too. Any (legal) psychological boost that can lift the rider to greater performances is worth the effort.

Personal support is important for many riders, but riders should also be prepared to be self-supportive. Sometimes a coach, friend or mentor cannot be present to offer comfort or encouragement. The rider must be empowered and

Figure 15.4 A clean bike is always a psychological boost and an opportunity to check over the components

confident enough to ride for himself, and not rely solely upon the encouragement of one or two close colleagues. Training alone, or riding events without extra support, is essential to provide the necessary psychological foundation required to cope with riding for hours, days or weeks on end. It will make those occasions where support is available much more significant, and will help the rider lift his performance for the special event.

Tips to get you through

Different people have different psychological strategies that work for them. Try some of the following which have been successfully tried and tested.

- Have a goal to focus on – such as a big, prestigious ride later in the year. This can help remind you why you are struggling up a 20% gradient into a headwind, taking a soaking in the rain, or sweating away on your turbo-trainer in a cold garage in December.
- Try reminding yourself about the training that you have already done, to prepare yourself for difficult times. 'I am prepared. By doing this I will become stronger. This is excellent training for my target event.'
- Some people keep up their morale by imagining themselves in a different place, riding like a 'pro'.
- Ride with others: you can encourage each other to keep going – and take your mind off any difficulties of the moment.
- Keep your energy reserves topped up by regularly taking plenty of fluid and carbohydrate.
- Maintain your equipment, and invest in quality whenever possible, so that you know you can rely on it.

- Divide any large task into manageable units. A ride of 600 km can be split into stages of 50–100 km at a time. Reward yourself for accomplishing each one – perhaps a brief rest or an extra food treat. Even parts of stages can be sub-divided, e.g. 'I'll give myself a two-minute rest when I reach the top of the next hill.'
- Before setting off, think about some 'what if' scenarios and what you could do to overcome these situations. Develop your lateral thinking and alternative strategies to any problems that you might encounter. You probably won't need to use them – the solution may involve minimising the possible risk in the first place – but it's always good to have a plan. For example: What if I get a puncture? I will use my spare inner tube. What if I get a second puncture? I will use my second tube. (Reminder – carry two spare inner tubes!) What if I puncture a third or fourth time? I will carry some repair patches and glue. (Reminder – add repair patches and glue to repair kit!) – and so on.
- Read about other people's adventures and hardships (mountaineering and exploration books are an excellent source of inspiration) and see how these people – often household names – have overcome adversity. This often puts your own problems into perspective!
- Relax. Do not impose unnecessary restrictions upon yourself (like 'I must finish in x hours'). Sometimes matters are beyond your control. You may have to re-focus your goal to something more appropriate, given the circumstances.

Almost invariably, riders look back on the 'hard times' with great satisfaction and this helps them in future situations.

16 Tours and events

Touring

One of the most satisfying ways to approach touring is to arrange your own multi-day tour – poring over maps to discover attractive routes and places, perhaps with assistance from an organisation like the CTC. Alternatively, you can join a touring party where all the planning is done for you.

If you decide to travel independently, you will need to consider accommodation. Test your capabilities with a short tour of three or four days before you embark on a longer journey. Why not use public transport to take you to the start of your journey, and then spend a few days riding home – perhaps staying with friends on the way, or at guest houses or hostels?

You may wish to pre-book your accommodation initially, but as you gain in confidence, you might be prepared to find a bed 'on spec'. Don't be over-ambitious with your distances at first. If you arrive too early, you can always leave your baggage at the guest house or hostel and go for an unladen ride in the area. If you find that you are arriving later than expected, you may need to re-calculate your capabilities, set off earlier, or make an effort to reduce rests and stops along the way and spend more time cycling.

Another option is to arrange a fixed-centre tour, staying in one place and then exploring the region in a series of loops each day. You can also mix your touring, perhaps riding from place to place one day and then spending a day or two in one place before loading your panniers once again to move on.

The Bolero 'bicycle bus' operates routes through the UK and into Europe (www.bike-express.co.uk), usually collecting and dropping riders at pre-agreed motorway junctions or service stations. Fitted with a large trailer, it takes all manner of bicycles safely and securely without the need for any dismantling or protective packaging (*see* Figure 16.1). Riders have a luxury coach to ferry them to destinations by a number of routes by day and night. You can pick and choose the stops as you wish, take the bus just one way, or use it to take you to two or three different areas during the course of a holiday.

An organised cycling tour removes the administration and hassle from cycle touring. Arrive at a pre-agreed point and the operator will (usually) have everything in hand. They may have a 'sag wagon' to take your luggage, provide a picnic lunch, or give a free ride for part of the route to the extra-weary cyclists. Hotels, motels and most meals will be covered in the cost and you know that you will be in the company of similarly minded riders. Obviously, you should check beforehand that the tour is suitable for you with regard to terrain and distances to be covered each day.

Figure 16.1 The Bike Express carries bikes in a special trailer and riders in a luxury coach on different routes from Britain into Europe (photo: Bike Express)

Randonnées: 100–1200 km

Entries and preparation

Randonnées and *sportive* rides are an excellent introduction to long-distance cycling. The basic distance is 200 km, but it's wise to develop some riding technique at shorter distances before tackling events of this length (*see* Chapters 12 and 13). This is a full day's ride, usually in the daylight, with other riders around and a series of checkpoints (often with food available so you do not have to burden yourself with extra luggage). The AUK Handbook details all of the randonnées in the UK (updates on www.audax.uk.net). You will need to sign an official entry form (with liability disclaimer). It's courteous to enter events at least two weeks beforehand, so that the organiser can ensure that he has the right number of brevet cards (*see* box) and deal with any catering arrangements. When the organiser receives your entry fee and two stamped addressed envelopes, he will send you a copy of the route sheet.

On these rides you are expected to be self-sufficient, so study the route sheet and follow the course on a map at home to get a good idea of where you will be going. (You may find a mistake on the route sheet which you can check with the organiser before you start. You're less likely to spot the error before it is too late when you are riding.)

The start

Aim to arrive at the start venue about 45 minutes before the start time. This will give you time to find it, park your car, assemble your bike and make any last-minute adjustments, visit the toilet (there may be a queue!) and collect your brevet card. Some organisers even provide pre-event tea! In UK randonnées, riders usually all start together. Take care at the start: some riders can be nervous or over-excited, which – coupled with poor bike handling skills – can cause accidents. Ensure that you take the correct route! It is far too easy to be riding strongly, perhaps in a big group, and miss a vital turn early on.

In Europe, the *sportive* events favour riders finishing closer together and so there is often a choice of starting times. Here, it is common to have the whole route arrowed, either by markings on the road, or with signs pasted or painted on to kerbs and street furniture. This makes navigation very simple, compared to providing route sheets and insisting on your navigational abilities (*see* Figure 16.2).

Controls

Not all European randonnées are big productions; many are much smaller than their British equivalents. UK organisers invariably arrange specific controls close to sources of food and shelter – especially if the ride covers remote areas and the hours of darkness. On the Continent, though, routes can be more vague, taking you to towns or villages where you have to find your own 'control' (e.g. *any* bar, café, supermarket or service station) and make your own arrangements for food and drink.

In all randonnées you must stop at specified controls and have your brevet card stamped, signed and timed by a controller. This might be an official sent there by the organiser, or the staff of a café or bar. Larger events now use magnetic swipe-cards (like credit cards): these eliminate the need to get cards stamped, and do not deteriorate with sweat or rain like regular brevet cards. Some events have introduced small transponders fixed to the bike to record riders' passage.

On some rides, to keep you on route, you may have to stop at an 'information control'. These are often used in less populated areas, where you will have to write the answer to a simple observation question (e.g. 'Name of the pub at the junction' or 'Year inscribed on village memorial'). You might be able to ride past without

Figure 16.2 Bordeaux–Paris randonnée, 2000: directions and *'ravitaillement'* (feed station) are painted on the road, and locals come out to cheer on the riders – even with a banner for one of the participating local factory workers! (photo: Ivo Miesen)

stopping – but you will need to remember the answer and write it into your brevet card before you finish the ride. So carry a pen or pencil too.

Pace yourself

You must be able to pace yourself over the required distance. Audax rides are very helpful in that they specify their maximum and minimum speeds. Remember, though, that these are overall speeds, and they include stopping time at controls or elsewhere. In reality, you will have to maintain a speed a little above the usual minimum of 15 kph to allow for eating and resting at controls, mechanical problems, or stopping to check the map (or retracing your route if you have gone off-course). The slower you ride, the less time you can afford to stop off the bike.

Table 16.1 Minimum and maximum speeds and times for randonnées of various lengths

Distance (km)	Max speed[1]	Min. time	Min. speed	Max. time
100	30 kph	3 h 20	14.3–15 kph[2]	6 h 40–7 h 00
200	30 kph	6 h 40	14.3–15 kph[2]	13 h 20–14 h 00
300	30 kph	10 h 00	14.3–15 kph[2]	20 h 00–21 h 00
400	30 kph	13 h 20	14.3–15 kph[2]	26 h 40–28 h 00
600	30 kph	20 h 00	14.3–15 kph[2]	40 h 00–42 h 00
700	30 kph	23 h 20	13.3 kph	52 h 40
1000	30 kph	33 h 20	13.3 kph	75 h 00
1200	30 kph	40 h 00	13.3 kph	90 h 00
1300	30 kph	42 h 20	12.0 kph	108 h 20
1400	30 kph	46 h 40	12.0 kph	116 h 40
1900	30 kph	63 h 20	10.0 kph	190 h 00
2000	30 kph	66 h 40	10.0 kph	200 h 00
2500	30 kph	83 h 20	200 kpd	12.5 days

[1]Organiser may set lower maximum speed.
[2]Minimum speed set at organiser's discretion. Lower minimum speeds are usually allowed for longer or more severe courses.

Unless the route is extremely hilly, most riders should be able to maintain a pace of 20 kph without too much difficulty. Your brevet card shows all the intermediate times of the controls opening and closing, using a maximum speed of 30 kph and minimum speed of 15 kph. If you arrive at each control with time in hand, you should complete the route without any problems. To be 'safe', aim to leave each one before 'closing time' too!

Some randonnées are more conducive to faster times than others. Hills, navigation, road surfaces, time of year, weather conditions, company and mechanical difficulties can all influence how long a ride will take. But that doesn't matter. It could be a particularly challenging ride boasting many tough hills (there are a few organisers and riders who revel in the tougher events). For the randonneur, a fast time should not be the prime objective. Completing the ride – perhaps in an area new to you, and maybe with old friends or in the company of new ones – is usually much more important.

For most randonées, self-sufficiency can be interpreted fairly loosely – although support cars are rarely permitted. You are free to stop when you like for rest or sustenance, but for reasons of mutual support it helps if you can ride with others. Ride within your 'comfort zone'. If you find the pace of others too hard, ease back and ride at your own speed. Sometimes if you arrive at a checkpoint in a large group you will lose time if there is a long queue of riders waiting to be served. It may be better not to stop at a 'control café' (except to get your card stamped), but to continue on a bit further instead. You can usually find a sandwich and can of coke at a store around the corner, or dip into the food you have brought with you, eating on the move. This way you can be on your way in a couple minutes instead of waiting 30–45 minutes before a group has been served (although you may wish to factor this in as a stop/rest session). You are not getting any closer to the finish if you're sitting in a café or waiting in a queue!

At the end of the event, check that all the details on your brevet card have been completed and hand your card to the controller. In due course this card will be returned to you, stamped by AUK's Validation Secretary, as a record of your achievement. Most organisers try to finish their events at a café or hall, close to the starting point and with refreshments available, so that you can see some of the other participants and unwind by sharing your experiences of the day. (*See* also, pp. 165–9.)

Night riding

Unless you are very fast, most randonnées over 200 km will involve some element of riding during the hours of darkness. (There are notable exceptions, such as rides in the north of Scotland in summertime.) You will need to carry lighting and some extra clothing with you. You may want to plan your ride to include a longer stop, possibly for some sleep, or just so that you will arrive somewhere at an hour where you know you will be able to get some food or a hot drink.

Some riders find great benefit from stopping to rest, eat or stretch (or sleep on longer events) and riding a little faster between controls. Others prefer to continue at a steady pace without taking any significant rest breaks. You have to discover what strategy works best for you. But be flexible – it may change from one ride to another.

There is no regulation set of start times for randonnées. They can begin at any hour of the day or night, at the organiser's whim, considering local traffic conditions and the availability of facilities. Rides beginning in the evening can pose serious problems later if you have spent all day awake, possibly at work, before travelling to begin an event at 9.00 or 10.00 p.m. You are beginning your ride just at the hour your body is normally winding down and preparing for sleep. An initial surge of adrenaline may take you through the early hours of the night but invariably you will feel extremely tired later. A few hours of sleep in the afternoon or evening prior to the start will make an enormous difference to your ability to cope with an evening start time.

On a long randonnée, you need to build up a buffer of time-in-hand if you want to sleep. With the reasonably generous time allowances this is not usually a problem. Quite how much sleep you take is up to you (*see* also pp. 105–9). Obviously, if you attempt to sleep but you are wide awake 20 minutes later, there is no point in trying to sleep for your pre-calculated time. Neural activity may be preventing you from sleeping. Faster riders can plan a longer night-time stop so they can have more sleep, and avoid riding in the dark almost completely.

Riding in company can be particularly beneficial at night, especially to help navigate the route. Be careful, though, of watching other riders too closely. Do not focus your eyes on their rear lights. Just as in daylight, keep your focus ahead of other riders and maintain an even distance from their rear wheels by keeping their tail-lights in your near vision.

Lights

Many riders angle their twin-lamps slightly differently, with one pointing further down the road for faster riding and the other focused closer to illuminate the road immediately ahead. Both beams can be employed in very dark areas or on fast descents. You might keep one lamp just slightly loose on its bracket so that you can point the beam to help read road-signs or to make oncoming traffic more aware of your presence. Alternatively, use a head-torch (*see* also pp. 47–9). These are ideal for reading your route sheet and computer or when fixing repairs in the dark.

Two rear lamps are considered essential by most night-time randonneurs. LEDs weigh so little that there is no problem in carrying a second one. They are very reliable too, but you never know when a battery might fail, water might affect the circuitry or a lamp might get damaged in a fall – or when someone else may need to borrow a lamp if theirs has failed. You may be required to carry spare batteries and spare bulbs on some events. A second front and rear lamp surpasses such ruling.

Clothing

Many riders 'forget' to dress for night-time conditions and they struggle to keep moving at a reasonable pace. You can ride comfortably in shorts and short-sleeves in daytime temperatures of >18°C, but at night the temperature usually drops to less than 15°C, perhaps even lower than 10°C. Leg-warmers, gloves and an extra top are almost essential for night-riding anywhere, but you may need more substantial clothing depending on the conditions.

If you feel too hot but the air temperature is too cold, undo the zips of the clothes nearest your skin, leaving the outer ones pulled up to prevent cold air from blasting down your chest. If you become too cold, it is very difficult to generate more heat in cold conditions – however many clothes you put on (*see* Figure 16.3).

You may be riding your randonnée with complete strangers, but once you've ridden through the night with them these people will be your friends for ever!

Figure 16.3 Cassie Lowe wrapped up to combat extreme cold but maintaining her fluid intake in the desert at night, RAAM 2000

Paris–Brest–Paris

This is the epitome of long-distance randonnées. At 1200 km it is not the longest event in the audax calendar, but it is the most prestigious, and this legendary race-route across northern France draws riders from all over the world.

Organised by Audax Club Parisien (ACP) once every four years, PBP attracts more than 3500 entries. The event's popularity has grown enormously over recent years and ACP has a strict regime of qualifying rides to weed out the less-prepared. Even so, ACP is always disappointed at the number of *abandonées* in their event and may change the rules to make entry more stringent and thus improve the statistics of successful participants.

The qualification rules for PBP do vary slightly from one nation to another, partly dictated by the numbers involved and by local climatic conditions. (It's unfair to insist that riders from Alaska complete their qualifying rides before the snows have cleared!) But usually, ACP demands that riders complete a Super Randonneur (SR) series of brevets: 200, 300, 400 and 600 km in the six months of the year prior to the end of June, as suitable pre-preparation. You will need to continue your preparation after your qualifying rides if you wish to avoid the problems of reversibility (*see* also p. 130). You will also need to supply a medical certificate stating that there is no reason to doubt your ability to complete the event. Towards the end of the year preceding PBP, Audax UK (or other national randonnée governing bodies) will be able to supply you with the full list of information giving the latest entry requirements.

Organisation

Apart from it being twice the distance that most randonneurs ever usually tackle, there is little to worry about in PBP. There are three start times: those who intend to complete the distance in 80 hours leave first at 8.00 p.m. on the Monday evening. This is the fast group, *les vedettes* ('stars'), with an open road ahead of them. Two hours later they are followed by the randonneurs allowing themselves the full 90 hours permitted for the 1200 km. At 5.00 a.m. the following morning, riders from the 84-hour group depart.

Because of the numbers participating, the organisers separate each time group into smaller groups. Invariably, even in the 90-hour group there are some riders who commence as if they are riding a road race. You need your wits about you not to get drawn into the pace, and to avoid the less skilled riders in a bunch of up to 500 riders.

Pace

An hour or two into the event and the police escort pulls over. Look back over your shoulder and you see a long line of white lights stretching back to the horizon. Ahead, the line is of red tail-lights. By this time the groups have settled down; later starters are pulling back the earlier getaways, and some of the early enthusiasts are already paying for their exuberance. Riders begin to form into smaller groups as the pelotons split on the gently rolling hills west of Paris. Stronger, more savvy riders ride in echelon (*see* also pp. 159–61), saving their energy and protecting one another from the wind. Cautious riders conserve their energy by riding at their own pace, knowing that they have nearly four days to complete this ride and there is a long way to go.

The usual maximum 30 kph applies to all except the *vedettes*. They have no upper pace limit, and the front-runners race the event, pacing and drafting one another, with helpers waiting for them with food, water and clothing at each control so that they do not lose any time. These riders forego sleep completely and attempt to finish the distance in less than 48 hours.

For the vast majority of entrants, the event's lower speed limit of 13.3 kph is quite manageable and even allows for reasonable amounts of sleep on the way if you maintain a moderate riding pace.

En route

PBP has atmosphere. France is steeped in cycling history and the people understand it and celebrate it. They have great respect for anyone on a bicycle and they give full credit to you whether you are a tourist, a racing cyclist or a randonneur. Everyone in France is, or has been, or knows someone who is a cyclist. Cycling is on the TV and reported in the newspapers and they know how hard it can be.

You ride through little villages, decorated with bicycles and flowers in recognition of the PBP ride. Children wait patiently at the roadside, hoping you will stop for them to fill your *bidon* with cold water. They run alongside to cheer you on and offer you sweets. Some have autograph books for you to sign. Messages of encouragement are painted on the road. In the dead of night you hear voices in the darkness, then clapping and cheering as villagers stay up all night having a PBP party to cheer you on. Some open up their homes to weary randonneurs, even offering a bed for a few hours, coffee or omelettes – often for free. Language is rarely a barrier. Everyone understands the needs of the randonneurs and riders from all nations are welcomed.

Generous as they are, it is unwise to plan your PBP expecting to find roadside hospitality from the locals just where you want it. The first control is about 150 km into the event and after that most are spaced every 80 km or so. Food is available canteen-style at all of these, and the route does pass through towns and villages where you can stop for provisions at any bar, café, supermarket or *boulangerie* if needed. Many of the controls also have provision for sleeping. This varies from dormitories equipped with camp beds and blankets, to space on the floor on a gym mat. If you're tired, you'll sleep anywhere!

You can organise your rest-stops by pre-booking a hotel room on the route beforehand. This way you know you can get a shower too and you can send ahead a change of clothes and other supplies to wait for your arrival. (Do make arrangements to have your dirty laundry sent back too!)

Your riding, eating and sleeping strategy needs to be flexible. You might travel further or less far than expected on any one day due to the weather, mechanical problems, fatigue or riding in a group, and so you may need to adjust your idea about where you might sleep. You could encounter long queues at a control and decide to press on instead, either eating your bonk rations on the move or looking for a restaurant further down the road. You could suddenly feel tired and sleepy, needing an immediate stop and rest. An hour or two shut-eye could be just what you need to revitalise yourself and get back on the road again.

The weather can play an important part in your success at PBP. If you have ridden your qualifying rides in a variety of conditions and you are equipped for any eventuality, you should have no problems. If you have only ridden flat rides in sunshine, then northern France at the end of summer could be a shock to you. This region has a maritime climate and may be cold and wet or hot and sunny at this time of year. Or all four – and windy!

The route is not difficult. There are no major climbs but the road rolls continuously and can be quite tiring, especially with some of the heavy chippings used on the tarmac. A good spread of gears is useful but very low gears are not necessary for most riders. Strong riders should have no problem with a bottom gear of 39×23, but tired riders with luggage may prefer something a little lower such as 39×28. If you have a triple chainset for touring you probably will not use the inner chainring on PBP. (*See* also Gearing, pp. 37–44.)

Equipment, clothing and supplies

PBP sees the whole spectrum of randonneurs: from the neo-racers on their stripped-down titanium and carbon-fibre racing bikes, to fat-tyred tourists with all their needs for four days packed into two pannier bags. With the facilities provided by the organisers you can easily ride this event without any outside support, and many argue that this is the spirit of the randonnée. Since you will be on your bike almost the whole time, you do not need to carry much with you and all your needs should fit quite comfortably into a saddlebag or rackpack.

Figure 16.4 Riders take a brief rest at Mortagne Au Perche, the first feeding point 140 km into PBP 1999

Although not essential, it is a good idea to have at least one full change of cycle clothing. Spare shorts, socks, track mitts, vest and jersey, together with a night jacket, leg-warmers, waterproof top, gloves and hat should be sufficient. Toiletries should include lip-balm, sunscreen, antiseptic cream for your shorts and a toothbrush. Antiseptic wipes are a good idea, used regularly to keep your saddle area clean and prevent sores from developing. Add in any bonk food you wish to take with you, plus the obligatory reflective vest and spare bulbs required by ACP – and you're away!

PBP has now become so big that a number of clubs and even commercial operators arrange motorised back-up. This ranges from a mini-van stacked with riders' bags containing their spare clothes, batteries and energy bars, to deluxe coaches with reclining seats or even beds and kitchen facilities with a masseur and mechanic at their service. Support vehicles are prohibited from following riders or meeting them along the route except at the controls. If the vehicle is supporting a number of riders it is best to have it stationed in just one or two pre-arranged locations so that even if the riders are spread out over a number of hours, they will all be able to meet the vehicle. This is also far less tiring for the support crew themselves, who need to be alert for the arrival of all their riders. In 1999, UK cycling holiday operator Graham Baxter had three coaches stationed on the course, whereby the 130 riders who had booked their travel arrangements with him could each leave a bag with spares, or a towel for a shower, at different controls along the course.

At the end of PBP, you will have a *mélange* of memories. It may be difficult to sort them into chronological order, and you may be tired and sore – but the usual lasting impression is about the atmosphere of the event. Hopefully you will also have taken the opportunity to bond with fellow randonneurs from around the world or people met on the route, perhaps exchanging addresses to send photographs when you get

home – and not necessarily just with those who speak the same language. Riding together through at least two days and two nights creates a special friendship between riders, as you help each other through the hard times, and share the camaraderie of the good times. Maybe that explains why so many riders repeat the experience so often.

RAAM

The Race Across AMerica is unlike any other event in the world. First run in 1982 as The Great American Bike Race, with just four competitors, it has grown in stature but never to the heights that it deserves. It's often said that 'If RAAM was easy then everyone could do it'. But it's not easy – in fact, more people have flown in outer space than have completed RAAM.

It is approximately 3000 miles (4800 km) across the USA. The record for the fastest solo crossing is currently held by Rob Kish (1992), at 8 days 3 hours 11 minutes. The women's record is held by Seanna Hogan (1995) with 9 days 4 hours 2 minutes – incidentally giving her the fastest average overall speed too (13.22 mph). The men's fastest overall speed (over a longer course than Kish's 1992 ride) is held by Pete Penseyres, who achieved 15.40 mph in 1986 – including his rest stops. His actual riding speed was in the region of 17.5 mph for 21 hours every day.

In the team event, each team usually consists of four riders. The riders can choose to ride together, pacing each other. Alternatively, and as is more usual, they can take it in turns to keep just one rider on the road at all times (for periods of perhaps 30 minutes to 2 hours) while the other three team members rest in the support vehicle before it is their turn again. The Kern Wheelmen currently hold the record of 5 days 6 hours 4 minutes, which they set in 1996.

Just like PBP (*see* pp. 187–91), there are strict qualifying guidelines just to start RAAM, laid down by the Ultra Marathon Cycling Association (UMCA). Hopeful RAAM racers need to ride an approved 'non-drafting' event of 500 miles or more and finish within the top 15% of the first previously non-qualified person's time within their own division (male or female). This figure is amended to 25% for riders over 50 years old. Anyone completing a minimum distance of 425 miles in a 24-hour race is also eligible – as is a sub-65-hour ride in the 750-mile (1200 km) Boston–Montreal–Boston randonneé (North America's answer to Paris–Brest–Paris), or completing an Elite PAC Tour across the USA, averaging 175 miles a day for 17 days.

These qualifications are the *minimum* standard. To be a successful RAAM finisher, riders need to be able to reach these standards without difficulty if they are going to survive riding for over 20 hours a day for 10 consecutive days (or thereabouts). Two to three hours sleep a night is the maximum that most riders expect over this event.

Many RAAM riders either stop work completely, or work part-time, so that they can concentrate all their time and efforts into training (and resting) in readiness for RAAM. It is a demanding event, and needs to be taken seriously if you want to be successful. It is also financially demanding: equipment, clothing, food, vehicles, fuel, medical care, transport to training events and races, etc. The riders are obliged to at least cover or contribute to their crew's accommodation, subsistence and travel costs during the event. Sponsorship certainly helps many riders, but there again, even the search for a kindly benefactor can be costly, time-consuming and energy sapping and needs full commitment if it is likely to be successful.

The route has always been West–East, but with different start and finish locations. In 2000, twice-winner and multiple trans-America record holder Lon Haldeman became Race Director and moved the race from its traditional July slot to the beginning of June with a new start point in Portland, Oregon, and finish in Pensacola, Florida. This route was far more mountainous than in previous years. An immediate 1737 m (5700') climb over Mt Hood in the first 100 km (60 miles) to spread out the field of 23 solo riders, and the Rocky Mountains of Utah and Colorado – including Tennessee Pass at 3120 m (10,400') – certainly made this a far tougher route than previous editions. The earlier date benefited the riders who experienced far less severe temperatures and humidity than usual, particularly in the southern states of Arkansas, Mississippi, Alabama and Florida.

Your crew

Your crew can't win the event for you, but they can lose it. The crew's job is to do everything for the rider except ride the bike: supplying food and water to ensure that the rider is properly fuelled at all times, maintaining the bike(s), attending to the rider's physical and emotional needs and being a motivator, supporter and friend.

The event takes it toll on crew members just as much as it does on the riders – not to quite the same physical extent, but certainly emotionally. It's very tiring, because of the long hours on duty. For the well-being of both the crew members and the rider it is important that everyone pulls together as a team. Everyone must understand the common objective and not lose sight of the goal. If the team falls apart, the rider will soon sense it and his performance will decline too.

RAAM rules allow a crew to be anything from two people to an unlimited number. One person must be appointed 'crew chief' for communications purposes, but in practice the crew may decide to work in a more co-operative manner and share the decision-making. Most riders have two or three support vehicles on the road manned by three or four people each. Smaller crews of 6–8 people tend to be more efficient as everyone has a task to do and no one is left idle. Larger crews consisting of 12–15 people contain a lot of personalities, multiplying the chances of people not getting along with one another.

It is always useful to have experienced people on the crew – preferably with an understanding of ultra-distance cycling gained through personal experience as a rider or supporter and through talking to others. They do not need to be great cyclists themselves, but they must understand the motivation for embarking on such an endeavour, and be aware of the trials and tribulations that they themselves will face along the way.

It is normal practice to have three crew members in the support car: a driver, a navigator, and a 'provisioner' who can anticipate, prepare and hand up the rider's needs as required. Between these three they should also be able to deal with minor mechanical problems on the bike and understand the rider's nutritional and medical needs. Although it is wise to have crew members who can multi-task, it is not necessary for everyone to be capable of everything. Each person should have their specific role but also be prepared to help with other tasks during the course of the event.

Communication is vital. Telephones and e-mail make this is easy today and a crew can literally be brought together from around the world, already knowing their individual roles and methods expected by the crew chief and rider. Communication must also continue during the race itself!

Most RAAM riders use radios to communicate with their crew to prevent the rider from straining his voice and getting a sore throat, and to maintain his spirits by knowing that he is always in contact on what can be a very long and lonely ride. For communication when the crews are reasonably close together (2–4 km), hand-held radios are cheap and convenient. For longer-distance calls and more secure communication (to prevent other crews eavesdropping your strategy or woes), mobile phones are almost essential. Be prepared for an astronomical telephone bill after the event! However, vast tracts of the USA are unpopulated and many areas have very poor cellphone coverage.

A good crew chief will delegate individuals or pairs to various tasks and arrange for each person to supply the various tools of their trade. For example, a masseur might cover all the medical requirements; a mechanic might organise tools and arrange any necessary spare components that need to be on hand. There may be other communal items required – buckets for cleaning purposes, blankets or towels, torches, maps, water carriers, food and kitchen paraphernalia. Someone has to co-ordinate these items, and it's best that such details be covered prior to arrival in the starting city.

Some advice for the crew

Emotions can fluctuate wildly in RAAM. The crew plays an essential role in lifting the rider when he is feeling tired, or losing concentration. Do not lie about distances or the positions of other riders, but concentrate instead on the success so far, the distance covered, perhaps the minimal difference in speed between one rider and another. Remind the rider about the training rides – how difficult some of those rides were, but how he managed them; how he has concentrated on this event for so long. This is probably the focus of his last year, perhaps an ambition he has harboured for many years. Do whatever you can to keep the rider moving as much as possible. Reassure him that others are going through bad patches, perhaps even worse! Convince him that he is going really well, and should not compare RAAM with the local 2-hour training bash.

Sometimes you need to divert the rider's attention away from the race completely. Some riders enjoy music, either over a PA system or through headphones. (If headphones are used, just one earpiece should be worn so the rider can hear traffic or instructions from the crew.) Others want to engage in conversation and this is quite simple with modern radio link-ups. Facts and figures can be used to encourage the rider. A calculator nearby is very useful: you may be feeling mentally fatigued when the rider asks 'How many miles do I need to do each day until the finish? What average speed is that? What speed is the rider ahead doing? How much climbing is there between here and the next time station?' and expects instant answers!

Figure 16.6 RAAM support vehicle: Steve Born's Dodge Caravan with a crew of three provides close support for Cassie Lowe's needs over the 3000-mile race. The vehicle is not allowed to pace or shelter the rider (photo: Carol Clark)

Vehicles and equipment

Vehicles have to be suitable for a 3000-mile journey, plus mileage to get to the start and home from the finish (*see* Figure 16.6). A full service, explaining to the garage mechanic exactly what the car will be undergoing, is a sound investment. (Don't expect him to understand *why* you want to drive for 21 hours a day at less than 15 mph for 10 days!) Check that your vehicle has the capacity to take all of your luggage.

Three people, their bags, all the rider's clothing, spare bikes, wheels, food and water supplies, medical needs and kitchen equipment take up a considerable amount of room. If the crew is going to survive the distance and cope with their allotted support tasks, they do not want to be travelling squashed between a pair of wheels, someone's dirty laundry and a week's supply of energy drink. If you hire vehicles on a one-way trip, be sure that whatever you book will be appropriate (and what you book will actually be what is supplied). Check too that your insurance is valid for RAAM.

Organising your kit

Good organisation is essential. Decide how many vehicles and crew you can cope with and the length of crew shifts. The usual approach is to have one 'pace car' to follow the rider closely at all times, and a second support vehicle for the off-duty crew. The second vehicle will then take chunks of rest, leap-frogging the rider and pace car as necessary. If the budget allows, a team in a third car may be employed for utility tasks such as shopping for supplies and doing laundry *en route*, perhaps checking out difficult sections of the route ahead and generally keeping the two crews supported.

Every item should have a home in one of the vehicles, and ideally the whole crew should know where each item lives to ensure that items go back to their allotted space, making them easier to find when next required. One of the best systems employed by three-time RAAM finisher Steve Born for Cassie Lowe[1] in the 2000 race, used a Dodge Caravan van. The rear seats were removed and a water cooler mounted behind the driver's seat. Behind that, facing the sliding door, the provisioner's seat was secured – a low, padded camping chair. A large cooler box sat behind the navigator's seat. The space to the side doorway was kept clear at all times. Food and water bottles were kept behind the provisioner, and behind the provisioner Steve had three sets of drawers – all clearly labelled for different clothing, medical supplies, nutritional supplements and a ready supply of batteries. Cassie's larger garments (waterproofs, cold weather tops and spare helmet) hung on a rail above the drawers. Space behind the drawers was used for extra water, a toolbox, spare bike parts and a pair of wheels. On the roof-rack sat one spare bike and four more spare wheels. An extra roof bar at the front of the vehicle was used for an external PA speaker system.

Cassie's second vehicle was a Roadtrek motorhome, easier to manoeuvre than a RV but quite large enough as a rest place when required. This had plenty of storage cupboards for the crew's personal kit, and more food and water, more spares and the mechanics' work kits. Another pair of wheels was kept in the motorhome, just in case it was needed as the pace vehicle.

[1] Cassie Lowe, from Sydney, was the only female entrant in RAAM 2000. She finished in 10 days 3 hours 9 minutes, in seventh place overall. Website: www.cassonbike.com. The overall winner in 2000 was Wolfgang Faschina of Austria, in 8 days 10 hours 19 minutes.

What to take

RAAM rules prevent following cars from sheltering riders from the wind, or assisting them by pacing, but cars are allowed to illuminate the road at night from behind the rider. For this reason, the RAAM rider does not need state-of-the-art lighting like the randonneur or the British 24-hour time-triallist does, though the rules do insist that bike lights work and that all bikes and wheels are suitably decorated with reflective tape for night riding (*see* also pp. 104–5).

In an event that spans 3000 miles from humid lowlands to high-altitude mountains, all sorts of climate can be expected. The riders need to be prepared for everything; from temperatures around 0°C in the Rockies at night, to the mid- and high-30s during the day in the southern states. Perhaps the worst scenario is rain, which makes everything cold and wet, necessitates more frequent clothing changes, and makes finding a Laundromat an essential task for the crew every day. Consequently, the rider must have enough suitable clothes and the crew must be organised to cope with whatever situation they encounter. Embrocation and baby oil may be called upon to protect joints and exposed flesh from the cold, followed later in the day by calls for high-factor sunscreen and lip-balm.

The crew needs to be well-equipped too since they will be operating in the same range of conditions as the rider; standing by the roadside in the cold, heat, rain or wind. Crew members will probably have to fit their needs for two weeks into one small bag. The crew chief should issue an equipment list to all personnel to ensure that they have adequate quantities of suitable clothing, that no one arrives with 'kit overload'. Soft bags are better than rigid cases as they fit into smaller and less uniform spaces much more easily.

Assuming that the laundry will be done two or three times during the event, crew members should take the following:

- 4 shirts or T-shirts
- 2 pairs shorts
- 1 pair long trousers
- 4 pairs underwear
- 4 pairs socks
- fleece jumper or similar
- stout footwear with closed toes
- sandals
- sun hat or cap
- cold weather hat
- lightweight gloves
- waterproof jacket[2]
- towel
- toiletries plus lip-balm and sunscreen
- torch or head-torch
- pen, marker pen, highlighter pen and notebook
- wristwatch
- travel alarm clock.

Flexibilty, adaptability and a sense of humour should probably go at the top of the list, but they don't take up any room in a duffle-bag.

[2]Do not skimp on this. If you encounter heavy rain you will appreciate a good-quality waterproof jacket that does not leave you soaking wet in less than an hour.

Trouble-shooting

The RAAM rider needs much more attention than most. The sheer length of the event means that minor problems which usually sort themselves out after a ride do not have the opportunity to be resolved. Through the rider's preparatory rides and discussion with crew members there should be everything in the vehicles to cover 97% of all eventualities. There is no way that every conceivable problem can be anticipated in an event of this nature. If you have covered as many potential situations as possible, the best way to deal with the unforeseen is not to worry about it but to find a solution when you need to. The crew may need to think laterally for a temporary solution, utilising items in a novel manner or deflecting the rider's attention to something else while you fix the problem. With adequate planning and preparation you should be able to avoid all but the unavoidable.

The rider's medical kit needs to cover everything from saddle sores and blisters to cracked lips, sunburn, puffy eyes, cramp, diarrhoea, constipation, indigestion, insect bites, cuts and bruises, sore throat, tight chest, hay fever and breathing difficulties. Little ailments that you could normally ignore completely can turn into major issues on a ride like this. A cut finger will feel more and more sore rubbing against the brake hoods for hour upon hour. Your mouth reacts to food and drink quite differently after two or three days, perhaps requiring a neutralising mouthwash solution. To help you prepare, seek the advice of an experienced rider or crew member to find out just how your body and mind is affected by extended exercise and sleep deprivation. Although crews on RAAM can be remarkably secretive – withholding information about their rider and race strategy from other competitors and their crews – they are usually very happy to help rookie riders prepare themselves for the ordeal. (The figures show that only about 50% of rookie riders succeed in their first RAAM. However, many return two or three seasons later with the knowledge from their first experience and usually go on to do very well.)

Figure 16.7 The RAAM rider needs more attention than most: crew chief Steve Born checks that Cassie Lowe is protected from the sun

Be grateful!

Anyone who supports riders in a marathon event like this should be commended on their graciousness and commitment in helping the competitors in their personal quest. Don't be too busy or too tired to thank your friends, colleagues and crews – even strangers met along the way – adequately. Remember, they may be conscripted again in the future.

Wilderness cycling

Despite the relentless advance and expansion of civilisation across the globe, there are still many remote areas in the world. Wilderness riding is a demanding cycling activity, as well as being extremely rewarding. For obvious reasons, however, it is not recommended that inexperienced riders attempt to tackle the most remote regions. Some riders desire to seek these places for the solitude and contrast to everyday life. Others relish nature's challenge. Some encounter the wilderness by accident and poor planning! Anywhere remote from people can be considered a wilderness – e.g. Exmoor, the Peak District or Scottish Highlands in Britain (especially in winter), or areas like the great deserts of the world (the Sahara or Gobi), the Australian outback or away from the big towns and cities of North America.

The mental strength to cope with riding a bicycle across terrain where you might not see another human being for days can be enormous. It is almost impossible to teach and not always possible to acquire. Anyone harbouring thoughts of riding around the world or into the remote regions of the world should test their abilities on shorter activities first. See if you can cope with managing for three or four days in a more remote part of your home territory as part a two-week cycling holiday. If you have problems now, they will be far greater when your expedition takes you deeper into the wilds where water, food supplies and home comforts are so much further away.

Will you be able to rise to greater challenges or would you be better advised to stick to the easier option of riding between more 'civilised' places? Bear in mind also that if you do encounter problems, help may be difficult to summon – you may have difficulty communicating if you do not speak a few words of the local language. Pre-event sorties are excellent for testing any new gear. It is alarming how many people take a new tent or stove on holiday or expedition for the first time, only to discover that they don't really know how to use it or that some parts are missing!

Research the areas you intend to pass through to give you a better appreciation and enjoyment of them, and to prepare you for most eventualities. Books, magazine articles and accounts from others who have been there before or made similar journeys are invaluable. Check the weather patterns before you leave home. Many people overlook the possibility of bad weather in holiday regions like Florida, USA, or the speed at which weather can change. Some fail to consider the very cold night-time temperatures of hot regions like north Africa, or the effects of riding at high altitude. Read charts carefully. For example in St Louis, Missouri, USA, the average temperature is a pleasant 13°C, but in the summer it's 31°C and in the winter it's -6°C, with highs and lows of 41°C and -27°C! Forewarned is forearmed.

Water supply is essential. If you intend to ride through a real desert region, do make provision for carrying enough water and high-energy food to last the journey (with some spare in case of emergency situations, or if you find the going slower than originally anticipated). Apart from that, perhaps the most important single item of equipment is a compass to at least help you keep travelling in the right direction. Don't rely on electrical GPS aids (batteries can fail). A compass is simple and reliable. (If you've done your research, you'll be aware if you will be crossing one of the few areas in the world where magnetic compasses aren't so reliable.)

For the truly independent long-distance traveller, the priority in choosing equipment has to be reliability. You may have to forego super-lightweight parts and components in favour of stronger equipment, particularly for vulnerable items such as frames, rear wheels, pannier carriers and seatposts. Simplicity is preferred – repairs may have to be executed by the road or trailside, or perhaps at a remote village. Consider if an item can double up in its uses, so that your kit weight can be kept to a minimum and in case something breaks or is lost – sometimes necessity takes over here. (*See* also Emergency repairs, pp. 114–17.)

Many people who do ride in the remote regions do so alone. For safety, this is not usually recommended, and it is preferable to have a minimum of three people on such journeys. However, it may be that cyclists are lone spirits or perhaps there are just not enough other adventurous people around to share the journey.

Often, it helps to have some small comfort or reminder from 'back home'. Different riders choose different items, but most will have at least one luxury (and indeed, such items are often recommended by psychologists). These luxuries vary from things like special foods for a treat or reward, a hip-flask of drink, small radio, talisman, inflatable pillow or a book to read. Anything to make the situation better is always welcome.

The prize for carrying a week's supplies, following trails swept away by time, sometimes navigating on a compass-bearing and seeing little or no indication of human life for days on end, is the self-satisfaction of overcoming the challenge. Wilderness cyclists experience something that few people in modern society can possibly understand, perhaps following the route of early merchants or pilgrims and witnessing parts of nature in their most natural state. The intimacy of a bicycle is perfect for reaping these rewards.

'Go!' – summary of key points

- You will improve your fitness and cycling abilities through training or practice. By following the seven principles of conditioning – adaptation, specificity, progression, variation, overload, reversibility and recovery – you can create an effective training programme. Remember, though, that everyone reacts slightly differently to training and your progress and what you can cope with may be different from that of another rider.

- Think about your goals and how you can effectively use your time to build up to, and achieve, the results you are seeking.

- A heart rate monitor is an excellent tool for tracking your training, especially for racing cyclists, but make sure that you know how to use it effectively, and do not let it distract you from your riding enjoyment.

- To develop proficiency as a long-distance cyclist you will need to ride a bike for hours at a time. However, if on occasions your time is limited you can benefit from other training activities such as turbo-training or gym work.

- Always be aware of your riding technique. Learn how to ride in a group and 'read the road' for efficient use of your energy.

- The schedules provided in this section are for guidance only. You are not expected to follow them to the letter – after all, everyone is different – but they should provide you with a sound foundation so that you can calculate what you need to do to train for specific events.

- Having the mental ability to cope with marathon activities is vital and you can develop your own strategy to deal with your mission. Most people divide the task into manageable sections and deal with each in turn to chip away at the bigger picture.

- This book touches on just some of the long-distance cycling opportunities. Enquire with some of the established cycling organisations to see what else is available to test yourself – whether that's following a recognised route at your own pace, breaking place-to-place records or participating in a major event or competition. Alternatively, you can look at a map and create your own challenge or adventure.

Selected glossary

aero-bars – handlebars specially shaped to bring a rider's arms in closer to the body for better aerodynamics

ACP – Audax Club Parisien, French cycle club which initiated, and now ratifies, all *allure libre* randonnées

allure libre (Fr) – randonnées where riders are free to ride at their own pace (within limits)

arrivée (Fr) – finish line. Also the title of AUK's quarterly magazine

ATB – All Terrain Bike or mountain-bike designed for off-road riding

audax (Lat) – bold. Associated with long-distance rides to be completed within certain time limits. In France, true audax events are speed controlled by a riding captain who dictates pace and stops

AUK – Audax United Kingdom, the long-distance cyclists' association governing audax rides (brevets) in the UK. Close links with ACP and LRM

BCF – British Cycling Federation, national governing body for most competitive cycle sport

bit and bit – method of sharing workload between a group of cyclists

brevet (Fr) – a certified ride, card carried on such a ride, award for successful completion of such a ride

bonk – state of total energy depletion

bonk bag – *see musette*

bonk rations – food carried to avoid the bonk

bpm – beats per minute (heart rate)

broom wagon – vehicle following behind race or event to sweep up riders who abandon (*see* also sag wagon)

bunch – collective noun for group of cyclists on the road

cassette – collection of rear wheel sprockets used on a hub with integral freewheel mechanism

century ride – 100 miles (occasionally 'metric century', 100 km)

chaingang – group of cyclists riding 'through and off' to maintain pace

chainring – toothed wheel attached to crank

chainset – chainring and cranks

chainwheel – *see* chainring

cleat (US) – *see* shoe-plate

clipless pedals – pedals with an integral mechanism to hold the shoe firmly in place (combine with cleats on shoe soles)

compact frame – reduced-size bicycle frame, usually with sloping top-tube for improved aerodynamics and better handling

control – designated place riders must visit to prove their ride

CTC – Cyclists' Touring Club, national organisation providing international touring information and campaigning for cyclists' rights in the UK

cyclo-sportive (or **sportif**) – sporting rider or activities but less intense than racing

départ (Fr) – start line of race or event

double butted (db) – refers to frame tubing or spokes where there is more material at the ends of the tube or spoke to provide extra strength and less material in the less stressed centre to reduce weight

double century – 200 miles (occasionally 'metric' 200 km)

drafting – *see* slipstreaming

echelon – diagonal cycling formation used by riders to shelter from cross-winds

evens – 20 mph

freewheel – ratchet mechanism contained either within the rear hub or set of sprockets allowing rear wheel to turn and pedals remain stationary

fondo (It) – like French randonnée

Gran Fondo (It) – more prestigious Italian randonnée

grimpeur (Fr) – climber, or very hilly or mountainous event

honk – to climb out of the saddle

HR – heart rate, usually expressed as beats per minute (bpm)

HRM – heart rate monitor, device for measuring heart rate, especially during exercise

LRM – Les Randonneurs Mondiaux, association of international long-distance cycling clubs

LH thread – left-hand thread, turn anti-clockwise to tighten. Typically found on all left-side pedals, and in RH bottom brackets on English threaded frames. (Most Italian frames have RH threads on both sides of the bottom bracket)

lo-pro (low-profile) – reduced-size bicycle frame to improve aerodynamics

MHR – maximum heart rate

micro-frame – *see* lo-pro

MTB – mountain-bike (*see* also ATB and VTT)

mudguard (US = fenders) – plastic or metal covering over tyres to protect rider from water or mud spray

musette (Fr) – lightweight cotton bag used to hand up food and drinks for riders in races

OS – Ordnance Survey, British map-makers

PAC Tour – Pacific-Atlantic Coast ride across USA. Other long-distance tours are also organised

PBP – Paris–Brest–Paris, 1200 km randonnée run every four years by ACP

peloton (Fr) – collective noun for a group of cyclists riding together

PG – plain gauge, usually spokes, universal thickness throughout their length. Can refer to frame tubing

QR – quick release, as in wheels or buckles, whereby items can be secured or undone by a cam lever instead of needing tools or other time-consuming procedures

RAAM – (Race Across AMerica), 3000-mile, non-stop, coast-to-coast race across the USA. Different categories for male and female, and teams, also categorised by age

randonnée (Fr) – literally a 'ramble', referring to long-distance rides with some form of maximum time limit. Also applied to walking, horse-riding or canoeing

randonneur (Fr) – one who rides randonnées

reliability ride – non-competitive ride with time limit, usually held in pre-competition phase, to test rider's fitness and stamina

RH thread – right-hand thread, turn clockwise to tighten. Most nuts and bolts have RH threads

RTTC – **Road Time Trials Council,** governing body for most time-trials in England and Wales

sag wagon – (*see* also broom wagon) support vehicle for touring group to carry luggage (or tired riders)

shifter – gear lever

shoe-plate – attachment to shoe sole to hold shoe firmly in place on the pedal (also cleat)

slipstreaming – to ride behind another rider (or vehicle) to reduce air resistance

SPD – **Shimano Pedalling Dynamics**, but colloquially used to refer to any 'clipless pedals' where the cleat is recessed into the shoe sole

soigneur (Fr) – 'carer', usually used to define a masseur but with wider duties to look after riders' well-being

sportive – *see* cyclo-sportive

Super Randonneur – rider who completes randonées of 200, 300, 400 and 600 km in one season

test, tester – slang term for time-trial, time-triallist

through and off – rapid, regular sharing of pace-making

toe-clip – cage attached to pedals to aid foot position

toe-strap – leather strap with quick-release buckle used with toe-clips

TT – time-trial, individual race against the clock. Riders start at 60-second intervals. The rider with the quickest time wins, or if held over set time the rider who covers the greatest distance in the time is the winner

TTT – team time-trial. As TT, but where riders from the same team (usually four or more) ride together

tri-bars – *see* aero-bars

vedette (Fr) – 'star riders'

VTT – **Velo Tout Terrain** (Fr), mountain-bike

wheel-sucker – derogatory term for a rider who drafts behind another without doing his share of the work

Useful addresses

Manufacturers

All addresses are UK unless otherwise specified

Manufacturer	Address	Website	Products
Reynolds Cycle Technology	PO Box 765 Redfern Road Tyesley Birmingham B11 2BS	www.reynoldsusa.com	Bicycle frame tubing
Easton Sports Inc (USA)	Bicycle Products Division 7855 Haskell Avenue Van Nuys CA 91406–1999 USA	www.eastonsports.com	Bicycle frame tubing and components
Easton Sports Inc	Extra (UK) Ltd PO Box 101 Wellingborough Northampton NN8 6ZZ	www.extrauk.co.uk	UK agent for Easton
Columbus Tubing	Ceeway Bike Building Supplies 80–82 West Street Erith Kent DA8 1AQ	www.framebuilding.com	Bicycle frame tubing
Deda Tubing	Italian Solutions 4 Birchall Road Liverpool	www.bikes-dolan.uk.com	Bicycle frame tubing and components
Deda Tubing (USA)	Sinclair Imports (USA)	www.dedacciai.com	
Rolf Wheels	Trek USA Maidstone Road Kingston Milton Keynes MK10 0BE	www.rolfwheels.com	Lightweight wheels
Rolf Wheels (USA)	801 West Madison Street Waterloo Wisconsin 53594 USA		
Alex Moulton Bicycles Ltd	Holt Road Bradford on Avon Wilts BA15 1AH	www.alexmoulton.co.uk	Lightweight small-wheeled bicycles
Campagnolo	Select Cycle Components PO Box 5788 Nottingham NG13 8LW	www.campagnolo.com	Lightweight cycle components
Campagnolo USA Inc	2105-L Camino Vida Roble Carlsbad CA 92009 USA		

Manufacturer	Address	Website	Products
Carradice	Westmoreland Works St Mary's Street Nelson Lancs BB9 7BA	www.carradice.co.uk	Cycle bags
Blackburn Inc	Madison Cycles plc (*see* below)	www.blackburndesign.com	Lightweight pannier carriers and accessories
Karrimor International Ltd	Petre Road Clayton le Moors Accrington Lancs BB5 6JP	www.karrimor.com	Cycle bags, clothing and Karrimats
Shimano	Madison Cycles plc Buckingham House East Buckingham Parade The Broadway Stanmore Middx HA7 4EA	www.shimano.com	Lightweight cycle components and wheels
Shimano America Corporation	One Holland Irvine CA 92618 USA		
Mavic	RJ Chicken and Sons Bisley Works Landpark Lane Kensworth Dunstable Beds LU6 2PP	www.mavic.com	Lightweight wheels and components
Mavic (USA)	Mavic Inc 17 Parkridge Road Haverhill MA 01835 USA		
TA	RJ Chicken and Sons (*see* Mavic)		Chainsets and replacement chainrings
S&S Machine (USA)	9334 Viking Place Roseville CA 95747 USA	www.sandsmachine.com	S and S couplings for dividing bicycles
E-Caps (USA)	PO Box 4010 Whitefish MT 59937 USA	www.e-caps.com *or* www.hammernutrition.com	Nutritional supplements
Blue Guides	A & C Black Ltd 37 Soho Square London W1D 3QZ	www.acblack.com	Guide books
Rough Guides	62–70 Shorts Gardens London WC2H 9AB	www.roughguides.com	Guide books
Lonely Planet Publications	10a Spring Place London NW5 3BH	www.lonelyplanet.co.uk	Guide books
Lonely Planet Publications (USA)	150 Linden Street Oakland CA 94607 USA	www.lonelyplanet.com	

Manufacturer	Address	Website	Products
Ordnance Survey	Romsey Road Maybush Southampton Hants SO16 4GU	www.ordsrvy.gov.uk	Maps and guides
Michelin Publications	The Edward Hyde Buildings 38 Clarendon Road Watford Herts WD1 1SX	www.michelin-travel.com	Maps, guides and bicycle tyres
Casio Electronics Co Ltd Casio Inc (USA)	Unit 6 1000 North Circular Road London NW2 7JD 570 Mount Pleasant Drive PO Box 7000 Dover NJ 07801 USA		Electronic gadgets
Sprayway Ltd	16 Chester Street Manchester M1 5GE		Outdoor clothing
Lowe Alpine Group (UK) Ltd Lowe Alpine (USA)	Ann Street Kendal Cumbria LA9 6AA	www.lowealpine.co.uk www.lowealpine.com	Outdoor clothing
Columbia Sportswear UK Ltd	Unit 1.03, Studio 1 Power Road Studios Power Road, Chiswick London W4 5PY	www.columbia.com	Outdoor clothing
Camelbak	Zyro plc Becklands Close Bar Lane, Roecliffe York YO5 9LS	www.zyro.co.uk	Hydration systems
Platypus	First Ascent Units 2–7 Lime Tree Business Park Matlock Derbyshire DE4 3EJ	www.firstascent.co.uk	Hydration systems
SIS (Science in Sport) Ltd	Ashwood Laboratories Brockhall Village Blackburn Lancs BB6 8BB	www.scienceinsport.com	Energy drinks and food
Nikwax Ltd Nikwax USA	Durgates Industrial Est Wadhurst East Sussex TN5 6DF PO Box 1572 Everett WA 98206 USA	www.nikwax.com www.nikwax-usa.com	Waterproofing technologies Waterproofing technologies
Dave Yates (or Steel Cycles)	2 Station Road South Gosforth Newcastle upon Tyne NE3 1QD	www.msteelcycles.co.uk	Custom-built lightweight frames and cycles

Clubs and associations

Club/Association	Address	Website	Subject
Audax UK (AUK)	Events 57 Hartwell Road Ashton Northampton NN7 2JR	www.aukhawk.demon.co.uk	Long-distance cyclists' association
Randonneurs USA	226 West Avenue Santa Cruz CA 95060 USA		Long-distance cyclists' association
Audax Club of Australia	PO Box 363 Whittlesea VIC 3757 Australia	www.audax.org.au	Long-distance cyclists' association
Audax Club Parisien (ACP)	13 rue Maryae Hilaz 75020 Paris France	www.audax-club-parisien.com	Governing organisation for PBP
Cyclists' Touring Club (CTC)	69 Meadrow Godalming Surrey GU7 3HS	www.ctc.org.uk	UK cycle touring and campaigning organisation
British Cycling Federation (BCF)	National Cycling Centre Stuart Street Manchester M11 4DQ	www.bcf.uk.com	UK governing body for most cycle sport
Moulton Bicycle Club	20 Mead Road Uxbridge Middlesex UB8 1AU		Moulton bicycle owners' club
British Human Power Club	7 West Bank Abbot's Park Chester CH1 4BD	www.bhpc.org.uk	Association for human-powered vehicle enthusiasts
Tandem Club	25 Hendred Way Abingdon Oxon OX14 2AN	www.tandem-club.org.uk	Association for tandem enthusiasts
Tricycle Association	24 Manston Lane Crossgates Leeds LS15 8HZ		Association for tricycle enthusiasts
Union Cycliste Internationale (UCI)	37 route de Chevannes Case Postale CH1000 Lausanne 23 Switzerland	www.uci.ch	International governing body for cycle sport
Bike Events	PO Box 75 Bath BA1 1BX		Organisers of London–Brighton and other charity rides
Road Time Trials Council (RTTC)	77 Arlington Drive Pennington Leigh Lancs WN7 3QP	www.rttc.org.uk	UK governing body for time-trials

Club/Association	Address	Website	Subject
Sustrans	35 King Street Bristol BS1 4DZ	www.sustrans.org.uk *or* nationalcyclenetwork.org.uk	UK cyclepath planner
Iditabike		www.iditasport.com	Extreme bicycle race across Alaska
Ultra Marathon Cycling Association	PO Box 18028 Boulder CO 80308-1028 USA	www.ultracycling.com	Long-distance cycle racing association
Youth Hostel Association (YHA)	Trevelyan House 8 St Stephens Hill St Albans Herts AL1 2DY	www.yha.org.uk	Hostel accommodation in England and Wales
American Youth Hostels	733 15th Street, NW Suite 480 Washington DC 20005 USA	www.ditech.w1.com	Hostel accommodation throughout USA
International Youth Hostels Federation		www.iyhf.org	International hostel organisation
European Bike Express – *aka* Bolero Bike Bus	31 Baker Street Middlesborough TS1 2LF	www.bike-express.co.uk	Bike transport
League of American Bicyclists	1612 K St, NW Suite 40 Washington DC 20006 USA	www.bikleague.org	US bicycle touring association
RAAM	PO Box 303 202 Prairie Pedal Lane Sharon WI 53585 USA	www.raceacrossamerica.org	Race Across AMerica
PAC Tour	PO Box 303 Sharon, WI 53585 USA	www.pactour.com	US long-distance cycle tour specialist
Graham Baxter Sporting Tours	21 Manor Gardens Pool in Wharfedale W Yorks LS21 1NB	www.sportingtours.co.uk	Commercial tour operator specialising in European cycling
UK Sport	40 Bernard Street London WC1N 1ST	www.uksport.gov.uk	Governing (and funding) body for most Olympic and other sports in UK

Further reading

Zinn and the Art of Road Bike Maintenance, Lennard Zinn (VeloPress, 2000)

Richard's 21st Century Bicycle Book, Richard Ballantine (Pan Books, 2000)

Journey to the Centre of the Earth, Richard and Nicholas Crane (Bantam Press, 1987)

Ultimate High: My Everest Odyssey, Göran Kropp with David Lagercrantz, English Edition (Discovery Books, 1999)

British Journal of Sports Medicine – www.bmjpg.com/data/jsm.htm

Journal of Exercise Physiology – www.css.edu/users/tboone2/asep/fldr/fldr.htm

Gatorade Sports Science Institute – www.gssiweb.com/index/html

National Sports Medicine Institute (UK) – www.nsmi.org.uk

Sports Science – www.sportsci.org

Also available from A & C Black's Sports and Fitness list:

The Cyclist's Training Bible
Joe Friel

Cycling for Fitness
Fitness Trainers series
Dave Smith

The Complete Guide to Cross Training
Fiona Hayes

The Complete Guide to Endurance Training
Jon Ackland

The Complete Guide to Sports Nutrition (THIRD EDITION)
Anita Bean

The Complete Guide to Stretching
Christopher M. Norris

Marathon Running
Richard Nerurkar

Appendices

Conversion tables

Distance	Multiply by
Inches to centimetres (cm)	2.54
Centimetres to inches (in. or ")	0.39
Feet to metres (m)	0.30
Metres to feet (ft or ')	3.28
Yards to metres (m)	0.91
Metres to yards (yd)	1.09
Miles to kilometres (km)	0.625
Kilometres to miles (m or ml)[1]	1.6

Weight	Multiply by
Ounces to grams (g)	28.35
Grams to ounces (oz)	0.035
Pounds to kilograms (kg)	0.45
Kilograms to pounds (lb)	2.21
16 oz = 1lb	

Volume	Multiply by
Litres to cubic inches	0.6
Cubic inches to litres	0.0165
Imperial gallons to litres	4.55
Litres to imperial litres	0.22
US gallons to litres	3.79
Litres to US gallons	0.26

Temperature
To convert °C to °F multiply by 1.8 and add 32
To convert °F to °C subtract 32 and multiply by 5/9 (or 0.5555)

Energy
1 kilojoule (kj) = 4.2 kilocalories (kcal) or 4.2 Calories (Cal)

Pressure
1 bar (or atmosphere) = 14.7 lbs per sq. inch (psi)

[1]Although the symbols m or ml for miles can be confused with metres or millilitres, it is usually obvious from the context, which measurement is being used

Imperial gear table for 26" wheels

Chainwheel size	\ Sprocket size → 11	12	13	14	15	16	17	18	19	20	21	22	23	24	25	26	28	30	32
54	127.6	117.0	108.0	100.3	93.6	87.8	82.6	78.0	73.9	70.2	66.9	63.8	61.0	58.5	56.2	54.0	50.1	46.8	43.9
53	125.3	114.8	106.0	98.4	91.9	86.1	81.1	76.6	72.5	68.9	65.6	62.6	59.9	57.4	55.1	53.0	49.2	45.9	43.1
52	122.9	112.7	104.0	96.6	90.1	84.5	79.5	75.1	71.2	67.6	64.4	61.5	58.8	56.3	54.1	52.0	48.3	45.1	42.3
50	118.2	108.3	100.0	92.9	86.7	81.3	76.5	72.2	68.4	65.0	61.9	59.1	56.5	54.2	52.0	50.0	46.4	43.3	40.6
48	113.5	104.0	96.0	89.1	83.2	78.0	73.4	69.3	65.7	62.4	59.4	56.7	54.3	52.0	49.9	48.0	44.6	41.6	39.0
46	108.7	99.7	92.0	85.4	79.7	74.8	70.4	66.4	62.9	59.8	57.0	54.4	52.0	49.8	47.8	46.0	42.7	39.9	37.4
44	104.0	95.3	88.0	81.7	76.3	71.5	67.3	63.6	60.2	57.2	54.5	52.0	49.7	47.7	45.8	44.0	40.9	38.1	35.8
42	99.3	91.0	84.0	78.0	72.8	68.3	64.2	60.7	57.5	54.6	52.0	49.6	47.5	45.5	43.7	42.0	39.0	36.4	34.1
40	94.5	86.7	80.0	74.3	69.3	65.0	61.2	57.8	54.7	52.0	49.5	47.3	45.2	43.3	41.6	40.0	37.1	34.7	32.5
39	92.2	84.5	78.0	72.4	67.6	63.4	59.6	56.3	53.4	50.7	48.3	46.1	44.1	42.3	40.6	39.0	36.2	33.8	31.7
38	89.8	82.3	76.0	70.6	65.9	61.8	58.1	54.9	52.0	49.4	47.0	44.9	43.0	41.2	39.5	38.0	35.3	32.9	30.9
36	85.1	78.0	72.0	66.9	62.4	58.5	55.1	52.0	49.3	46.8	44.6	42.5	40.7	39.0	37.4	36.0	33.4	31.2	29.3
34	80.4	73.7	68.0	63.1	58.9	55.3	52.0	49.1	46.5	44.2	42.1	40.2	38.4	36.8	35.4	34.0	31.6	29.5	27.6
32	75.6	69.3	64.0	59.4	55.5	52.0	48.9	46.2	43.8	41.6	39.6	37.8	36.2	34.7	33.3	32.0	29.7	27.7	26.0
30	70.9	65.0	60.0	55.7	52.0	48.8	45.9	43.3	41.1	39.0	37.1	35.5	33.9	32.5	31.2	30.0	27.9	26.0	24.4
28	66.2	60.7	56.0	52.0	48.5	45.5	42.8	40.4	38.3	36.4	34.7	33.1	31.7	30.3	29.1	28.0	26.0	24.3	22.8
26	61.5	56.3	52.0	48.3	45.1	42.3	39.8	37.6	35.6	33.8	32.2	30.7	29.4	28.2	27.0	26.0	24.1	22.5	21.1
24	56.7	52.0	48.0	44.6	41.6	39.0	36.7	34.7	32.8	31.2	29.7	28.4	27.1	26.0	25.0	24.0	22.3	20.8	19.5

Imperial gear table for 27" wheels

Chainwheel size	Sprocket size																		
	11	12	13	14	15	16	17	18	19	20	21	22	23	24	25	26	28	30	32
54	132.5	121.5	112.2	104.1	97.2	91.1	85.8	81.0	76.7	72.9	69.4	66.3	63.4	60.8	58.3	56.1	52.1	48.6	45.6
53	130.1	119.3	110.1	102.2	95.4	89.4	84.2	79.5	75.3	71.6	68.1	65.0	62.2	59.6	57.2	55.0	51.1	47.7	44.7
52	127.6	117.0	108.0	100.3	93.6	87.8	82.6	78.0	73.9	70.2	66.9	63.8	61.0	58.5	56.2	54.0	50.1	46.8	43.9
50	122.7	112.5	103.8	96.4	90.0	84.4	79.4	75.0	71.1	67.5	64.3	61.4	58.7	56.3	54.0	51.9	48.2	45.0	42.2
48	117.8	108.0	99.7	92.6	86.4	81.0	76.2	72.0	68.2	64.8	61.7	58.9	56.3	54.0	51.8	49.8	46.3	43.2	40.5
46	112.9	103.5	95.5	88.7	82.8	77.6	73.1	69.0	65.4	62.1	59.1	56.5	54.0	51.8	49.7	47.8	44.4	41.4	38.8
44	108.0	99.0	91.4	84.9	79.2	74.3	69.9	66.0	62.5	59.4	56.6	54.0	51.7	49.5	47.5	45.7	42.4	39.6	37.1
42	103.1	94.5	87.2	81.0	75.6	70.9	66.7	63.0	59.7	56.7	54.0	51.5	49.3	47.3	45.4	43.6	40.5	37.8	35.4
40	98.2	90.0	83.1	77.1	72.0	67.5	63.5	60.0	56.8	54.0	51.4	49.1	47.0	45.0	43.2	41.5	38.6	36.0	33.8
39	95.7	87.8	81.0	75.2	70.2	65.8	61.9	58.5	55.4	52.7	50.1	47.9	45.8	43.9	42.1	40.5	37.6	35.1	32.9
38	93.3	85.5	78.9	73.3	68.4	64.1	60.4	57.0	54.0	51.3	48.9	46.6	44.6	42.8	41.0	39.5	36.6	34.2	32.1
36	88.4	81.0	74.8	69.4	64.8	60.8	57.2	54.0	51.2	48.6	46.3	44.2	42.3	40.5	38.9	37.4	34.7	32.4	30.4
34	83.5	76.5	70.6	65.6	61.2	57.4	54.0	51.0	48.3	45.9	43.7	41.7	39.9	38.3	36.7	35.3	32.8	30.6	28.7
32	78.5	72.0	66.5	61.7	57.6	54.0	50.8	48.0	45.5	43.2	41.1	39.3	37.6	36.0	34.6	33.2	30.9	28.8	27.0
30	73.6	67.5	62.3	57.9	54.0	50.6	47.6	45.0	42.6	40.5	38.6	36.8	35.2	33.8	32.4	31.2	28.9	27.0	25.3
28	68.7	63.0	58.2	54.0	50.4	47.3	44.5	42.0	39.8	37.8	36.0	34.4	32.9	31.5	30.2	29.1	27.0	25.2	23.6
26	63.8	58.5	54.0	50.1	46.8	43.9	41.3	39.0	36.9	35.1	33.4	31.9	30.5	29.3	28.1	27.0	25.1	23.4	21.9
24	58.9	54.0	49.8	46.3	43.2	40.5	38.1	36.0	34.1	32.4	30.9	29.5	28.2	27.0	25.9	24.9	23.1	21.6	20.3

Metric gear table for 700 x 25 tyre
(wheel circumference = 2.142 m)

Chainwheel size	\ Sprocket size	11	12	13	14	15	16	17	18	19	20	21	22	23	24	25	26	28	30	32
54		10.52	9.64	8.90	8.26	7.71	7.23	6.80	6.43	6.09	5.78	5.51	5.26	5.03	4.82	4.63	4.45	4.13	3.86	3.61
53		10.32	9.46	8.73	8.11	7.57	7.10	6.68	6.31	5.98	5.68	5.41	5.16	4.94	4.73	4.54	4.37	4.05	3.78	3.55
52		10.13	9.28	8.57	7.96	7.43	6.96	6.55	6.19	5.86	5.57	5.30	5.06	4.84	4.64	4.46	4.28	3.98	3.71	3.48
50		19.74	8.93	8.24	7.65	7.14	6.69	6.30	5.95	5.64	5.36	5.10	4.87	4.66	4.46	4.28	4.12	3.83	3.57	3.35
48		19.35	8.57	7.91	7.34	6.85	6.43	6.05	5.71	5.41	5.14	4.90	4.67	4.47	4.28	4.11	3.95	3.67	3.43	3.21
46		8.96	8.21	7.58	7.04	6.57	6.16	5.80	5.47	5.19	4.93	4.69	4.48	4.28	4.11	3.94	3.79	3.52	3.28	3.08
44		8.57	7.85	7.25	6.73	6.28	5.89	5.54	5.24	4.96	4.71	4.49	4.28	4.10	3.93	3.77	3.62	3.37	3.14	2.95
42		8.18	7.50	6.92	6.43	6.00	5.62	5.29	5.00	4.73	4.50	4.28	4.09	3.91	3.75	3.60	3.46	3.21	3.00	2.81
40		7.79	7.14	6.59	6.12	5.71	5.36	5.04	4.76	4.51	4.28	4.08	3.89	3.73	3.57	3.43	3.30	3.06	2.86	2.68
39		7.59	6.96	6.43	5.97	5.57	5.22	4.91	4.64	4.40	4.18	3.98	3.80	3.63	3.48	3.34	3.21	2.98	2.78	2.61
38		7.40	6.78	6.26	5.81	5.43	5.09	4.79	4.52	4.28	4.07	3.88	3.70	3.54	3.39	3.26	3.13	2.91	2.71	2.54
36		7.01	6.43	5.93	5.51	5.14	4.82	4.54	4.28	4.06	3.86	3.67	3.51	3.35	3.21	3.08	2.97	2.75	2.57	2.41
34		6.62	6.07	5.60	5.20	4.86	4.55	4.28	4.05	3.83	3.64	3.47	3.31	3.17	3.03	2.91	2.80	2.60	2.43	2.28
32		6.23	5.71	5.27	4.90	4.57	4.28	4.03	3.81	3.61	3.43	3.26	3.12	2.98	2.86	2.74	2.64	2.45	2.28	2.14
30		5.84	5.36	4.94	4.59	4.28	4.02	3.78	3.57	3.38	3.21	3.06	2.92	2.79	2.68	2.57	2.47	2.30	2.14	2.01
28		5.45	5.00	4.61	4.28	4.00	3.75	3.53	3.33	3.16	3.00	2.86	2.73	2.61	2.50	2.40	2.31	2.14	2.00	1.87
26		5.06	4.64	4.28	3.98	3.71	3.48	3.28	3.09	2.93	2.78	2.65	2.53	2.42	2.32	2.23	2.14	1.99	1.86	1.74
24		4.67	4.28	3.95	3.67	3.43	3.21	3.02	2.86	2.71	2.57	2.45	2.34	2.24	2.14	2.06	1.98	1.84	1.71	1.61

Metric gear table for 26 x 1.4 tyre (wheel circumference = 1.978 m)

Chainwheel size	\ Sprocket size																		
	11	12	13	14	15	16	17	18	19	20	21	22	23	24	25	26	28	30	32
54	9.71	8.90	8.22	7.63	7.12	6.68	6.28	5.93	5.62	5.34	5.09	4.86	4.64	4.45	4.27	4.11	3.81	3.56	3.34
53	9.53	8.74	8.06	7.49	6.99	6.55	6.17	5.82	5.52	5.24	4.99	4.77	4.56	4.37	4.19	4.03	3.74	3.49	3.28
52	9.35	8.57	7.91	7.35	6.86	6.43	6.05	5.71	5.41	5.14	4.90	4.68	4.47	4.29	4.11	3.96	3.67	3.43	3.21
50	8.99	8.24	7.61	7.06	6.59	6.18	5.82	5.49	5.21	4.95	4.71	4.50	4.30	4.12	3.96	3.80	3.53	3.30	3.09
48	8.63	7.91	7.30	6.78	6.33	5.93	5.58	5.27	5.00	4.75	4.52	4.32	4.13	3.96	3.80	3.65	3.39	3.16	2.97
46	8.27	7.58	7.00	6.50	6.07	5.69	5.35	5.05	4.79	4.55	4.33	4.14	3.96	3.79	3.64	3.50	3.25	3.03	2.84
44	7.91	7.25	6.69	6.22	5.80	5.44	5.12	4.84	4.58	4.35	4.14	3.96	3.78	3.63	3.48	3.35	3.11	2.90	2.72
42	7.55	6.92	6.39	5.93	5.54	5.19	4.89	4.62	4.37	4.15	3.96	3.78	3.61	3.46	3.32	3.20	2.97	2.77	2.60
40	7.19	6.59	6.09	5.65	5.27	4.95	4.65	4.40	4.16	3.96	3.77	3.60	3.44	3.30	3.16	3.04	2.83	2.64	2.47
39	7.01	6.43	5.93	5.51	5.14	4.82	4.54	4.29	4.06	3.86	3.67	3.51	3.35	3.21	3.09	2.97	2.76	2.57	2.41
38	6.83	6.26	5.78	5.37	5.01	4.70	4.42	4.18	3.96	3.76	3.58	3.42	3.27	3.13	3.01	2.89	2.68	2.51	2.35
36	6.47	5.93	5.48	5.09	4.75	4.45	4.19	3.96	3.75	3.56	3.39	3.24	3.10	2.97	2.85	2.74	2.54	2.37	2.23
34	6.11	5.60	5.17	4.80	4.48	4.20	3.96	3.74	3.54	3.36	3.20	3.06	2.92	2.80	2.69	2.59	2.40	2.24	2.10
32	5.75	5.27	4.87	4.52	4.22	3.96	3.72	3.52	3.33	3.16	3.01	2.88	2.75	2.64	2.53	2.43	2.26	2.11	1.98
30	5.39	4.95	4.56	4.24	3.96	3.71	3.49	3.30	3.12	2.97	2.83	2.70	2.58	2.47	2.37	2.28	2.12	1.98	1.85
28	5.03	4.62	4.26	3.96	3.69	3.46	3.26	3.08	2.91	2.77	2.64	2.52	2.41	2.31	2.22	2.13	1.98	1.85	1.73
26	4.68	4.29	3.96	3.67	3.43	3.21	3.03	2.86	2.71	2.57	2.45	2.34	2.24	2.14	2.06	1.98	1.84	1.71	1.61
24	4.32	3.96	3.65	3.39	3.16	2.97	2.79	2.64	2.50	2.37	2.26	2.16	2.06	1.98	1.90	1.83	1.70	1.58	1.48

Index

Bold numbers denote illustrations.